UNISA

MICROECONOMICS

R P Viljoen

University of South Africa
Pretoria

First edition, first impression

ISBN 1 86888 095 8

Published by Unisa Press
University of South Africa
PO Box 392, 0003 Pretoria
Electronic origination by PG&A, Johannesburg
Printed and bound by National Book Printers, Goodwood, Western Cape

House editors: Liz Stewart, Sarie Moolman
Cover design and layout: Erica de Wet

CONTENTS

PREFACE

Microeconomics is traditionally regarded by students as a difficult subject, often because they cannot see the wood for the trees – too many less important matters distract their attention from the bigger picture. This book tries to avoid this problem. All the important aspects of microeconomics which an undergraduate student is supposed to note are discussed. At the same time I attempted to be concise and to the point and not to fall into the temptation of being sidetracked by inessentials.

This book is aimed at students who want to obtain an intermediate knowledge of microeconomics, but it is also written in such a way that students or readers with no preknowledge of the subject can understand it. It starts with basic principles, then more advanced issues are attended to. The approach is non-mathematical, and graphs are mostly used to explain the models.

Microeconomics was written mainly for students at distance-education institutions and may therefore contain more repetition of important facts than would otherwise be necessary. Other students should, however, also benefit from this approach. No microeconomics course can avoid the technical aspects, but here the aim was to keep the analysis as digestible as possible. Practical examples are given where appropriate, without distracting the student from the main argument. Boxes are sometimes used to highlight such practical examples or to supply additional explanations.

The book focuses on basic concepts such as demand, supply, price formation, consumer behaviour, production functions and the decision-making of firms under different market conditions (perfect competition, monopoly, monopolistic competition and oligopoly). The last chapter contains an introduction to general equilibrium analysis and the theory of welfare economics. The contents are, therefore, based mainly on conventional neo-classical theory, as usually presented in undergraduate courses. Price formation of production factors is not discussed – the reason being that the topic is offered mostly as a separate course (eg labour economics).

An introduction at the beginning of each chapter gives a résumé of the chapter and puts the subject matter in perspective. Study objectives draw the attention of the reader to the most important aspects. A list of important concepts appears at the end of each chapter, more or less in the order in which they appear in the text. These are followed by model questions which give an indication of the type of question that can be set in an examination paper.

The book is published in both English and Afrikaans. Symbols and abbreviations typical of each language are used in the different editions.

Acknowledgements

A book like this is not written in isolation. A special word of thanks to Louis Fourie who read everything and provided valuable comments. Also a word of thanks to Koos le Roux, Martin Marais and Mike Louw who all made suggestions about the contents of some of the chapters.

Thank you to Sarie Moolman, Liz Stewart, Anita Engelbrecht and Erica de Wet from Unisa Press. Without their expertise and willingness to help it would have been much more difficult to publish this book.

The following people assisted in translating the contents of the book from Afrikaans to English: Moya Joubert, Sandra Mills, Liza Niedermeier and Piet-Hein van Eeghen. Thank you to all of them.

Lastly, a special word of thanks to my wife, Carolé. Her contribution entailed more than any job description could have outlined, or do justice to.

Roelie Viljoen

Pretoria

October 1998

1

INTRODUCTION TO MICROECONOMICS

Without microeconomics we would have no explanations for most of the important economic questions that crop up. Microeconomics equips us to make sense of and find solutions to economic events and questions – not only about the South African economy but also any other economy. Microeconomics supplies the answers to questions such as the following: Why is it that when a country spends more on defence, it will probably have to reduce its expenditure on housing? Why is beef more expensive than chicken? Why did the world price of oil rise sharply during the seventies, and drop during the eighties? Why do actuaries earn more than teachers? Why are certain goods and services provided by the government instead of the private sector? Why do some countries use a large number of labourers and relatively little machinery for a particular production process, whereas it is the other way round in other countries? These are simply a few of the questions to which answers and solutions can be found with the aid of microeconomic theory.

Microeconomics also explains some of the anomalies we come across in our daily lives. An entrance ticket for an ordinary soccer match in South Africa might cost R15, but a ticket to an important World Cup match overseas is exorbitantly expensive. One person may pay R980 to fly from Johannesburg to Cape Town, but the passenger in the next seat may only be paying R499. A public servant might earn around R50 000 per year, but a golfer could receive over R1m for winning a single important tournament. Telephone calls cost less in the evenings than during the day. These are just a few examples of the numerous issues on which microeconomics can shed more light.

Microeconomics also provides the theoretical background for most of the applied fields of economics, such as development economics, international trade, public finance, labour economics, regional economics and agricultural economics. These specialisations cannot be mastered without a thorough knowledge of microeconomic theory. Students are therefore usually expected to study microeconomics before they tackle any of the other fields.

A knowledge of basic economic theory, combined with the ability to apply it, is undoubtedly a huge advantage to any citizen who wants to gain an insight into the numerous social and economic questions of the day and into the economic phenomena which we can see taking place around us. Such knowledge is also useful in helping us to predict what is likely to happen in the world around us when economic changes take place. The manager or manufacturer who has to plan ahead, the marketer who wants to know how markets work and how they differ from one another, the entrepreneur who is engaged in strategic planning, the banker or broker who has to advise clients – in fact anyone who works in a dynamic environment – will benefit from a sound knowledge of economics.

In courses such as this one the emphasis is on how a consumer could spend his or her income to the best advantage, how a firm should go about keeping production costs as low as possible and maximising profits, how a particular market structure (perfect competition, monopoly, monopolistic competition and oligopoly) comes into being and how this influences the welfare of the community, how the prices of factors of production are determined, and how the government can influence social welfare by means of taxes and subsidies.

In this introductory chapter we explain what microeconomics is and where it fits into economics as an area of study. The scarcity problem, which every society faces all the time, is discussed first. The basic economic functions which have to be fulfilled by any economic system are then studied. The way these functions are fulfilled in a market economy such as the South African economy is also examined. The operation of the economic process is explained with reference to the circular flow diagram. The role of economic models is then discussed and lastly a few concepts and assumptions that you ought to know before you begin the course are briefly dealt with.

It is unavoidable in a chapter such as this that concepts will be mentioned that will only become clear at a later stage. One such concept is the market economy, which is the system on which the South African economy is based (as indeed are the economies of most countries in the world) and which is also the system studied in microeconomics. We should mention at this stage that the most important characteristics of a market economy are that the government permits private ownership, individuals and firms are allowed to take their own economic decisions and there is competition.

After having studied this chapter, you will

- understand and be able to explain the nature and importance of microeconomics
- be able to explain the scarcity problem
- know the difference between economic goods and free goods
- be able to distinguish between final goods and intermediary goods
- be able to describe the function of the economic system
- be able to explain how an economy works, using the circular flow diagram
- be able to write an essay on the use of economic models
- understand the concepts *ceteris paribus* and equilibrium

THE NATURE OF MICROECONOMICS

Economics is divided into two broad sections: microeconomics and macroeconomics. The prefix 'micro' is derived from the Greek word *mikros*, which means small. Microeconomics is the section of economics which deals with the actions of individual decision-making units such as consumers, firms, entrepreneurs and the owners of factors of production. Briefly, microeconomics is concerned with all the individuals or separate units which play a part in the functioning of the economy. These separate elements of the economy are placed under a microscope, figuratively speaking, and studied in detail. Microeconomics explains how and why these decision-making units take particular decisions. For example, it explains how consumers take certain purchasing decisions and how their choices are influenced by changes in prices and income. Microeconomic theory also explains the principles according to which firms decide how many workers to employ, the quantity of goods to produce and at what price to sell the goods. Stated more formally, *microeconomics involves a study of the way in which individual decision makers, functioning as consumers or producers, use their limited resources in an attempt to achieve their respective economic goals, namely the maximisation of utility and profit*. Through the study of the behaviour and interaction of individual firms and consumers, microeconomics also provides explanations for the origin and functioning of industries and markets, the way they differ from each other and how they are influenced by government policy or developments in the global economy.

Micro-economics

Naturally, the analysis of consumer and producer behaviour patterns is not simply carried out for interest's sake. These behaviour patterns are used to *explain* what is happening in the economy, to *predict* what could possibly happen, and to help policy makers to choose or develop the most suitable *economic policy*. The application of microeconomic theory is therefore ultimately a practical matter.

Macroeconomics, the other important section of economics, deals with the economy as a whole. The prefix 'macro' is derived from the Greek word *makros* which means 'large'. The emphasis therefore falls on the broad perspective, the big picture, so to speak. The economic behaviour of large groups of participants is studied and an image of the total economic system is developed. Topics such as total production, total income and total expenditure in the economy, economic growth, unemployment and inflation are studied. The dividing line between microeconomics and macroeconomics is not always very distinct, however, because macroeconomics also involves the analysis of markets – an analysis of the total (or aggregate) market for goods and services in a country is one example. In order to understand the total magnitudes, one has to begin by understanding the behaviour of the firms, consumers, workers and investors that collectively make up the market. In the end we find that the big picture is made up of a whole lot of smaller parts.

To sum up, while microeconomics studies the operation of the economy at the level where basic decisions are taken, macroeconomics concentrates on total economic behaviour and the performance of the economy as a whole. In this book the emphasis falls on microeconomics.

THE SCARCITY PROBLEM

In the previous section microeconomics was defined as a study of the way in which individual decision makers, functioning as consumers or producers, use their limited resources in an attempt to achieve their respective economic goals, namely the maximisation of utility and profit. The fact that there are only 'limited resources', in other words that scarcity does exist, forms the basis for the study of economics in general and microeconomics in particular.

Scarcity is something which each of us encounters daily. Every student would like to have more time to spend on his or her studies, but would also like more time for sport or recreation. Similarly, most students would like to study full time, but would also like to work full time in order to earn a salary. Most of us would appreciate a luxury car, but at the same time we want enough money for overseas travel. We all experience the feeling of wanting to buy certain things but knowing we can't afford them. The question is: Why can't we always have *more* of these things? The answer is, first, that the material wants of society, that is the material needs of individuals and institutions, are unlimited and can never be fully satisfied; and second, economic resources (ie the resources used to produce goods and services) are limited or scarce.

Unlimited wants

Wants

What is meant by 'material wants' in the paragraph above? First, the term indicates the needs of consumers to obtain various goods and services which provide utility. (Utility is the term economists use for satisfaction or pleasure.) A broad spectrum of goods would provide utility for consumers: houses, cars, groceries, clothing, television sets – the list is endless. The goods which are capable of satisfying people's wants are usually divided into two groups: first, there are the essentials (eg clothing, housing and food) and second, there are the luxuries (eg expensive jewellery, perfume). It is self-evident that what may be a luxury for Jones could be an essential for Smith, or that a product which is considered an essential these days was regarded as a luxury a few years ago.

Services also satisfy consumer wants. A haircut, an operation, repairs to a car, legal advice – all these are examples of services which satisfy people's wants. The difference between goods and services is not always as clear as it may appear at first sight. Many goods, such as cars and washing machines, are bought for the sake of the service they give their owners.

Material wants include those of businesses and the state. Businesses (firms) require factory buildings, machinery, trucks, storage space, communication systems and numerous other items that will help them to reach their production targets. The state, which reflects the collective needs of society and also has needs of its own, would like to acquire more schools, hospitals, roads, military equipment and so on.

Seen as a whole, the material wants of society are unlimited or insatiable for all practical purposes, which naturally means that they can never be met in full. Although an individual's wants regarding a specific product or service can be satisfied (we could all probably make do with one appendectomy) they can never be satisfied for goods and services in general. Suppose we were each asked to draw up a list of goods and services we would like to have but do not have at present. If we spent a bit of time on it we would probably come up with impressively long lists. Over a period of time we might satisfy some of the wants on our lists, but we would continually be adding new ones. Material wants seem to breed like rabbits. The rapid development of new products has created new wants among people and institutions, and extensive advertising ensures that consumers stay right up to date with what is available. A few years ago products such as personal computers, light beer, digital watches and microwave ovens did not even exist and consumers did not appear to miss them. The minute the products appeared on the market, however, consumers began to want them and started buying them. Also, it is part of human nature not to be content when basic wants are satisfied – the acquisition of a black-and-white TV set often leads to a desire for a colour set; owning a small car leads to a desire for a bigger or more luxurious model.

To sum up, we can say that at any given time the individuals and institutions that make up society have innumerable unfulfilled wants. Some of the wants (eg food, clothing and housing) have a biological origin. Other wants are influenced by the customs and standards of the society of which the individual or institution is a part. For example, the specific types of clothing, food and housing which people want are determined mainly by the social and cultural environments in which they live. Wants change and multiply over time – a process which is aided by the development of new products and extensive advertising and sales promotion.

It is important to note that the goal of all economic activity is to satisfy all these divergent material wants.

Limited resources

We shall now turn our attention to the fact that economic resources are limited or scarce. Precisely what does the term 'economic resources' mean? In general it refers to all the natural, human and manufactured resources which are used to manufacture goods and services. Another term for 'economic resources' would be factors of production. Clearly, many different things are included: all types of labour; factory buildings, machinery and equipment which are used to produce or process manufactured goods or agricultural produce; various means of transport and communication; land, and marine and mineral resources. Economic resources are usually divided into the following four categories: natural resources, labour, capital and entrepreneurial ability. We shall now briefly examine each of the factors of production (and the fact that they are limited in extent).

- The term *natural resources* is an umbrella term – it refers to all the 'gifts of nature' which can be used in the production process. These include agricultural land, natural forests, minerals, water, vegetation, oil reserves, marine resources and other forms of animal life. Natural resources occur in limited quantities, and when a resource has been exhausted it cannot be replaced easily. This has given rise to a great deal of concern, so much so that big international conferences have been held on this subject.

- *Labour* is a broad term which refers to all the human physical and mental abilities which can be used to produce goods and services. (Entrepreneurial ability is such a special talent that it is not included here but is regarded as a special category.) The contributions made by everybody, from the humblest to those working in the top professions, are classified as labour: street sweepers, woodcutters, clerks, professional sportsmen, nuclear physicists – all fall into this category. The amount of labour available in a country is determined by the size of the population and the portion of the population that is able to and wants to work. The quality of the labour force is even more important than its sheer size. As you will readily understand, there are limits to both the quantity and the quality of labour, especially in the short term.

- *Capital* or capital goods refers to all manufactured resources which are used to produce goods and services and get them to the consumers. This category includes machinery, tools, equipment, factory buildings, storage space, as well as transport and distribution facilities.

  Two points are important here. First, capital goods differ from consumer goods in the sense that consumer goods satisfy consumer needs directly, whereas capital goods do so indirectly by making the production of consumer goods possible. Second, the term 'capital' as it is defined here can be confusing because the word is not used in a financial or monetary sense and therefore does not refer to money. When we refer to capital as a production factor we mean all tangible things used to manufacture other goods. It is true that when they speak of 'capital', businessmen, bankers and accountants are often referring to money. However, money on its own cannot produce anything. Real capital (machinery, tools and other equipment) is an economic resource (ie production factor) but financial capital or money is not regarded as an economic resource.

Capital goods do not have an unlimited life. Wear and tear and technological obsolescence make it necessary to replace capital goods from time to time. The capital goods of a country that is progressing economically will increase over time, but nevertheless at any given time only a certain quantity will be available. Like all other factors of production, therefore, capital goods are scarce.

- *Entrepreneurial ability*, as we have already said, is a very special talent and it plays an extremely important role in the market economy. Entrepreneurs are people who have the ability to take the initiative and have the drive to combine the factors of production of capital, labour and natural resources in such a way that goods and services are produced. Entrepreneurs take the important business decisions that shape the course taken by an enterprise. Entrepreneurs are innovative in their thinking – they see new opportunities, introduce new products, use new production methods and also develop new management methods. The nature of their activities makes entrepreneurs risk takers. An entrepreneur cannot be certain in advance that his or her enterprise will be a success; in fact the reward for the entrepreneur's time, trouble and talents may be either high profits, or losses, or even bankruptcy.

  Because entrepreneurial ability is such a special talent, it is self-evident that true entrepreneurs are rare. It has often been cited as a major problem that South Africa has too few entrepreneurs.

The income that owners of factors of production can earn by using them for the production of goods and services is the following: *rent* (natural resources), *wages* and *salaries* (labour), *interest* (on capital) and *profit* (entrepreneurial ability).

Economic goods and free goods

An economic good is a good (product) which is produced at a cost by using scarce factors of production. Economic goods are therefore also known as scarce goods. Most goods are economic goods and are traded at a price. A free good is a good which is not scarce and therefore has no price. Air, sunshine and seawater at the coast are usually regarded as free goods. As a result of pollution, fresh air and clean seawater are not always so freely available, however, and in some cases they could even become a scarce product. The gifts of nature are sometimes regarded as free goods because they are not produced by man, but often time and trouble are required to make these gifts available to people. Minerals have to be mined at high cost and the storage and distribution of water is a very expensive process.

Economists are naturally interested in economic goods, that is goods where there is a scarcity problem. As indicated in the previous paragraph, this would include virtually the whole spectrum of goods and services.

Final goods and intermediary goods

Final goods are goods used by individuals, households and firms. In households, food and clothing are good examples of final goods. Intermediary goods, on the other hand, are goods which are sold for use as inputs in the production of other goods. It is characteristic of intermediary goods, therefore, that they have to be processed before being sold to the end-consumers. Steel would be an intermediary product for car manufacturers.

Final and intermediary goods will both be the subject of discussion in the further chapters of this book. In the chapter in which consumer behaviour is discussed we are obviously concerned with final goods. When it comes to the analysis of the behaviour of firms under various market conditions, the firms could be producers of either final goods or intermediary goods – the analysis would not be affected.

THE TASK OF THE ECONOMIC SYSTEM

Any society, from the most primitive to the most developed, has the constant problem of scarcity: the unlimited wants of society have to be supplied from restricted economic resources. Because resources are scarce, it is self-evident that they have to be used as efficiently as possible. In the process of meeting the wants and needs of society as far as possible, answers to the following three important questions have to be obtained:

- What should be produced?
- How should it be produced?
- For whom should it be produced?

We shall now examine each of these questions and also consider how the price mechanism in a market economy succeeds in solving them. (We mentioned in the introduction that an important characteristic of a market economy is that government allows individuals and firms to take their own economic decisions.)

What

What should be produced means what goods and services, and what quantities of those goods and services, should be produced. Because no society is able to produce all the goods and services for which there is a need, choices have to be made as to which goods and services should be produced and which should not. In a market economy these important issues are decided by the price mechanism. That is to say, only those goods and services will be produced for which consumers are able and prepared to pay a price which is at least high enough to cover all production costs. For instance, vehicle manufacturers would not manufacture cars which cost R1m if there was no market for them. Consumers can prompt firms to manufacture more of a certain product by being willing to pay a higher price. On the other hand, a reduction in the price which consumers are prepared to pay for a product usually means that less of that product will be produced. For example, a rise in the price of chickens and a drop in the milk price would be a sign (signal) to farmers to produce more poultry and less milk.

How *How it should be produced* refers to the way economic resources are combined to produce the goods and services consumers want. Questions such as the following must be answered: Should clothing (or any other product) be produced by using a lot of capital and a small amount of labour in the production process, or should a lot of labour and a small amount of capital be used? Because resources are scarce, it is important that whatever resources are available should be used as efficiently as possible. In a market economy the way in which the economic resources are combined in the production process is determined by the price mechanism. The prices of resources are a reflection of their relative scarcity and firms combine the economic resources they use in such a way that costs are kept to a minimum. By doing so firms are able to utilise resources in the most efficient and productive manner possible in order to produce the goods which society most desires and values. If the price of a resource rises, firms try to use less of it in the production process and to replace it with cheaper resources in order to keep their production costs as low as possible. For example, an increase in minimum wages would encourage firms to mechanise and use machinery instead of labour.

For whom *For whom should goods be produced?* This refers to the way in which the output (production) is distributed among the members of the community. This is also decided by the price mechanism. Income is the source of expenditure and consumers 'vote' for what they want by expending their income on particular goods and services. Individuals who have unusual skills or who possess a larger quantity of other economic resources will earn higher incomes and be able to pay more for products. Such individuals will therefore have a greater ability to prompt firms to produce more of the products they want. Their greater financial clout enables them to ensure that more of their wants are satisfied. For example, in a society more goods and services are produced for the average actuary than for the average clerk, simply because actuaries earn far more than clerks.

The pure market system is not without defects – for example it contains a tendency towards inequality and instability. Adjustments sometimes have to be made to compensate for the defects and the government has to take responsibility for such adjustments. But on the whole the market mechanism is a remarkable economic instrument. It is almost incredible that a complicated economic system can function fairly smoothly without any agency to coordinate the millions of disparate decisions which are taken daily by the various participants. Further attention is given in Chapter 2 to the operation of the market mechanism.

THE ECONOMIC CIRCULAR FLOW

We mentioned previously that microeconomics focuses on the actions of individual decision-making units in the economy; these decision-making units can be divided into two broad categories, namely households (ie consumers) and firms.

Interaction There is a continuous interaction between households and firms, an interaction that is so important that it forms the core of the market economy. Two kinds of markets play an important part in this interaction: the market for factors of production and the market for goods and services (see Fig 1-1). The part played by these two kinds of markets can be explained as follows: households are the owners of factors of production which are required by firms to produce goods and services. The households offer these factors of production to firms in the market for factors of production; in exchange the households receive payment (wages and salaries, rent, interest and profits) from the firms. The firms combine the factors of production to produce goods and services which are then sold to households on the market for consumer goods. The income from the households is also the expenditure of the firms on production. The expenditure of the households on goods and services equates to the income of the firms.

This is the origin of a circular flow in the economy between households and firms. On the one hand there is a flow of goods and services from firms to households via the goods market, with a monetary flow in the opposite direction. On the other hand there is a flow of factors of production from households to firms via the factor market, with a monetary flow in the opposite direction.

This explanation, which is illustrated in Figure 1-1, is a much simplified representation of the way a country's economy works, but it is important because it gives us an idea of how the various pieces of the economic jigsaw fit together. It therefore also gives us a general impression of the framework within which microeconomic activities take place. In this course we will concentrate on an analysis of the goods market, the behaviour of households (consumers) and the way firms operate under different market conditions. The market for factors of production (eg labour) is studied in other courses and has therefore been omitted here.

ECONOMIC MODELS

The most important aim of microeconomic theory is to explain and predict the economic behaviour of individual consumers and firms, and the operation of markets, with a view to policy making. It is no easy task because in any large economy there are millions of separate decision-making units, each making individual decisions. How is it possible to make any sense out of such a complicated situation? The answer is that we approach the study of economics by using models. A model can be regarded as the formal representation of a theory. The use of models is not confined to economics; models are used in other disciplines as well. Models are simplifications or abstractions of reality – their purpose is to make sense of an extremely complicated world by emphasising only the most important factors, while omitting all unimportant details. Stephen Hawking, the world-famous theoretical physicist, said: 'A theory is a good theory if it satisfies two requirements: It must accurately describe a large class of observations on the basis of a model that contains only a few arbitrary elements, and it must make definite predictions about the results of future observations.' A road-map is a good example of a simple model. If you were driving from Messina to Cape Town the last thing you would want is a realistic picture of the route, showing every turn-off, stream, koppie and farmhouse. That kind of map would be so confusing (and big) that it would be totally impractical. What you would need is a map that is a simplification of reality and shows only the main routes, towns and cities.

Models

Figure 1-1

The economic circular flow diagram

This illustrates the flow of goods and services from firms to households, and the flow of factors of production from households to firms. In each case there is a monetary flow in the opposite direction.

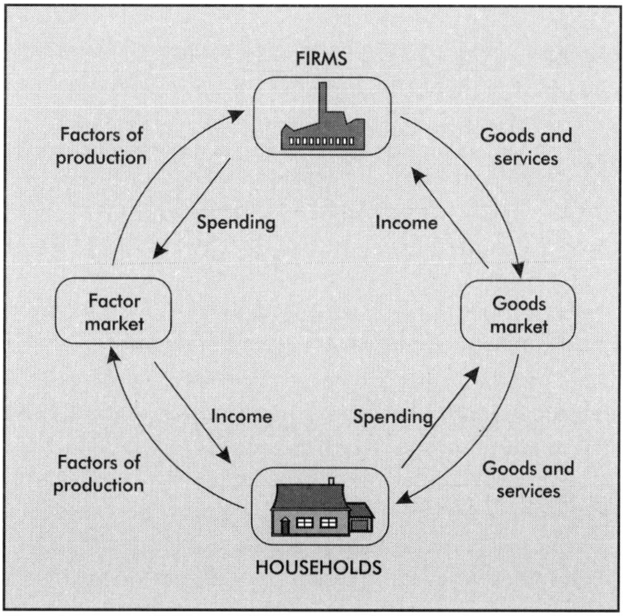

A model consists of a number of assumptions which can be used to draw conclusions (or make predictions). Suppose an astronomer wanted to build a model of our solar system. He could represent each of the planets as a dot on a sheet of paper, show their orbits as elliptical circles, and make the assumption that their positions relative to the sun will change in accordance with certain mathematical equations. With the aid of a model of this kind it is possible to predict events such as solar eclipses. We have already mentioned that, in order to be useful, a model should be a simplification of reality. The assumptions should obviously be related to the purpose for which the model will be used, but those assumptions need not necessarily reflect reality exactly in all respects. In the example of the astronomer's model the fact that planets are not dots would make no difference. What is more, if the mathematical equations representing the movements of the planets were not one hundred per cent correct it would not make much difference either, provided the model was able to predict events so reliably that it was still useful despite any inaccuracies.

In both the social and the natural sciences models based on simplified (and sometimes idealised) conditions have very useful applications. The assumptions sometimes relate to variables that cannot even be directly measured, such as the concept of 'utility' in economics. That it cannot be measured does not mean that such a variable has no function or application. Its value is that it could lead to the development of models that are powerful and able to produce accurate predictions.

A theory or model is usually the result of an observation made in society. We could make the observation, for example, that consumers generally buy less of a product when the price rises. Before this kind of theory about consumer demand can be accepted, however, we have to test it in practice. We would have to make sure beyond all doubt that individuals in different environments, over different periods of time, and as a group do buy less of a product when the price rises. Only after numerous successful tests have been carried out and in the absence of contradictory results, could the theory be accepted. It could then be used in further analyses to explain and predict consumer behaviour. But if the test results were to contradict the model, it would have to be rejected and a new model formulated.

It is understandable that all sciences make attempts to formulate generally acceptable models. A model that is able to predict the general behaviour of consumers in the economy is of more value than one that can only predict the behaviour of Sarah Smith or John Jones. Economists in particular are interested in models that are generally applicable to consumers, firms, etc. However, the more generally applicable a model is, the more difficult it becomes to make accurate predictions. It is relatively easy to design a model that does not have a general application. For example, if we were to study a specific person's eating habits it should be possible to design a model that would predict what he would have for breakfast fairly accurately. It would be far more difficult, however, to design a model that would be able to predict with the same degree of accuracy the choice of any kind of breakfast food by any consumer in the economy.

Models (and theories) can be expressed by means of mathematical symbols and equations. They can also be explained in words (orally or in writing). Graphs or numerical tables are also sometimes used to explain models. In this course we mainly use graphs and verbal explanations to describe the behaviour of consumers and firms and their interaction in the various markets. The models used are generally those that have repeatedly been proved to be correct. In a course on microeconomics we are not so much concerned with testing theories and models as with their presentation, usefulness and applications.

OTHER IMPORTANT CONCEPTS

Ceteris paribus

Economists, like other scientists, use the *ceteris paribus* assumption when designing models. This means that economists assume that all variables other then the one they are specifically dealing with will remain unchanged. *Ceteris paribus* is a Latin expression which means 'all other things being equal'. This technique makes it easier to design economic theories and models because it isolates the relationship that is being studied. Suppose an economist wants to determine the relationship between the price of product A and the quantity of product A that is sold. It makes the investigation easier if the assumption is made that only the price of product A has changed, while all the other factors that could influence the sales of A (eg the price of other goods, consumer incomes and tastes) have remained constant. The economist is then able to concentrate on the relationship between price and sales, without other variables playing a part. In the short term the *ceteris paribus* assumption is a reasonable one. However, the longer the period in question, the more difficult it is to leave other factors out of account. To enable economists to make fairly accurate predictions, they have to know what factors have been taken as constant, why this has been done, and over what period of time the *ceteris paribus* assumption will be applied.

Equilibrium

The concept of equilibrium plays an important part in economic theory and is one you will encounter frequently in any book on microeconomics. Equilibrium refers to a situation which, once it has been reached, tends to persist. It therefore refers to a situation in which there is no reason for any of the participants to alter his or her behaviour. Equilibrium can also be described as a situation in which all opposing forces are in balance. This does not mean that the situation of equilibrium will *never* change, but that there is a reluctance to change. If the amount of a product that consumers are willing to buy is exactly equal to the amount producers are offering on the market, we say that supply and demand are in equilibrium. If a consumer is in a position where he or she is obtaining maximum utility, we say the consumer is in equilibrium. When a firm is in a situation where it is maximising profit, the firm is in equilibrium.

Prices

Prices play an extremely important role in economics. In macroeconomics absolute prices (in rands and cents) are important because of the phenomenon of inflation. In microeconomics relative prices (ie the relationship between the price in question and the price of other products) are important. Relative prices also play an important role in the market system because individuals react to changes in relative prices rather than absolute prices. When the relative price of a product rises, it is an indication for consumers and suppliers that the product in question has become relatively scarcer. Relative prices are therefore also the signals that regulate the allocation of resources. This happens in the following way: if the relative price of a product rises, the producers would probably see in the price rise the possibility of making bigger profits and in time more resources would be channelled into the production of that particular product. The 'message' of relative scarcities which is conveyed by the relative prices therefore influences the allocation of resources. This forms one of the cornerstones of the market system.

Rational individuals

It is assumed in economic theory that all individuals will behave rationally, that is to say that they will always try to see that they are as well off as possible, given the limitations to which their actions are subject. In microeconomics this means that consumers will always try to maximise their utility, and entrepreneurs to maximise their profits. The actions of individuals are taken to be logical and reasoned in all instances. One could say that people behave consistently and 'according to the dictates of common sense'.

Male or female?

Because of the emphasis placed on the equality of the sexes, you will often find that books such as this one contain sentences such as: 'The consumer is in equilibrium if *he or she* is in a position…' or: 'The producer could, if *he or she* wished…' The continuous use of 'he or she' can become a real irritation. While 'he or she' is used quite frequently in this book, we usually speak simply of 'he'. This is merely for practical reasons and is in no way intended to give offence to women.

IMPORTANT CONCEPTS

- Microeconomics
- Macroeconomics
- Scarcity problem
- Unlimited wants
- Limited resources
- Economic goods and free goods
- Final goods and intermediary goods
- Task of the economic system
- Circular flow diagram
- Economic models
- *Ceteris paribus*
- Equilibrium
- Rational individuals

QUESTIONS

(1) Explain the difference between microeconomics and macroeconomics. (5)

(2) Define microeconomics. (3)

(3) Explain the task that the economic system in a country performs with regard to the following questions: How, what and for whom must goods be produced? (6)

(4) Draw the circular flow diagram and use it to explain how the economic process works. (10)

(5) Explain in your own words what is meant by an 'economic' model. (8)

2

DEMAND AND SUPPLY

The demand and supply model forms the corner-stone of microeconomic analysis. Sir Arthur Lewis, winner of the Nobel Prize for economics in 1979, went so far as to say that there are few things in economics that cannot be explained by means of demand and supply. The interaction between the forces of demand and supply occurs in numerous markets for goods and services in an economy; this interaction (also known as the market mechanism) forms the central theme of the chapter. Markets play a central role in the determination of prices in a free market economy; consequently they also determine the way in which the factors of production are employed (they indicate for which goods there is significant demand). The chapter begins by explaining exactly what is meant by a market. Then attention is given to the demand side of the market where concepts such as the market demand curve and elasticity are discussed. This will be followed by a discussion of the supply side. The interaction between market demand and market supply and the determination of the equilibrium price and equilibrium quantity of a product will also be studied. Finally, the way in which the equilibrium price and the equilibrium quantity of a product are affected by changes in the demand for and supply of the product will be determined. The demand and supply model (ie the market model) is applicable over a wide field and a sound knowledge of its workings is imperative for someone interested in economics.

After you have studied this chapter, you will be able to

- explain how market demand and market supply are determined
- explain how the equilibrium price comes into being
- describe the effect of changes in demand and supply
- calculate price elasticity of demand and supply by means of formulae
- calculate elasticity using Marshall's method
- explain the relationship between price elasticity and revenue
- calculate income elasticity of demand by means of formulae
- calculate cross elasticity of demand by means of formulae

MARKETS

Because markets play a vital role in determining prices it is important to investigate from the outset exactly what is meant by a market. The concept is not as obvious as it may sound, since markets are often ill defined in terms of geographical space or physical appearance. One definition of a market is that it comprises individuals or groups who come into contact with one another with the aim of buying or selling. Stated more formally: a market is an institution or mechanism which brings together buyers (demanders) and sellers (suppliers) of goods and services. This does not necessarily mean that every person in a market has to be in contact with every other person – a person or a firm can be part of a market even if contact is limited to a section of the other individuals or firms in the market.

Markets

Markets vary considerably in terms of size and operation. The local vegetable or flower market, the filling station on the corner, the kiosk where instant food is sold, a farm stall – these are all examples of markets. The Johannesburg Stock Exchange is an example of a highly sophisticated market where buyers and sellers of shares and equities from all over the world come into contact with one another. Auctioneers also bring together potential buyers and sellers of, inter alia, second-hand goods, works of art and fixed property. Personnel agents bring work seekers and employers into contact with each other. All these examples where buyers and sellers come into contact with each other represent markets. As you can see, some markets are local, others are national, or even international in nature. For some household goods all the consumers of the good will be in the same geographical area, for example within the borders of a town or country. For other goods, for example Van Gogh paintings, only a few collectors, dealers and museums which are spread across the globe form the market. In principle all markets consist of buyers and sellers, although middlemen such as agents and brokers may also form part of the market. Mostly it is the seller who proposes the price of a product, but there may be exceptions.

The assumption of perfect competition

In this chapter we generally accept that a market consists of a large number of buyers and sellers and that none of them has the ability to significantly influence the price. Stated more formally: we assume that markets are perfectly competitive, which means that no individual buyer or seller can influence the price (ie only the interaction between demand and supply determines the market price), products are homogeneous (identical), factors of production are perfectly mobile and buyers and sellers have perfect knowledge about market conditions. In later chapters these assumptions of perfect competition will be relaxed.

THE DEMAND SIDE OF THE MARKET

The market demand curve

The market for any given product has a demand side and a supply side. The demand side can be depicted by means of a table which shows the quantity of the product that will be bought at various prices. Suppose, for example, that the market demand for frozen fish in an area (eg a province) is as depicted in Table 2-1 on a particular day. (The method used for determining the demand curve using the individual demand curves of all the participants in the market is explained in Box 2-1.)

Table 2-1
Market demand for frozen fish

Price per kilogram (Rand)	Quantity demanded ('000 kg per day)
8	0
7	1
6	2
5	3
4	4
3	5
2	6
1	7
0	8

Law of demand

According to Table 2-1 (the figures are imaginary, but are merely used for illustration) no frozen fish will be demanded at a price of R8 per kilogram. At R7 per kilogram 1 000 kilograms will be demanded on that particular day. At R6 per kilogram 2 000 kilograms will be demanded, etc. The table reflects the *law of demand* which states that *the higher the price of a product the lower the quantity demanded (or the lower the price of a product the higher the quantity demanded) provided that all other things remain constant (ceteris paribus).*

Another way of representing the information in Table 2-1 is by a demand curve on a graph. Price in Rand (per kilogram) is depicted on the vertical axis and the quantity per day on the horizontal axis. Figure 2-1 provides a graphical representation of the market demand for frozen fish given in Table 2-1.

Figure 2–1

The market demand curve

It is obtained by horizontally adding all the individual demand curves of consumers comprising the market. (See Box 2–1.)

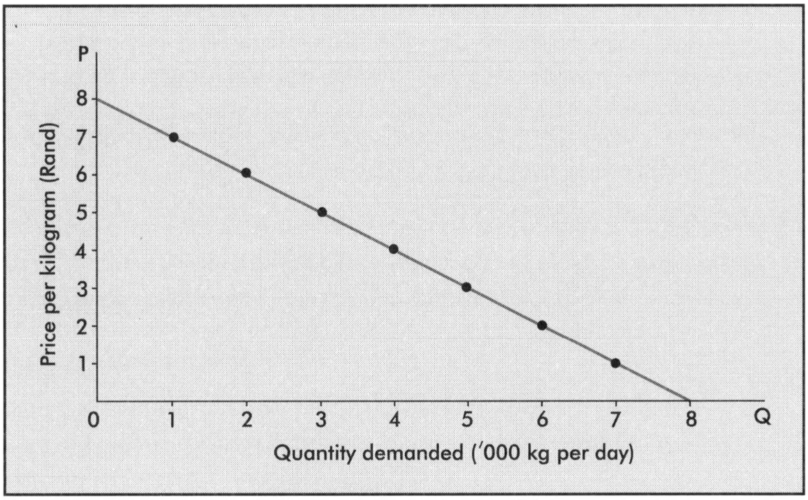

Box 2–1

MARKET DEMAND CURVE

The market demand curve for a specific product is obtained by adding horizontally all the individual demand curves which constitute the market.

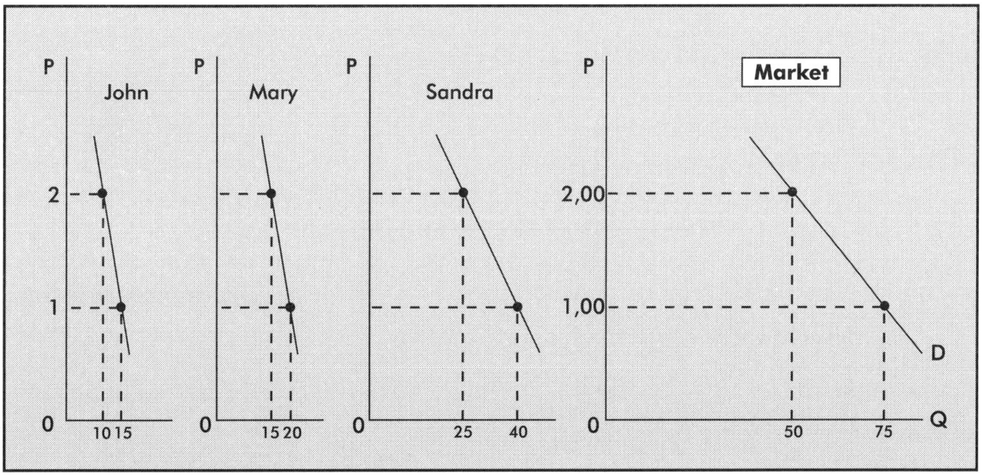

Refer to the above figure. Suppose that the market consists of only three consumers, namely John, Mary and Sandra, and that the individual demand curves for a certain product are the ones shown above. At a price of R2 the quantity demanded by the whole market will be 50 units (that is 10 + 15 + 25). At a price of R1 the total quantity demanded will be equal to 75 units (that is 15 + 20 + 40). This information is depicted or the right side of the figure. The market demand curve is thus a horizontal summation of the individual demand curves making up the market.

The market supply curve is arrived at in a similar manner – that is to say by adding together all the individual supply curves which make up the market.

In this course this technique of horizontal summation is often used – therefore ensure that you understand it. Note that the scale of the figure representing the market must be greater than the one in which John's, Mary's and Sandra's individual demand curves appear.

Two important properties of the demand curve illustrated in Figure 2-1 must be highlighted. First, the market demand curve is downward sloping, in other words the quantity of frozen fish demanded increases as the price decreases. This is true of the demand curves of most products – almost always the demand curve slopes downwards from left to right. (In the following chapter you will come across the exception to the rule, but at this stage you do not have to worry about it.) Second, the market demand curve in Figure 2-1 refers to a specific time period – in our example it is a day. It is important to note that any demand curve refers to a certain time period (day, month, year) and that the length of the period can influence the shape and position of the demand curve.

Shift of demand curve

There are various other factors that can have an important influence on the position of the demand curve and they can cause the demand curve to move to the left or to the right. The tastes of consumers are one of the factors that can influence the position of the market demand curve. If consumers develop an increasing preference for a product, the demand curve will shift to the right – this means that consumers will want to buy more at each price (see Fig 2-2). On the other hand, if consumers' preferences for a product decline, the market demand curve will shift to the left, since consumers will be willing to buy less at each price. This is reflected in Figure 2-3. (Naturally the usual *ceteris paribus* principle applies, that is to say that here only consumers' tastes change whereas all other factors remain constant. In the rest of the discussion the *ceteris paribus* principle also applies.)

Another factor that can influence the position of the market demand curve for a product is the income level of consumers. For some products the market demand curve shifts to the right when income per capita increases, whereas for other products the market demand curve shifts to the left when income per capita increases. Attention will be paid to this in the next chapter. It is important at this stage to know that changes in per capita income can affect the demand curve.

Figure 2-2

An increase in market demand

If the demand for a product increases, the market demand curve shifts to the right.

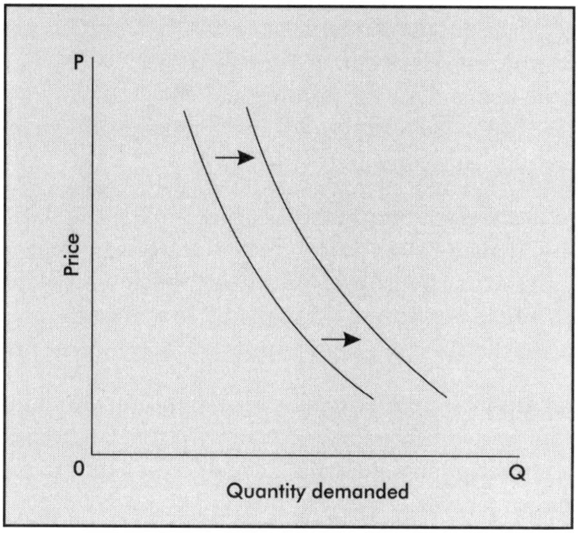

Figure 2-3

A decrease in market demand

If the demand for a product decreases, the market demand curve shifts to the left.

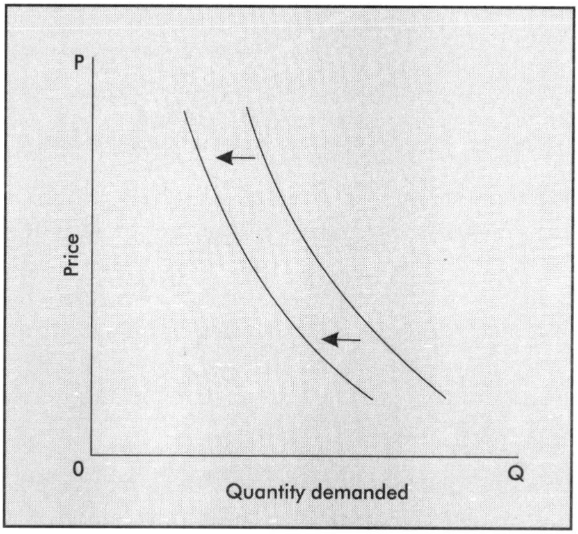

A further factor that can influence the position of a market demand curve is the price level of other goods. For example, because chicken is a substitute for beef, the demand for chicken, to a certain extent, will be influenced by the price of beef. If beef becomes very expensive and consumers do not expect the price to decrease and chicken is cheaper, there will be an increased demand for it – this will result in the market demand curve for chicken shifting to the right. The opposite of course can also occur.

The size of the population which is served by a certain product is also an important determinant of the demand for the product. The larger the population the greater the demand for the product and *vice versa.* An increase in the population will therefore cause a rightward movement of the demand curve if all other factors remain unchanged.

If there is a redistribution of income among the various households in an economy, demand can also be affected. If, for example, income is redistributed from high income households to low income households, then the demand for a product which is primarily bought by low income households will increase, whereas the demand for goods bought by high income households will decrease.

Expectations play an important role in economic decision making. If consumers expect the price of a product to become relatively cheaper, they will be inclined to reduce their present demand and prefer (if other factors remain constant) to wait until such time as they can buy more at a lower price. Similarly, expected price increases can lead to an increase in present demand.

These factors can result in a movement of the demand curve to the left or to the right. There may be other factors, but those discussed above are the most important,

It is now important to be able to distinguish between a shift of the demand curve and a movement along the curve.

A shift of a demand curve and a movement along a demand curve

In the previous paragraphs it seemed as if changes in non-price factors such as tastes, income levels, the prices of other goods and the size of the population could result in a shift of the demand curve. (They are called non-price factors because they are determinants of demand other than price.) Such a movement can be to the left or to the right, depending on the circumstances. A shift to the right means that demand has increased and more will be demanded at every price; a shift to the left means that demand has decreased and less will be demanded at every price.

In contrast to the above, any change in the price of a product would result in a mere movement along the demand curve and a change in the quantity demanded. In Figure 2-1 it can be seen that if the price of frozen fish drops from R7 per kilogram to R6 per kilogram, the quantity demanded increases from 1 000 kilograms to 2 000 kilograms. Consumers will therefore move along the demand curve from the original price-quantity combination to a new price-quantity combination, but the demand curve will not shift.

The differentiation between a shift of the demand curve and a movement along the demand curve is important. Ensure that you understand the difference.

Price elasticity of demand

The shape of demand curves for products differ from one product to another and from one market to another. It is particularly important to note that market demand curves also differ in terms of the sensitivity of the quantity demanded to price. For some goods a relatively small price change will result in a relatively large change in the quantity demanded, whereas with other goods a relatively large change in price will only lead to a relatively small change in the quantity demanded. To indicate the sensitivity of the quantity demanded to a change in price, economists use a measurement known as the price elasticity of demand.

Demand elasticity

The price elasticity of demand (abbreviated to demand elasticity) is defined as the percentage change in the quantity demanded caused by a 1 per cent change in price.

To illustrate, let us assume that a 1 per cent drop in the price of petrol results in a 1,2 per cent increase in the quantity of petrol demanded. According to our definition the price elasticity of demand for petrol is 1,2. It is common practice to reflect the price elasticity as a positive number, although the price change is negative and the change in the quantity demanded is positive. The price elasticity of demand generally changes from one point to the next along a demand curve. For example, the price elasticity of demand may be higher if the price of petrol is very high. The price elasticity of demand may also vary from one market to the next. In Canada the price elasticity of petrol will be different from that in, for example, South Africa.

An important factor that must be taken into account is that the price elasticity of demand is expressed in terms of relative changes (that is to say percentage changes) in the price and quantity demanded – and not absolute changes. The reason is that absolute changes in prices are expressed in money units (rand, dollar, etc) and absolute changes in quantity are expressed in physical units (kilograms, litres, metres, etc). If percentage changes are used, the units in which prices and quantities are measured do not affect the results.

A mistake which is often made is simply to equate price elasticity with the slope of the demand curve – the measurements which are used on the axes can result in the demand curve appearing to be elastic when it may really be inelastic. In addition, the elasticity of a linear demand curve varies from one point to another, as explained in Box 2-2. It is always safer to calculate the elasticity before arriving at any conclusions about price sensitivity. (See Appendix 1 for the situation in which two demand curves intersect each other, which allows their elasticities to be compared.)

Assume we have a market demand schedule (Table 2-1 is an example of one) which depicts the quantity demanded of a product at different prices. How is the elasticity of demand calculated? Let ΔP represent a very small change (in percentage terms) in the price of a product whereas ΔQ_d depicts the change in the quantity demanded (as a result of the change in price.) The formula used to calculate the price elasticity of demand at a point on a demand curve (known as point elasticity of demand in its abbreviated form) is

$$e_d = \frac{\text{percentage change in the quantity demanded}}{\text{percentage change in the price}}$$

$$= \frac{\Delta Q_d}{Q_d} \div \frac{\Delta P}{P}$$

A minus sign should actually be on the right-hand side of the above figure but, as has already been mentioned, it is common practice to reflect elasticity as a positive number – economists are more interested in its absolute value. The practice is therefore followed here also.

Table 2-2 can serve as an example where the data reflects small percentage changes in the price and quantity of a product.

Table 2-2
Quantity demanded at different prices
(small percentage changes in price)

Price (Rand per unit)	Quantity demanded (number of units)
99	1 005
100	1 000
101	995

Should we wish to calculate the price elasticity of demand in the above table if the price increases from R99 to R100, the following result will be obtained (if the minus sign is omitted):

$$e_d = \frac{\Delta Q_d}{Q_d} \div \frac{\Delta P}{P}$$

$$= \frac{5}{1\,005} \div \frac{1}{99}$$

$$= 0{,}49$$

In the above diagram we assumed P to be R99 and Q_d 1 005. If we allow the price to drop from R100 to R99 and therefore take P to be R100 and Q_d to be 1 000 we get almost the same result, namely:

$$e_d = \frac{\Delta Q_d}{Q_d} \div \frac{\Delta P}{P}$$
$$= \frac{5}{1\,000} \div \frac{1}{100}$$
$$= 0{,}5$$

In the above example the price change was very small in percentage terms and for all practical purposes we arrived at the same answer. If, however, we have a table reflecting a large percentage change in price and the percentage change in the quantity demanded is also large, then the answers will vary considerably depending on which values of P and Q_d are used. Take, for example, the demand schedule shown in Table 2-3.

Table 2-3

Quantity demanded at different prices

(large percentage changes in price)

Price (Rand per unit)	Quantity demanded (number of units)
7	1 000
6	2 000
5	3 000

Suppose that the price decreases from R7 to R5 and we take P to be R7 and Q_d to be 1 000. The price elasticity of demand is then:

$$e_d = \frac{\Delta Q_d}{Q_d} \div \frac{\Delta P}{P}$$
$$= \frac{2\,000}{1\,000} \div \frac{2}{7}$$
$$= 7$$

If we do the opposite, namely allow the price to change from R5 to R7 and we therefore take P to be R5 and Q_d to be 3 000, then the price elasticity of demand will be as follows:

$$e_d = \frac{\Delta Q_d}{Q_d} \div \frac{\Delta P}{P}$$
$$= \frac{2\,000}{3\,000} \div \frac{2}{5}$$
$$= 1{,}67$$

The difference between the last two answers is huge. In a case such as this, where the price change is proportionately large, it is advisable to use another method, namely to calculate the arc elasticity of demand. When the arc elasticity of demand is calculated the average values of P and Q_d are used as shown in the following formula:

$$e_d = \frac{\Delta Q_d}{(Q_{d1} + Q_{d2}) / 2} \div \frac{\Delta P}{(P_1 + P_2) / 2}$$

$$= \frac{\Delta Q_d(P_1 + P_2)}{\Delta P(Q_{d1} + Q_{d2})}$$

where P_1 and Q_{d1} are the original values of price and quantity and P_2 and Q_{d2} are the second set of values. If we apply this adapted formula for a price change from R7 to R5 (or *vice versa*) we get:

$$e_d = \frac{2\,000\ (12)}{2\ (4\,000)}$$

$$= 3$$

What the above method actually amounts to is that the elasticity is calculated halfway between the two prices (R7 and R5).

Box 2-2

MARSHALL'S METHOD

Besides using formulae there is another handy method of calculating elasticity if the demand curve is a straight line which touches both the vertical and horizontal axes. This method was developed by the British economist Alfred Marshall (1842–1924), who incidentally also coined the term 'price elasticity of demand'. Refer to the following diagram. Marshall showed that the price elasticity of demand can be determined at a point such as B by calculating the ratio BE/AB. To determine the elasticity at a point such as D the ratio DE/AD is calculated. It is not even necessary to calculate the distances on the demand curve, because the elasticity coefficient e_d can also be determined by using the corresponding measurements on the price axis or the quantity axis. At B the elasticity coefficient is therefore BE/AB or H0/AH (if the price axis is used) which works out to be 8/2 = 4. If we calculate e_d at B by using the quantity axis, then it works out to be IE/0I which amounts to 80/20 = 4 which is the same as the previous answer.

By using the same method we can calculate the elasticity coefficient at point D. The following result is obtained by using the quantity axis: KE/0K = 20/80 = 0,25. If we were to use the price axis we would arrive at the same answer, namely 0F/AF = 2/8 = 0,25.

If we calculate the elasticity coefficient at C which is the midpoint of the demand curve the result is $e_d = 1$ (that is, JE/0J = 50/50 = 1 or 0G/AG = 1).

The above results illustrate an important fact, namely that the elasticity coefficient of a linear demand curve is greater than 1 above the midpoint and less than 1 below the midpoint. At exactly the midpoint the coefficient is equal to 1. This general rule does not apply to demand curves which are not linear (in other words are not straight lines).

Marshall's method can also be used to calculate the elasticity coefficient at any point along a non-linear demand curve. The coefficient can be obtained by drawing a tangent to the demand curve at the point at issue and by using the same technique as the one above.

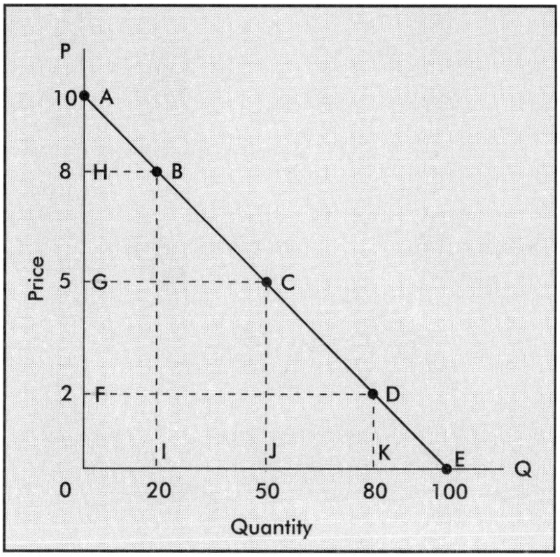

Price elasticity and total revenue (or expenditure)

Economists say that the demand for a product is elastic if the demand elasticity is greater than 1. If the demand elasticity is less than 1, demand is price inelastic. If the demand elasticity is equal to 1, then unitary elasticity is said to apply. (See Appendix 2 for two more cases of elasticity.)

Important decisions are made in the business world as well as in political circles based on the price elasticity of demand. One reason is that the price elasticity of demand determines whether a change in the price of a product will result in an increase or a decrease in the total expenditure on the product. This is of utmost importance for firms – or for the authorities who are sometimes in the same position – who need to make decisions as to whether they should increase or decrease the price of their products.

Which aspects of price elasticity should a firm take into account when considering a price change? To illustrate how the elasticity of demand will influence the spending of consumers (and in so doing the income of the firm or the government) on a product, we will use the information supplied in Table 2-4. In the table the different quantities demanded of a product are illustrated for prices that vary between R0 and R8. The total revenue depicted is merely the price multiplied by the quantity demanded – if the price is R8, none of the product is sold and the total revenue is therefore also zero. At a price of R7 the number of units sold is 1 000 and the total revenue is R7 000 (that is R7 × 1 000) etc.

Table 2-4
Price, quantity demanded and total revenue

Price per kilogram (P_x in Rand)	Quantity demanded (Q_x per day)	Total revenue ($P_x \times Q_x$)
8	0	0
7	1 000	7 000
6	2 000	12 000
5	3 000	15 000
4	4 000	16 000
3	5 000	15 000
2	6 000	12 000
1	7 000	7 000
0	8 000	0

The information in Table 2-4 is also provided in Figure 2-4. In Figure 2-4 the elasticity of the demand curve is depicted according to the calculations which were done in Box 2-2: $e_d = 1$ exactly at the midpoint, below the midpoint e_d is less than 1 and above the midpoint e_d is greater than 1. Total revenue (P × Q) is also shown in the bottom section of the figure. The information reflected in the bottom section of Figure 2-4 is very important. Assume that the demand for a certain product of a firm is price elastic, that is to say it is greater than 1 – which also means that the firm finds itself with a price somewhere along the top half of the demand curve in Figure 2-4. If the firm reduces its price in the elastic section of the demand curve from, say, R7 to R6, the total revenue of the firm will increase from R7 000 to R12 000, as depicted in the bottom section of the diagram (the opposite will also apply: a price increase leads to a decrease in revenue). In fact, price decreases will lead to increases in total revenue up to the midpoint of the demand curve in Figure 2-4 where $e_d = 1$. On the other hand, if the firm reduces the price of a product in the inelastic range of the demand curve from, say, R2 to R1, the total revenue will decrease from R12 000 to R7 000, as depicted in the bottom section of the diagram (once again the opposite also applies).

Elastic demand

Stated more generally, we can say that if the demand for a product is elastic, then if the price is reduced, the percentage increase in the quantity demanded will be greater than the percentage decrease in the price (this follows from the definition of elasticity of demand). Consequently a price decrease will lead to an increase in the revenue of a firm (ie expenditure by consumers) whereas a price increase will lead to a decrease in revenue.

Inelastic demand

On the other hand, if the demand for a product is inelastic, then if the price is reduced, the percentage increase in the quantity demanded will be less than the percentage decrease in price (this once again follows from the definition of price elasticity of demand). Therefore a price decrease will lead to a decrease in the revenue of the firm, while a price increase will lead to an increase in revenue.

It is easy to understand that if a firm wishes to change the price of its product it is of utmost importance to know whether the demand for the product is elastic or inelastic. If the demand is elastic, a price increase can, for example, have serious negative consequences on total revenue (income), whereas with an inelastic demand a price increase would lead to an increase in revenue. Firms often know from experience whether the demand for their product is elastic or inelastic. Numerous studies have also been carried out to calculate elasticity – these figures can serve as a guideline for firms. In Box 2-3 a table with this type of information is provided. Study it carefully.

To conclude this section: if the demand curve is a rectangular hyperbole, then $e_d = 1$ at any point along the curve. In such a situation, that is to say when unitary elasticity applies, price increases or decreases will not affect total revenue. This means that firms which are confronted with this type of demand curve cannot increase or decrease their total revenue by increasing or decreasing the price of the product. In both cases the percentage change in price will be offset exactly by the percentage change in the quantity demanded (which will be in the opposite direction to the price change). Total revenue (P × Q) will therefore remain unchanged. Understandably this is a highly exceptional instance.

Figure 2–4

The relationship between the price elasticity of demand and total revenue (income)

When demand is elastic, a price drop leads to an increase in TR (total revenue) and a price rise to a decrease in TR. When demand is inelastic, a price decrease leads to a decrease in TR and a price increase to an increase in TR. This applies for all linear demand curves with a negative slope.

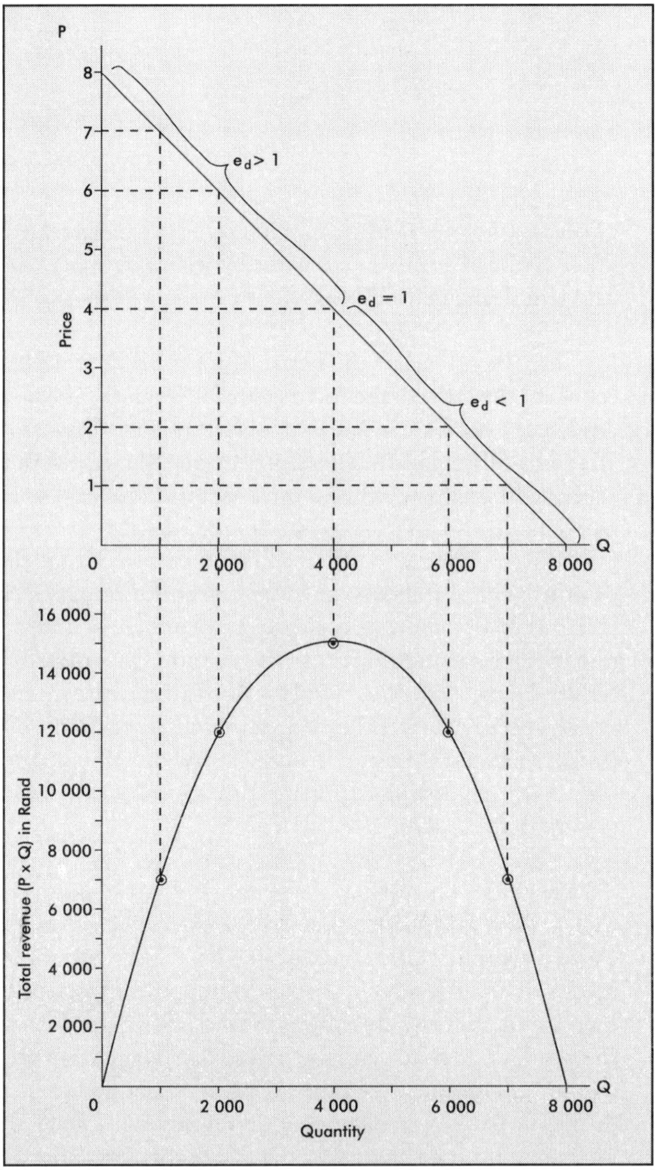

Box 2-3

Approximate price elasticities of demand for selected products

(The figures apply to the USA)

Product	Price elasticity
Electricity	1,20
Beef	0,92
Sugar	0,31
Wheat	0,08
Potatoes	0,31
Fish	2,20
Tyres	1,20
Movie tickets	3,70

Source: E Mansfield, 1991, *Microeconomics*, Seventh edition, New York: Norton.

Other demand elasticities

The quantity of a product demanded does not depend only on the price of the product. It is therefore also possible to calculate other demand elasticities. In this section attention is briefly paid to two such demand elasticities, namely the *income elasticity of demand* and the *cross elasticity of demand.*

Income elasticity of demand

The income of consumers also has an important influence on the quantity of a product demanded. Should consumers' income increase, the quantity demanded will usually increase (if all other things remain constant). The question is by how much will it change relative to the change in income? The *income elasticity of demand* (e_y) measures the sensitivity of the quantity demanded to changes in income. By applying the general definition of elasticity, it can be defined as the percentage change in the quantity demanded as a result of a 1 per cent change in consumers' income, that is to say

$$e_y = \frac{\text{percentage change in the quantity demanded}}{\text{percentage change in consumers' income}}$$

The income elasticity of demand can be positive or negative. If the increase in income is accompanied by an increase in the quantity demanded of the product concerned, then the income elasticity of demand is positive (or a decrease in income is accompanied by a decrease in the quantity demanded). Goods with a *positive income elasticity* of demand are referred to as *normal goods.* A negative income elasticity of demand implies that an increase in income will lead to a decrease in the quantity demanded of the product concerned (or that a decrease in income would lead to an increase in demand). Goods with a *negative income elasticity of demand* are referred to as *inferior goods*. Paraffin and candles for example, are regarded as inferior goods among low income households in South Africa (refer to Box 2-4).

Normal goods are subdivided into luxury goods and necessities. If the *income elasticity is greater than one,* that is to say when the percentage change in quantity demanded is greater than the percentage change in income, the product can be classified as a *luxury product*. Furniture and electrical appliances are typical examples. If the elasticity of demand is *positive but less than one*, that is to say, when the percentage change in the quantity demanded is less than the percentage change in income, the product is referred to as a *necessity*. Staples such as brown bread, maize meal, rice and fresh milk fall into this category (once more refer to Box 2-4).

Box 2-4

Estimated income elasticities of demand in South Africa, 1985

Product	Income elasticity of demand	
	High-income households	Low-income households
Brown/full grain bread	0,25	0,23
Maize meal	0,31	0,00
Rice	0,02	0,60
Cakes and biscuits	0,78	2,27
Meat	0,32	0,90
Biltong	1,36	1,11
Fresh fish	0,51	1,61
Fresh milk	0,21	0,66
Cheese	0,46	2,01
Pure fruit juice	0,83	2,03
Tea	0,21	0,25
Ladies' fashions	0,98	1,14
Men's clothing	0,99	1,26
Paraffin	0,55	-0,51
Candles	0,82	-0,20
Transport	1,26	1,25
Medical care	0,65	0,98
Furniture	1,40	1,30
Electrical appliances	1,06	2,18
Normal radios	0,88	-0,56
Television sets	0,37	1,65

Source: Philip Mohr, Louis Fourie *et al*, 1996, *Economics for South African students*, First edition, Pretoria: Van Schaik.

The income elasticity is important for the suppliers of goods and services. They want to know what will happen to the quantity demanded of goods and services that they produce if consumers' incomes increase. During the post-war economic upheaval, developing countries which exported agricultural products fared relatively badly as a result of the low income elasticity of demand for basic foodstuffs. The demand for basic foodstuffs did not keep pace with the increase in income and the demand for manufactures. On the other hand, countries which exported goods with high income elasticities (eg electronic equipment and cars) fared well because the quantity demanded of these goods increased faster than the income of consumers.

Cross elasticity of demand

The quantity demanded of a particular product also depends on the *price of related products* such as *substitutes* and *complements*. The cross elasticity of demand measures the sensitivity of the quantity demanded of a specific product to changes in the price of a related product. By applying the general definition of elasticity, the cross elasticity of demand e_c can be defined as the percentage change in the quantity of a product demanded as due to a 1 per cent change in the price of a related product, that is to say

$$e_c = \frac{\text{percentage change in the quantity demanded of product A}}{\text{percentage change in the price of product B}}$$

When two products are not related to each other (eg computers and shoes) the cross elasticity of demand is zero. With *substitutes* (eg coffee and tea) the cross elasticity of demand is *positive*. A change in the price of one good (eg coffee) leads to a change in the same direction of the quantity demanded of the substitute product (tea). For example, if the price of coffee rises, more tea will be demanded, *ceteris paribus,* since consumers convert to tea, which is relatively cheaper.

With *complements* (eg cars and petrol) the cross elasticity of demand is *negative*. A change in the price of one product (eg cars) leads to a change in the opposite direction of the quantity demanded of the complementary product (petrol). If the price of cars falls, more cars will be demanded and consequently more petrol will also be demanded.

THE SUPPLY SIDE OF THE MARKET

The market supply curve

Every market has both a supply side and a demand side. The supply side can be represented by means of a market supply schedule, which is a table representing the quantities of a product supplied at various prices. Assume for example that the market supply of frozen fish is represented by Table 2-5.

Table 2-5
Market supply for frozen fish

Price per kilogram (Rand)	Quantity supplied ('000 kg per day)
6	8
5	6
4	4
3	2
2	0

At a price of R6 per kilogram 8 000 kilograms will be supplied on the market; at a price of R5 per kilogram 6 000 kilograms will be supplied on the market, etc. The information supplied in Table 2-5 can also be represented by means of a supply curve. The vertical axis of a graph depicts the price of the product, whereas the horizontal axis shows the quantity supplied per time period (month, year,etc). Figure 2-5 shows the market supply curve for frozen fish as reflected in Table 2-5.

Figure 2-5
The market supply curve

It is obtained by horizontally adding all the supply curves of the producers in the market together.

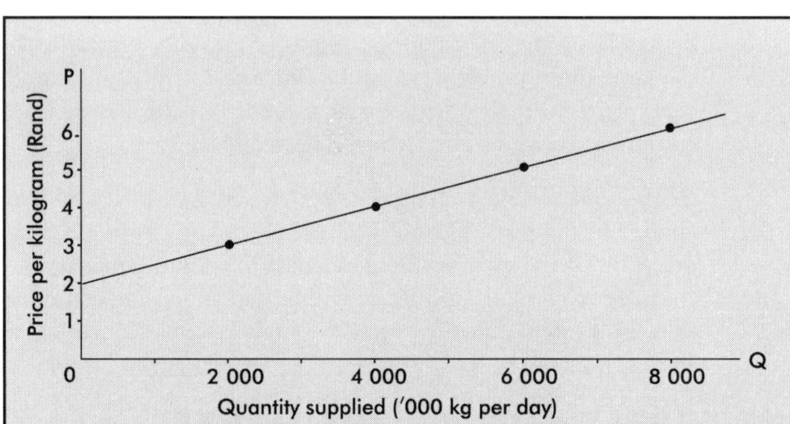

Two important comments must be made about Figure 2-5. First, the market supply curve for frozen fish slopes upwards from left to right; in other words the quantity of frozen fish supplied on the market increases as the price of frozen fish increases. This is because suppliers of frozen fish have a greater incentive to supply their product at a higher price. Empirical studies have shown that the market supply of most goods has this characteristic, namely that it rises from left to right. (In later chapters the supply curves of various market forms are studied in more detail.) Second, the market supply curve in Figure 2-5 refers to a specific time period – in our example it is a day. Any market supply curve refers to a certain time period (day, month, year) and the shape and position of the curve is affected by the time period. If we determine the market supply curve of frozen fish for, say, the first month of the year, it will look different from that for the year as a whole. This can partly be explained because producers can adapt their supply to price changes if the period under consideration is longer.

Other factors

Besides the length of time for which the supply curve is calculated other factors influence the shape and position of the market supply curve. One important factor is technological change – as new machines and production techniques are developed, it becomes cheaper to manufacture products, which means that firms are often in a position to offer goods at a lower price than before. Technological change, therefore, often gives rise to a rightward shift of the supply curve. If the suppliers of frozen fish, for example, develop better ways of catching, handling and packaging fish, a rightward shift of the supply curve will result, as depicted in Figure 2-6.

Another factor which affects the shape and position of the market supply curve is the price of factors of production (eg labour, capital and land) which are used to produce the product. Decreases in the price of inputs make it cheaper to produce the goods, which puts firms in a position where they are able to offer a certain quantity of goods at a lower price than before. A drop in the price of factors of production will also cause a rightward shift of the supply curve. On the other hand, increases in the price of inputs can cause the supply curve to shift leftwards, as depicted in Figure 2-7.

A shift of the supply curve and a movement along the supply curve

As in the market demand curve it is important to differentiate between a shift of the curve and a movement along the curve. In essence the principle is the same: in the market supply curve factors such as technological change and changes in the price of factors of production will cause the market supply curve to shift to the left or to the right depending on the circumstances (see Figs 2-6 and 2-7). On the other hand, if only the price of the product changes, there will merely be a movement along the supply curve and the quantity supplied will change. In Figure 2-5 it can be seen that if the price of frozen fish increases from R5 per kilogram to R6 per kilogram the quantity supplied will increase from 6 000 kilograms to 8 000 kilograms per day.

Figure 2–6

An increase in market supply

If the supply of a product increases, the market supply curve shifts to the right.

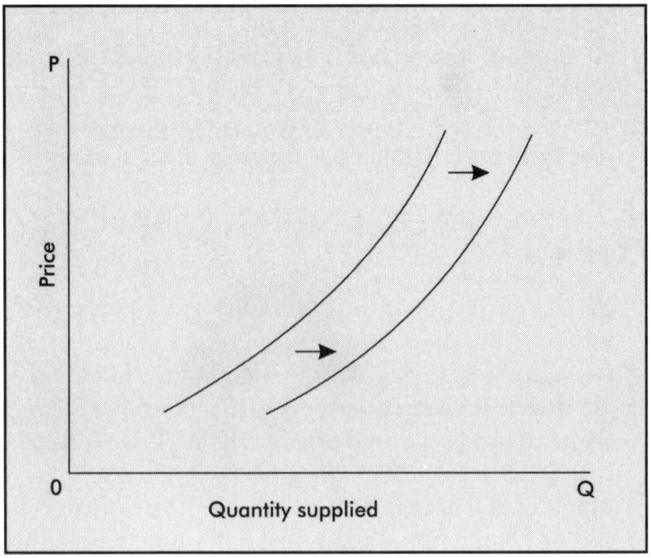

Figure 2–7

A decrease in market supply

If the supply of a good decreases, the market supply curve shifts to the left.

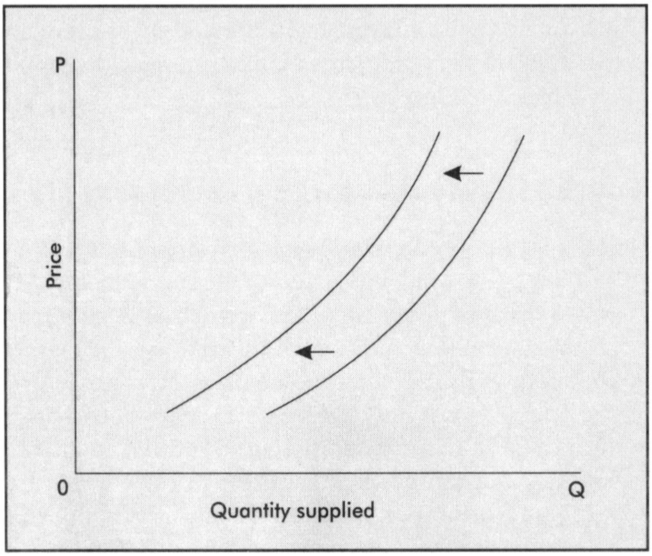

Price elasticity of supply

Like market demand curves, market supply curves have various shapes. Their difference is due in particular to the sensitivity of the quantity supplied to price. For some products, a small change in the price will result in a large change in the quantity supplied, whereas with other products a large change in price will only lead to a small change in the quantity demanded. As with demand, economists make use of the elasticity principle when it comes to supply in order to calculate the elasticity of supply. The price elasticity of supply (abbreviated to supply elasticity) is defined as the percentage change in the quantity supplied which results from a 1 per cent change in price. Therefore if a 1 per cent change in the price of coffee leads to a 0,75 per cent increase in the amount of coffee supplied, then the price elasticity of supply is 0,75.

Elasticity of supply

It should be clear that the price elasticity of supply has a lot in common with the price elasticity of demand. Like the latter, supply elasticity is expressed in terms of relative changes and not absolute changes in price and quantity and should therefore not merely be equated with the slope of the supply curve. Price elasticity of supply also usually differs from one point to the next along the supply curve – for example the supply elasticity of coffee may be higher when the price of coffee is very low compared to when the price is high. (At high prices coffee producers are probably already offering most of their production on the market, with the result that they cannot react very much if the price increases by another 1 per cent.) In general we can assume that the price elasticity of supply will increase if the period of time which the supply curve represents increases. The reason is the same as for the previous section – if the time period is longer, producers of products will be in a better position to adjust their production to price changes.

If we have a table which shows the quantity of a product supplied at various prices, then the price elasticity of supply can be calculated. Let ΔP represent a very small change (in percentage terms) in the price of the product whereas ΔQ_s represents the change in the quantity supplied (as a result of the price change). The formula for the price elasticity of supply at a point on a supply curve is therefore:

$$e_s = \frac{\text{percentage change in the quantity supplied}}{\text{percentage change in the price}}$$

$$= \frac{\Delta Q_s}{Q_s} \div \frac{\Delta P}{P}$$

If ΔP is not very small in percentage terms, the arc elasticity of supply should be calculated by using the average values of P and Q_s. The calculation is done in the same way as the arc elasticity of demand. The formula is as follows:

$$e_s = \frac{\Delta Q_s}{(Q_{s1} + Q_{s2}) / 2} \div \frac{\Delta P}{(P_1 + P_2) / 2}$$

$$= \frac{\Delta Q_s(P_1 + P_2)}{\Delta P(Q_{s1} + Q_{s2})}$$

PRICE DETERMINATION

The equilibrium price

In a free market economy prices are important determinants of what is going to be produced, how it is to be produced and who is going to buy it. In the previous two sections we noted two basic concepts which form the basis of the market mechanism, namely supply and demand. Logically speaking, the next step would be to see how prices are determined in a free market economy. In order to do this it is important to define the equilibrium price of a product. You will often encounter the equilibrium concept in this book; it is an important concept in economics (as in many other study fields).

Equilibrium price

Equilibrium is a situation where there is no tendency towards change; in other words it is a condition which can continue existing. Equilibrium can also be described as a situation of balance, that is a situation where all opposing forces cancel each other out. An equilibrium price is therefore a price that can be maintained. Any price that is not an equilibrium price cannot be maintained for very long, because there will be basic forces in operation which will give rise to a change in price. To illustrate this, in Table 2-6 we combine the information on the market demand for and supply of frozen fish which we have already come across (see Tables 2-1 and 2-5). The same information also appears in Figure 2-8, which you will recognise as the market demand and supply curves discussed earlier in the chapter (see Figs 2-1 and 2-5).

Table 2-6

Market demand for and supply of frozen fish

Price per kilogram (Rand)	Quantity demanded ('000 kg per day)	Quantity supplied ('000 kg per day)
6	2	8
5	3	6
4	4	4
3	5	2
2	6	0

From Table 2-6 as well as Figure 2-8 it can be seen that 6 000 kilograms of frozen fish are supplied at a price of R5 per kilogram, whereas 3 000 kilograms are demanded. There is therefore disequilibrium between the quantity demanded and the quantity supplied – in this instance, at a price of R5 per kilogram there is an excess supply of 3 000 kilograms of frozen fish per day. A portion of the frozen fish will therefore not be sold and as the producers' stocks increase, they will be inclined to decrease their price in order to get rid of their superfluous stock. A price of R5 will therefore not be maintained for very long and therefore cannot be regarded as the equilibrium price.

Figure 2-8
Equilibrium price
It is the price at which the quantity demanded is equal to the quantity supplied.

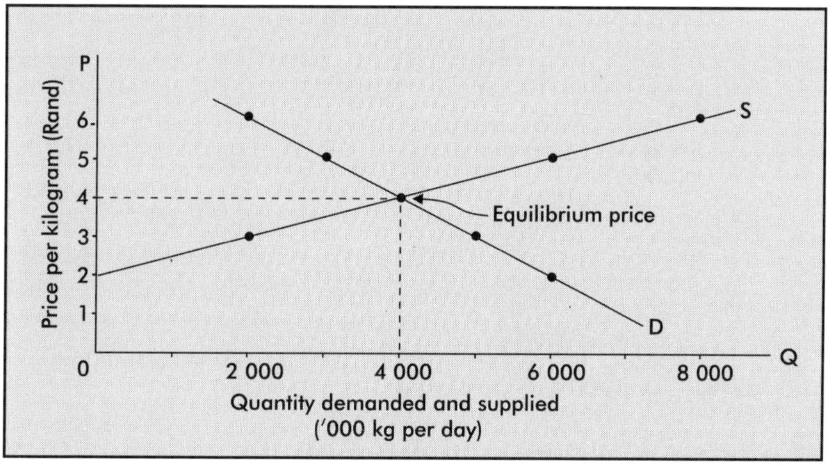

At a price of R3 per kilogram the opposite applies. The quantity demanded by consumers will be 5 000 kilograms per day whereas 2 000 kilograms will be supplied by producers per day. At R3 per kilogram there is therefore an excess demand of 3 000 kilograms per day on the market. Some consumers will be left empty-handed because there is not enough to cater to their demands. Producers will therefore find it profitable to increase their prices. This, accompanied by competition among consumers, will push prices up. A price of R3 per kilogram will therefore not last for very long either and cannot be regarded as an equilibrium price.

The equilibrium price can be defined as the price at which the quantity demanded is equal to the quantity supplied. It is obvious that it is the only price at which there is no disequilibrium between the quantity supplied and the quantity demanded – as a result it is the only price which can be maintained for some time. In Figure 2-8 a price of R4 is the price at which the quantity demanded is equal to the quantity supplied, that is where the demand and supply curves intersect each other. Under the given circumstances R4 per kilogram is the equilibrium price of frozen fish, whereas 4 000 kilograms is the equilibrium quantity.

Prices in practice

The prices which are encountered in practice are market prices or real prices. Our aim in the explanation of demand and supply is not to determine the equilibrium price as such, but to explain how market prices change in practice. In general economists accept that the market price will move in the direction of the equilibrium price because the underlying forces will propel it in that direction.

In the previous section we saw that if the market price is above the equilibrium price, then the forces will operate in such a way that it will move downwards in the direction of the equilibrium price. Likewise, if the market price is below the equilibrium price, there are forces which will force it upwards in the direction of the equilibrium price. If the demand and supply curves remain relatively stable for some time, then the market price should move closer to the equilibrium price. Such a change will not necessarily occur quickly – it may take some time before the market price approaches the equilibrium price. Sometimes the market price never even reaches the equilibrium price because by the time that it has come close the equilibrium price has changed due to changing circumstances. It can be said with certainty, however, that the market price will move in the direction of the equilibrium price. This conclusion is valuable in terms of both theory and practice. In many instances it is not the equilibrium price itself which is important, but it is important to be able to predict whether prices will move upwards or downwards as a result of changed circumstances.

The effect of a change in demand

It has already been shown that the demand for a product changes in reaction to changes in tastes, income and the prices of other products. Any supply and demand diagram, such as Figure 2-8, is a representation of a situation during a specific time period, for example a day, a week, a month or a year. The question now is what will happen to the equilibrium price of a product if the demand curve changes?

Assume that consumers' tastes change in favour of a product such as the frozen fish in our example – this will cause a rightward shift of the demand curve. Such a situation is depicted in Figure 2-9 where the demand curve shifts from D to D_1. It is easy to see the resultant effect on the equilibrium price. When D is the demand curve, the equilibrium price is P, but when the demand curve shifts to D_1 there is a shortage of $Q_2 - Q$ at a price of P. This means that at a price of P demand exceeds supply by a quantity of $Q_2 - Q$; consumers will therefore be prepared to pay more for the product. Suppliers of the product will therefore increase their price and see how the market reacts to this – after a few adjustments back and forth the price will be inclined to settle at P_1, the new equilibrium price, whereas the quantity will settle at Q_1.

Figure 2-9

A change in demand and the equilibrium price

If all other things remain constant, a shift of the demand curve to the right results in a price increase; a shift to the left (D_2) results in a price decrease.

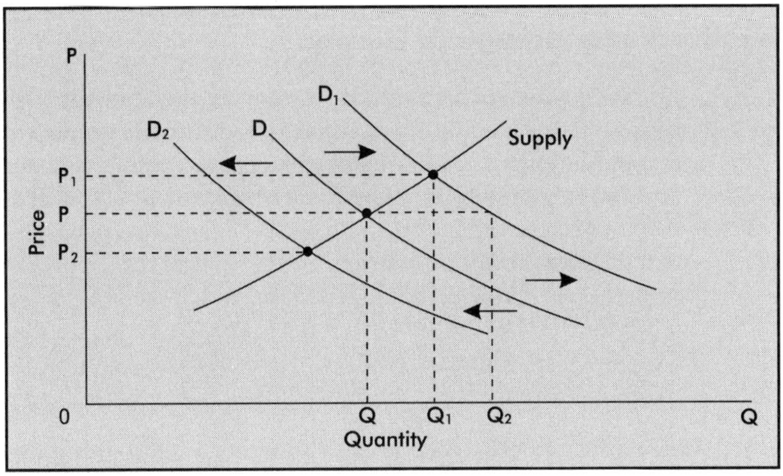

On the other hand, suppose that instead of the above situation occurring, the opposite takes place, namely that consumer demand for a certain product (such as frozen fish) drops – this could be as a result of a drop in the price of another product (for example chicken) which is a good substitute for it. The demand curve in Figure 2-9 will shift to the left, that is from D to D_2. The effect of this would be that the equilibrium price will drop to P_2 where the new demand curve now intersects the supply curve.

This model can be illustrated by numerous practical examples. One of the most dramatic examples in South African history is the big change in the demand for ostrich feathers in the first quarter of the 20th century. There was an enormous global demand for ostrich feathers around 1900, mainly in the fashion world, with the result that ostrich farmers in the Outshoorn district became extremely wealthy. A few years later fashions changed dramatically and in addition the First World War broke out, which just about wiped out the world demand for ostrich feathers. This resulted in many ostrich farmers going bankrupt. Theoretically speaking the demand curve initially moved far to the right, which resulted in high prices, then the curve shifted so far to the left that farmers could not sell their product at prices at which they could economically continue. (Many years later the industry came back on track and today it is an important part of the farming activity in the Outshoorn district.)

In general a rightward shift of the demand curve will lead to an increase in the equilibrium price, whereas a shift to the left would lead to a decrease in the equilibrium price. This is obvious from Figure 2-9. The conclusion, of course, depends on the assumption that the supply curve rises from left to right which, as has already been noted, is usually so. Furthermore, the supply curve itself does not shift as a result of the change in demand.

The effect of a change in supply

Shift of supply curve

Just as demand curves shift, supply curves also shift for various reasons. What happens to the equilibrium price of a product if the supply curve shifts? Suppose that technological advancement gives rise to producers being prepared and in a position to supply more of a certain product than before at any price. In Figure 2-10 this is represented by a shift of the supply curve from S to S_1. The result is that the equilibrium price drops from P (where the supply curve S intersects the demand curve) to P_3. Should it so happen that the price of factors of production increases, the result could be that the supply curve would shift from the original S to S_2 – from Figure 2-10 it is obvious that the equilibrium price will increase from P (where the supply curve S intersects the demand curve) to P_4.

The price of personal computers provides a good illustration of the result of a rightward shift of the supply curve. When personal computers came onto the market in the early eighties, their prices were relatively high. New producers, however, entered the market quickly and this, together with technological advancement, resulted in the price of personal computers falling. Today's personal computers are not only more powerful but, if inflation is eliminated, they cost a lot less than the models of yesteryear.

Figure 2-10

A change in supply and the equilibrium price

A shift of the supply curve to the right (other things remaining the same) leads to a price decrease; a shift to the left (S_2) leads to a price increase.

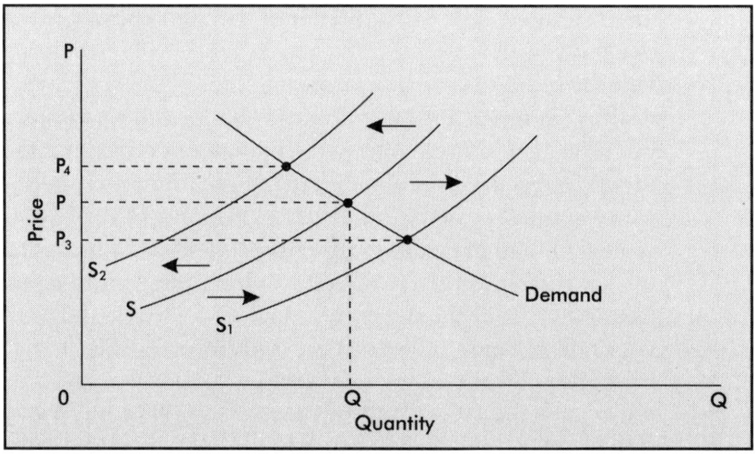

In general a shift to the right of the supply curve will lead to a drop in the equilibrium price, whereas a shift to the left would lead to an increase in the equilibrium price. This is also illustrated in Figure 2-10. This conclusion is naturally based on the assumption that the demand curve slopes downwards from left to right – which as has already been noted is usually so. Furthermore, the demand curve itself does not shift.

The effect of simultaneous changes in demand and supply

Previous analyses have shown that if only demand changes or only supply, it is possible to predict what will happen to the equilibrium price and quantity. If demand and supply change simultaneously it is impossible to predict exactly what the result will be. The reason is that the changes may have opposite effects on the market.

We have seen that an increase in demand leads to an increase in the equilibrium price and that a decrease in supply also leads to an increase in the equilibrium price. If a simultaneous increase in demand and decrease in supply take place, the equilibrium price of the product will increase – but exactly what is going to happen to the equilibrium quantity cannot be said with certainty. An increase in demand increases the equilibrium quantity, *ceteris paribus*, whereas a decrease in supply will reduce the equilibrium quantity, *ceteris paribus*. In so far as the equilibrium quantity is concerned the two forces are working in opposite directions and the result will depend on the relative size of the changes in demand and supply.

Simultaneous change

To illustrate the uncertainty when demand and supply change simultaneously, we look at the situation when demand increases and supply decreases at the same time. Assume that D and S are the original supply and demand curves in Figure 2-11. If demand increases from D to D_1 and supply decreases by the same amount from S to S_1, the equilibrium price will increase from P_0 to P_1, whereas the equilibrium quantity will stay the same, namely Q_0. If demand shows a larger increase (D to D_2) than the decrease in supply (S to S_1), however, then both the equilibrium price and quantity will increase (see the price and quantity represented by point B). On the other hand, if demand shows a smaller increase (D to D_1) than the decrease in the supply (S to S_2) then the equilibrium price will increase, but the equilibrium quantity will decrease (see point C). It is clear that the result will depend on the relative sizes of the changes in demand and supply.

Similar problems are encountered under other circumstances. For example, if demand and supply both decrease it is possible to predict what will happen to the equilibrium quantity (it will decrease), because both forces have the same effect on the equilibrium quantity. The combined effect on the equilibrium price however, is uncertain, because a decrease in demand will decrease the price, *ceteris paribus*, whereas a decrease in supply will increase the price, *ceteris paribus*. The equilibrium price can therefore increase, stay the same or decrease, depending on the relative sizes of the changes in demand and supply.

Figure 2-11

Simultaneous changes in demand and supply

Equilibrium price can increase, remain the same or decrease, depending on the relative sizes of the changes in demand and supply.

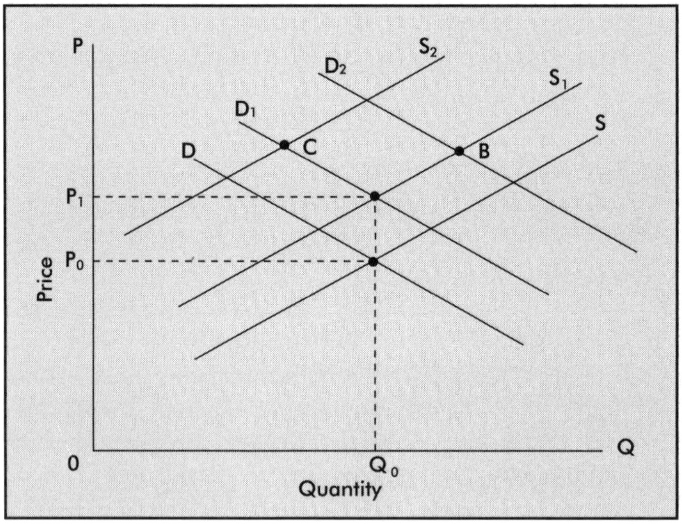

There are a few possibilities whereby simultaneous changes in demand and supply can occur: both can increase, both can decrease, demand can increase while supply decreases, or demand can decrease while supply increases. You can show the different combinations by means of your own diagrams based on the example in Figure 2-11. The following table is a summary of the results you should obtain.

Table 2-7

Simultaneous changes in demand and supply

Change in demand	Change in supply	Change in price	Change in quantity
Increase	Decrease	Rise	Uncertain
Decrease	Decrease	Uncertain	Drop
Increase	Increase	Uncertain	Rise
Decrease	Increase	Drop	Uncertain

IMPORTANT CONCEPTS

- Perfect competition
- Market demand
- Changes in market demand
- Price elasticity of demand
- Marshall's method
- Price elasticity and revenue
- Income elasticity of demand
- Cross elasticity of demand
- Market supply
- Changes in market supply
- Price elasticity of supply
- Equilibrium price
- Effects of changes in demand/supply
- Simultaneous changes in demand/supply

QUESTIONS

(1) Define a market. (2)

(2) Define the law of demand. (3)

(3) Name four factors that may influence the shape and location of a market demand curve. (4)

(4) Define the price elasticity of demand. (3)

(5) Use a demand curve with numerical values to explain that the price elasticity of demand differs at two different points on the curve. (10)

(6) Explain what will happen to total revenue if the price of the product is increased in the elastic part of the demand curve. (5)

(7) Explain what will happen to total revenue if the price of the product is increased in the inelastic part of the demand curve. (5)

(8) Define cross elasticity of demand. (3)

(9) Name four factors that influence the shape and location of the market supply curve. (4)

(10) Define price elasticity of supply. (3)

(11) Define an equilibrium price. (2)

(12) Explain what will happen if there is a temporary surplus demand in a market. (5)

(13) Explain, with the aid of a figure, what will happen to the equilibrium price and quantity if there is a decrease in demand and an increase in supply. (8)

APPENDIX 1

We referred to the fact that price elasticity of demand cannot merely be equated with the slope of a demand curve. When two demand curves intersect each other, however, it is possible to determine the relative elasticities of the curves at the point of intersection by looking at the slopes. For example, you can refer to the diagram below and calculate the elasticities using Marshall's method. At a price of P the elasticity of the demand curve BE is equal to 0P/PB = 2/1 = 2. In contrast the elasticity of demand curve CD at a price of P is equal to 0P/PC = 2/2 = 1. At a price of P the flatter demand curve BE is therefore more elastic than the steeper demand curve CD. In general it can be said that the demand curve which intersects the vertical axis closest to the origin (ie the flatter one) is more elastic at any price. It is important to note that the demand curves *must intersect each other* to be able to compare the two.

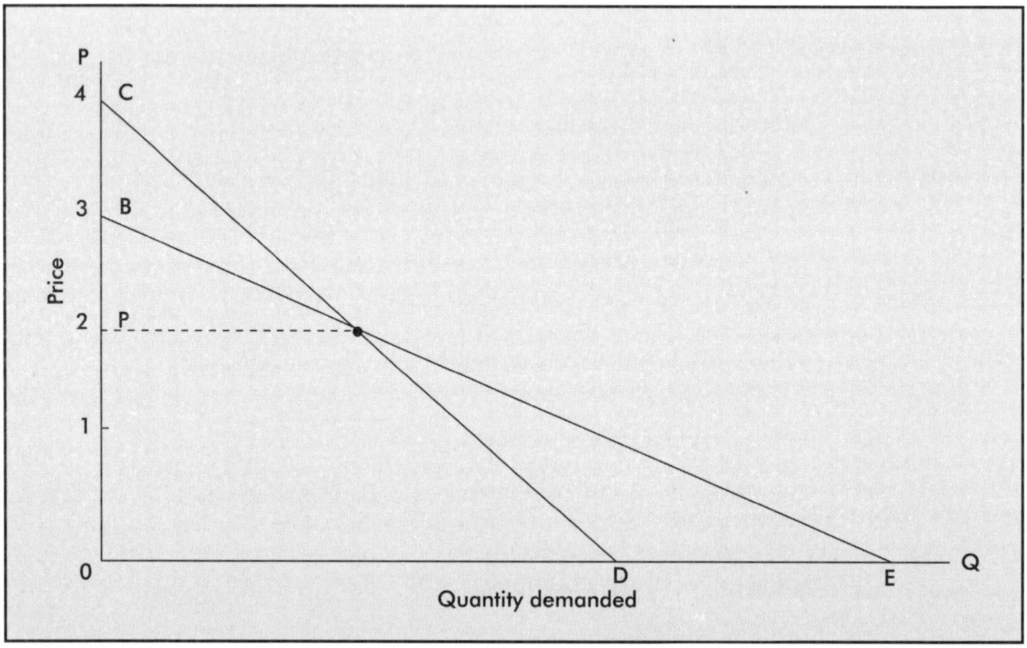

APPENDIX 2

Besides the three types of elasticity (elastic, inelastic and unitary elastic) which have already been mentioned, there are two other types.

Perfectly inelastic demand is represented by a vertical demand curve, that is to say a straight line parallel to the price axis, such as DD in the figure below. The quantity demanded of the product remains unchanged when the price of the product changes, that is to say a fixed amount is demanded irrespective of the price. In such a situation the price elasticity of demand is equal to zero. A practical example is life-supporting medicine – the consumer will have to buy the product irrespective of the price.

Perfectly inelastic demand

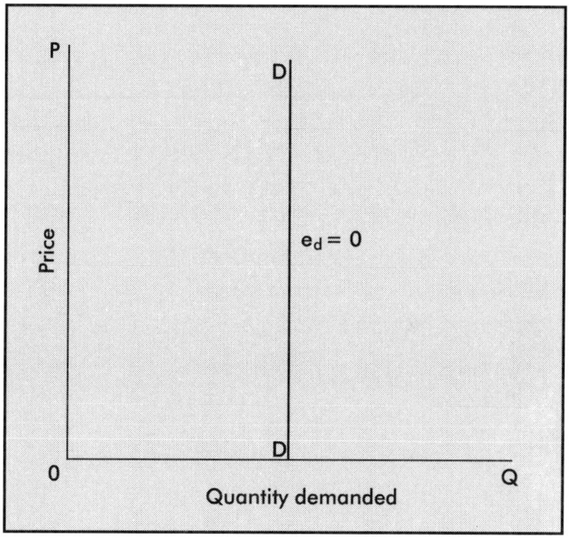

If the demand for a product is perfectly inelastic, producers can increase their incomes by increasing the price of the product. As has already been explained, producers' total revenue is equal to P × Q. When P increases and Q remains the same, total revenue will increase.

Perfectly elastic demand is represented by a horizontal demand curve like D′D′ in the next figure. Such a demand curve has an elasticity coefficient of infinity. A producer can sell any quantity at a price of P_1, but if the price of the product is increased slightly, nothing will be sold. An example of perfectly elastic demand is provided in Chapter 5, where the position of an individual firm in a perfectly competitive market is analysed.

Perfectly elastic demand

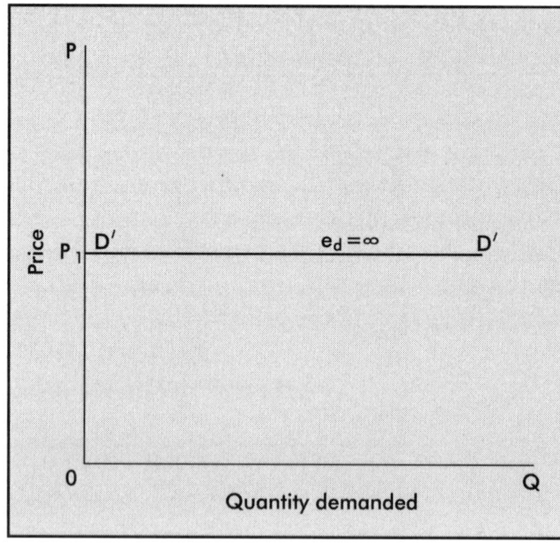

3

CONSUMER BEHAVIOUR: THE INDIFFERENCE APPROACH*

Microeconomics studies the behaviour of the individual decision making units in the economy, of which the consumer is one of the most important. The importance of the role of consumers is apparent from the fact that in South Africa about 60 per cent of all goods and services is purchased by consumers. (The rest is purchased mainly by the government or private enterprises, or exported.) It is therefore easy to understand why economists pay so much attention to the behaviour of consumers. Consumer behaviour is also important for marketers of consumer goods who want to know how a typical consumer would react and behave under different circumstances.

In the analysis of demand and supply in Chapter 2 it was assumed that the demand curves of consumers usually slope downwards from left to right. This is in accordance with the law of demand, which states that the quantity demanded of a good will increase if its price decreases, and will decrease if its price rises *(ceteris paribus)*. In this chapter consumer behaviour is analysed in more detail. In doing so it we explain why demand curves slope downwards from left to right. In this chapter the indifference approach is used, which is an alternative to the marginal utility approach which is usually encountered in introductory microeconomic courses. An important difference between the marginal utility approach and the indifference approach is that the indifference approach does not require the measurement of marginal utility. The two approaches nevertheless yield the same results.

The indifference approach was devised towards the end of the 19th century by a famous Italian economist, Vilfredo Pareto (1848–1923), and developed further by 20th-century economists such as the Nobel Prize winner Sir John Hicks.

The indifference approach has definite advantages over the traditional utility approach in analysing consumer behaviour. First, many students (and economists) are not impressed by the notion that consumer satisfaction or utility can be measured and that changes in utility can be compared. Second, indifference curves allow us to distinguish between the income effects and substitution effects of a change in the price of a product. Third, the indifference curve technique is an extremely useful tool which can be used to

---

* The author based this chapter to a large extent on a chapter which he has contributed to the book *Economics for South African students* by P Mohr *et al*, which was published in 1996 by Van Schaik.

analyse a variety of other choices, apart from consumers' choices between different goods and services. This is done in Chapter 4.

In this chapter we first explain what indifference curves are, and indicate their important properties. We then introduce the budget line and combine it with indifference curves to explain consumer equilibrium. This is followed by an investigation of the effects of changes in income and prices. The income and substitution effects of a price change are separated and different demand curves are derived.

Once you have studied this chapter you should be able to

- explain what indifference curves are and list their important properties
- define the budget line and explain consumer equilibrium
- examine the effects of changes in income or prices
- distinguish between the income and substitution effects of a price change (for normal, inferior and Giffen goods)
- derive the demand curve for normal, inferior and Giffen goods by using indifference curves
- explain the backward-bending labour supply curve

INTRODUCTION

The utility approach to the analysis of consumer behaviour, which usually forms part of an introductory course in microeconomics, is based on the assumption that a consumer can assign values to the amount of satisfaction (utility) that he or she obtains from the consumption of each successive unit of a consumer good or service. It is also assumed that it is possible to compare the utility of different consumer goods and services quantitatively. In this chapter the indifference approach is used to analyse consumer behaviour. This is an alternative, more modern approach to the analysis of consumer behaviour, which rests on more acceptable assumptions than the utility approach.

Cardinal and ordinal utility

Whereas the utility approach is based on the notion of *cardinal utility*, the indifference approach employs the notion of *ordinal utility*.

We can explain the difference between cardinal and ordinal magnitudes by considering the measurement of length. The metric scale is an example of a cardinal scale. It enables us to measure distances and allows us to compare different distances with each other. For example, if distance A is 75 kilometres and distance B 225 kilometres, then we know that B is exactly three times as long as A. We also know that the difference between A and B is exactly 150 kilometres. An ordinal scale, on the other hand, simply indicates that some distances are shorter than, longer than, or the same as other distances. Such a scale enables us to rank the distances, say, from shortest to longest, but it does not enable us to determine precisely how the distances compare. In contrast to cardinal numbers, the size relationship of ordinal numbers cannot be established.

The cardinal utility approach is based on the assumption that satisfaction (utility) is somehow measurable on a cardinal scale and that differences in utility can be precisely quantified. For example, if the marginal utility of coffee is 5 utils and the marginal utility of beer is 10 utils, then the marginal utility of beer is twice as large as the marginal utility of coffee. It is also possible to say exactly what the difference in the marginal utility of the products is.

Ordinal utility, on the other hand, simply means that the satisfaction which a consumer obtains from consuming different products or bundles of products can be *ranked* or *ordered*. The consumer can rank different products or combinations of products in order of preference but can say nothing about the absolute level of satisfaction that each product or combination of products yields. *The size of the utility differences cannot be established.* The consumer can only rank things from highest to lowest, best to worst, most satisfying to least satisfying, and so on. The indifference approach to consumer behaviour is based on this less stringent (or more plausible) notion of utility. It is also confined to comparing different combinations or bundles of goods and services with each other, and therefore cannot be used to analyse the consumption of one good or service in isolation. Nevertheless, the indifference approach yields essentially the same results as the utility approach.

Three basic assumptions

The indifference approach is based on three basic assumptions: the assumption of completeness (or law of comparison), the assumption of consistency (or transitivity) and the assumption of non-satiation (or non-satiety). These assumptions may sound complicated, but they are actually quite simple. As you will see, they are also very reasonable and plausible assumptions.

Completeness

- The assumption of *completeness* simply means that it is assumed that a consumer is able to rank *all* possible combinations (or bundles) of goods and services in order of preference. Consider two bundles of consumer goods: bundle X consists of two portions of meat and five litres of milk, while bundle Y consists of one portion of meat and eight litres of milk. A consumer must then be able to say whether he or she prefers X to Y, prefers Y to X or is indifferent between them (ie values them both equally). The consumer must be able to do the same for all other possible combinations of products.

Consistency

- The assumption of *consistency* (or *transitivity*) simply means that consumers are assumed to act consistently. Consider three bundles, A, B and C. If the consumer prefers A to B and prefers B to C, then he or she (according to this assumption) must also prefer A to C. If not, then the consumer will sometimes act inconsistently and his or her behaviour cannot be analysed.

Non-satiation

- The assumption of *non-satiation* (or *non-satiety*) simply states that consumers are not yet fully satisfied and always *prefer more to less*. Thus, if bundle A contains two kilograms of meat and two dozen bottles of beer and bundle B contains two kilograms of meat and three dozen bottles of beer, the consumer is assumed to always prefer B to A.

The assumption of non-satiation has implications which are illustrated in Figure 3-1. In the figure, meat (in kilograms) is shown on the vertical axis and beer (in dozens of bottles) on the horizontal axis. Point A shows the combination of three kilograms of meat and two dozen bottles of beer. By drawing a horizontal and a vertical line through point A we divide the area between the axes into four areas. Any point north-east of A (ie the area labelled I) is preferable to point A since the points in this area represent combinations of more meat and/or more beer than A. At worst the consumer will get more of at least one of the products while getting the same quantity of the other product.

Figure 3-1

A comparison of combinations of meat and beer

Point A represents a combination of 3 kilograms of meat and 2 dozen bottles of beer. Any point in quadrant I will be preferable to A, while A will be preferable to any point in quadrant III. In quadrants II and IV the position is uncertain. At some points in these quadrants the consumer will achieve the same satisfaction as at A.

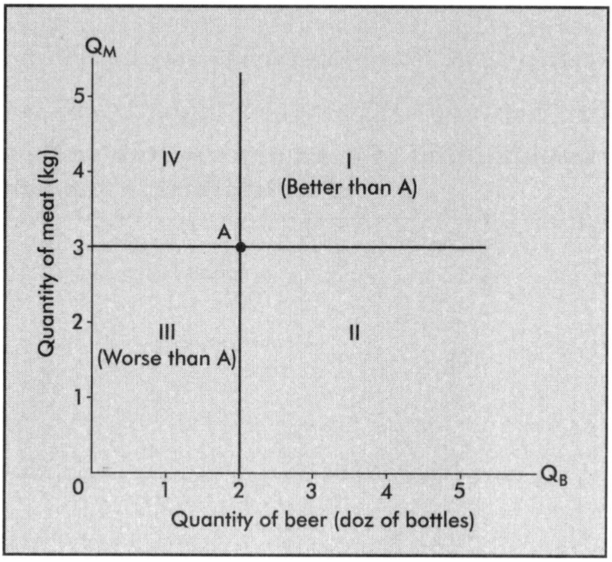

As in the previous case, point A will be preferable to any point in area III (the area to the southwest of A). But what about areas II and IV? Here we cannot make any deductions with certainty since these areas represent points where the consumer gets more of one good but fewer of the other. It is most likely that somewhere in these areas there will be points that will represent the same level of satisfaction as A. For the consumer these points are indifferent to point A. If we combine all these points between which the consumer is indifferent (because they represent the same level of utility) we obtain an indifference curve.

INDIFFERENCE CURVES

Given the three basic assumptions disussed in the previous section, a consumer's tastes and preferences can be indicated by means of an indifference curve.

Definition *An indifference curve is a curve which shows all the combinations of two products that will provide the consumer with equal levels of satisfaction or utility.* The combinations are equally desirable and the consumer is thus indifferent between them.

An example

To explain indifference curves, we consider an imaginary consumer, Jan Burger, who consumes only two products, meat and vegetables. Jan decides that it does not matter to him whether he gets one portion of meat and six portions of vegetables per week or two portions of meat and three portions of vegetables. These two combinations provide him with the same amount of satisfaction, that is, he is indifferent between them. Jan also indicates some other combinations of meat and vegetables that will yield the same level of satisfaction or total utility as the previous two. The different combinations are shown in Table 3-1.

Table 3-1

Combinations of meat and vegetables that yield the same level of satisfaction to Jan Burger

Combination	Meat (portions per week)	Vegetables (portions per week)
A	1	6
B	2	3
C	3	2
D	4	1½

The information in Table 3-1 is shown graphically in Figure 3-2, with vegetables (portions per week) on the vertical axis and meat (portions per week) on the horizontal axis. Each of the combinations A, B, C and D in the table is represented by a single point in the figure. The points listed in Table 3-1 are by no means the only points between which Jan is indifferent – there are also other (intermediate) combinations (eg between A and B) which yield the same level of satisfaction. A curve drawn through points A, B, C and D is called an *indifference curve*. The points on the curve (including those between A, B, C and D) represent different combinations of the two goods that are equally desirable or attractive to Jan – he will derive the same total satisfaction or utility from each of these combinations.

Law of substitution

The indifference curve in Figure 3-2 bulges towards the origin – we say that the curve is *convex* when it is viewed from the origin. As we move downwards to the right along the indifference curve (ie as the portions of vegetables decrease and the portions of meat increase), the curve becomes flatter (ie its slope decreases). This illustrates the *law of substitution* which is similar to the law of diminishing marginal utility encountered in the utility approach to consumer behaviour. The law of substitution states that *the scarcer a good becomes, the greater its substitution value will be.* In other words, the marginal utility of the good that becomes less plentiful rises in relation to the marginal utility of the good that becomes more plentiful. This can be explained by considering the various combinations listed in Table 3-1. The difference between combinations A and B indicates that Jan is willing to sacrifice three portions of vegetables for a second portion of meat. However, between points B and C he is only prepared to sacrifice one portion of vegetables for an extra (third) portion of meat. Moreover, he is prepared to sacrifice only half a portion of vegetables to obtain a fourth portion of meat (points C and D). The fewer his portions of vegetables (ie the less plentiful vegetables become) the less portions of vegetables he is willing to swop for an additional portion of meat.

Marginal rate of substitution

The rate at which Jan is prepared to substitute or exchange bread for meat between different points is given by the slope of a straight line between the points. For example, between A and B in Figure 3-2 the slope of such a line is 3 (ignoring the negative sign); between points B and C it is 1, and so on. At any point on the indifference curve the exchange ratio or substitution ratio between the two goods is given by the slope of a tangent to the indifference curve (ie a line which just touches the curve at that particular point). The slope of the tangent (which is also the slope of the indifference curve at that point) indicates the rate at which the consumer is prepared to sacrifice a small quantity of one good (vegetables) for a little more of the other good (meat). This rate is called the *marginal rate of substitution* (MRS).

Figure 3-2
An indifference curve

A, B, C and D are all combinations between which the consumer (Jan Burger) is indifferent. The indifference curve derived in this way represents combinations of the two products which yield the same level of consumer satisfaction.

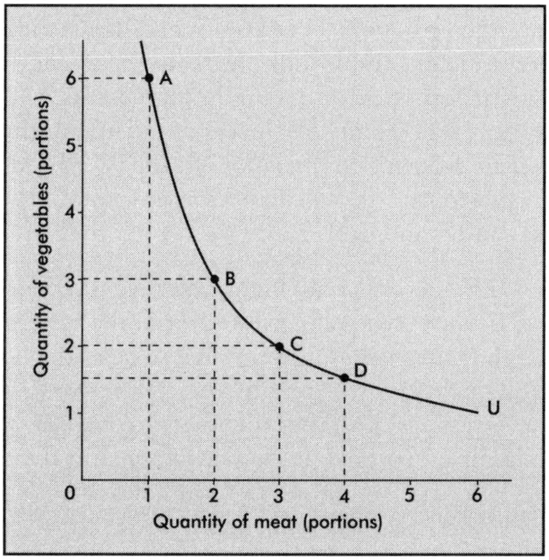

We can now restate our previous conclusion as follows. As we move downwards from left to right along an indifference curve, the marginal rate of substitution (which is equal to the slope of the curve) decreases. The law of substitution can therefore also be called the *law of the diminishing marginal rate of substitution.*

We shall return to the significance of the marginal rate of substitution later. But first we examine some properties of indifference curves and the consumer's equilibrium position.

Box 3-1

TWO EXTREME CASES

Complements are goods which complement each other in the satisfaction of consumers' wants. Examples are cars and petrol, tobacco and pipes, tables and chairs, etc. If two goods are *perfect complements* it means that they can only be used together (ie in fixed proportions). A normal, two-legged person, for example, can only use one left shoe with one right shoe. If he or she has only one left shoe, then more than one right shoe will yield no additional satisfaction. Similarly, if the consumer has only one right shoe, then the second, third or fourth left shoe will not increase his or her total utility. In perfect complements the indifference curves will therefore be L-shaped, as in the figure below.

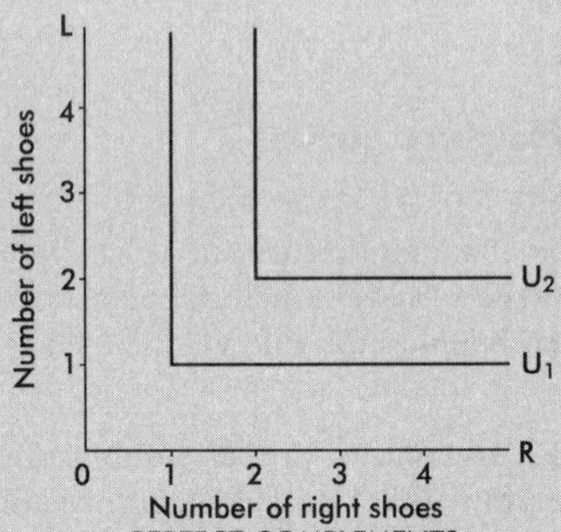

PERFECT COMPLEMENTS

The other extreme case of indifference curves occurs when the two goods are regarded as *perfect substitutes.* Substitutes are goods which satisfy the same wants and needs of consumers and which can therefore easily be substituted for one another. Examples are coffee and tea, butter and margarine, beef and mutton, etc. For example, if a consumer regards Shell petrol as a perfect substitute for Caltex petrol, then one litre of Shell petrol will always yield the same consumer satisfaction as one litre of Caltex petrol. In perfect substitutes the indifference curve is a straight line which slopes downward from left to right as in the figure below. Note that 'normal' indifference curves, such as the one illustrated in Figure 3-2, lie between the two extremes of perfect complements and perfect substitutes.

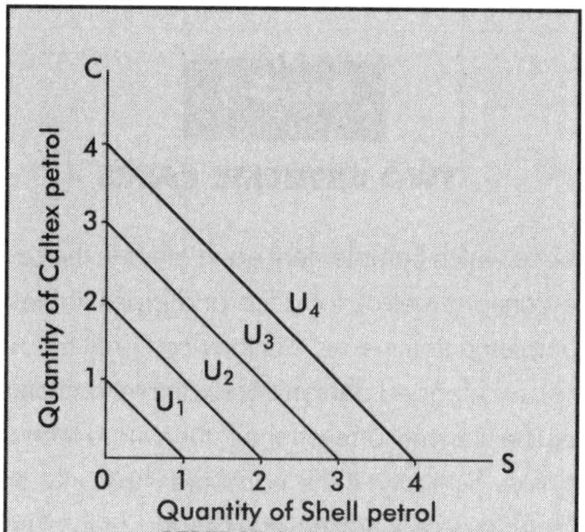

PERFECT SUBSTITUTES

Properties of indifference curves

The exact shape of an indifference curve will vary from one consumer to the next, but indifference curves usually slope downwards from left to right. (In Box 3-1 two exceptions to this rule are discussed.)

Indifference map

An indifference curve shows various combinations of two goods or services which yield the same level of satisfaction or total utility to a particular consumer. For each level of satisfaction there will be a unique indifference curve, showing the various combinations which yield that particular level of satisfaction to the consumer. In principle it is therefore possible to draw an infinite number of indifference curves for any consumer's choice between two goods. Such a *collection of indifference curves* is called an *indifference map*. Table 3-2 contains two additional sets of combinations of vegetables and meat that yield equal satisfaction to Jan Burger. These data can be used to plot two more indifference curves, U_1 and U_3, in Figure 3-3. The original indifference curve in Figure 3-2 is also shown and is labelled U_2.

Table 3-2
Two further sets of combinations of meat and vegetables between which Jan Burger is indifferent

U_1		U_3	
Meat (portions per week)	Vegetables (portions per week)	Meat (portions per week)	Vegetables (portions per week)
½	6	1½	6
1	4	2	4½
2	2	3	3
3	1	4½	2½

Figure 3-3
An indifference map

U_1, U_2 and U_3 are three indifference curves. Each indifference curve represents a certain level of satisfaction. As we move away from the origin, the level of satisfaction increases. U_3 represents the highest level of satisfaction and U_1 the lowest.

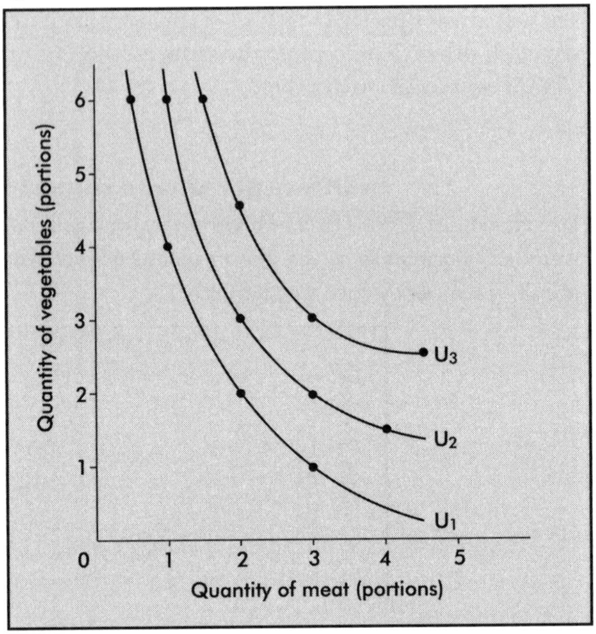

Figure 3-3 is an example of an indifference map containing three indifference curves (U_1, U_2 and U_3). The further we move away from the origin, the larger the combinations of the two goods become and therefore the greater the level of consumer satisfaction, as illustrated by the indifference curve. Given our assumption that the consumer is not satiated (ie not satisfied fully), it follows that he or she will derive greater utility from consuming more of both goods, as illustrated by a movement to a higher indifference curve (further away from the origin). Although we cannot quantify the amount of consumer satisfaction represented by each indifference curve, we can say that U_2 in Figure 3-3 represents a higher level of satisfaction than U_1, and that U_3 represents a greater level of satisfaction than either U_1 or U_2.

Another important property of indifference curves is that they never intersect or touch each other. This can be explained with the aid of Figure 3-4, which shows two 'indifference curves' that intersect each other. It can easily be proved that such an intersection is impossible, given our assumptions. According to the definition of an indifference curve, all combinations of meat and vegetables on a particular curve will yield the same level of satisfaction or total utility to the consumer. This means that combinations B and C on curve I represent the same level of satisfaction. Similarly, B and H on curve II provide the consumer with the same level of satisfaction. If B and C (on curve I), and B and H (on curve II) yield the same level of satisfaction, then C and H should also yield equal satisfaction. However, it is obvious that H represents a combination of more meat and vegetables than C. We have assumed that consumers prefer more to less and it is therefore impossible for the consumer to be indifferent between C and H – he or she will always prefer H to C. This proves that indifference curves cannot intersect each other. You can use the same method to prove that indifference curves cannot ever touch each other.

Figure 3-4

Indifference curves cannot intersect

By comparing B, C and H it can be shown that I and II cannot be indifference curves. If I and II were both indifference curves, then the consumer would have to be indifferent between C and H, which clearly cannot be the case.

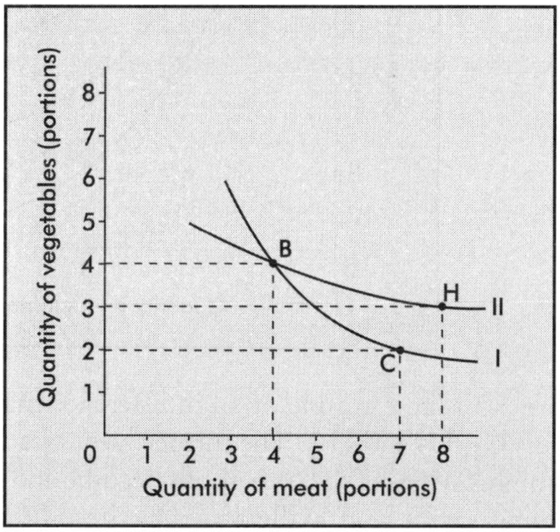

THE BUDGET LINE

Now that we have considered the satisfaction the consumer obtains from various combinations of goods, we turn to the other element of the consumer's decision, namely the combinations that he or she *can afford.*

We return to Jan Burger's choice between meat and vegetables. We assume that he has a fixed amount of R12 per week to spend on meat and vegetables, and that vegetables cost R2 per portion and meat R3 a portion. With his R12 Jan can afford a maximum of 6 portions of vegetables (and no meat) or 4 portions of meat (and no vegetables). Table 3-3 indicates some of the ways in which Jan can spend his R12 on vegetables and meat, on the assumption that he always spends the full amount.

Table 3-3
Affordable combinations of vegetables and meat

Combination	Meat (portions per week)	Vegetables (portions per week)
a	0	6
b	1	4½
c	2	3
d	3	1½
e	4	0

The combinations in Table 3-3 (as well as the intermediate combinations, such as 5¼ portions of vegetables and half a portion of meat) are illustrated graphically in Figure 3-5 by the straight line Q_VQ_M which runs through points a to e. At a Jan spends all his income on vegetables, while at e he spends everything on meat.

Budget line

This line is called the *budget line*, since it indicates all the combinations of the two products that the consumer (Jan Burger) can afford to purchase with the amount of income at his disposal. The budget line is sometimes called the *consumption-possibilities curve, expenditure line* or *budget constraint.* All that is required to construct a budget line are the intercepts on the two axes (ie the maximum number of each good which the consumer can afford by spending the available amount of money on that good only). In Figure 3-5 the intercepts are 6 portions of vegetables and 4 portions of meat.

The slope of the budget line (Q_VQ_M) is 6/4 (ie 3/2), which is the same as the ratio of the price of a portion of meat (R3) to the price of a portion of vegetables (R2). It is easy to understand why this is so. If Jan wants to purchase one more portion of meat, he must sacrifice 1½ portions of vegetables. The exchange ratio between meat and vegetables is thus 3:2, which is the same as the ratio between the price of meat and the price of vegetables. This is, of course, also equal to the *opportunity cost* of meat in terms of vegetables (ie the portions of vegetables that are sacrificed to gain one more portion of meat).

We now combine indifference curves and the budget line to determine the consumer's equilibrium position.

Figure 3-5
The budget line

The line Q_VQ_M illustrates all the possible combinations of vegetables and meat that Jan can afford to purchase for R12, if the price of vegetables is R2 and that of meat R3 per portion, respectively. Points a to e correspond to the combinations in Table 3-3.

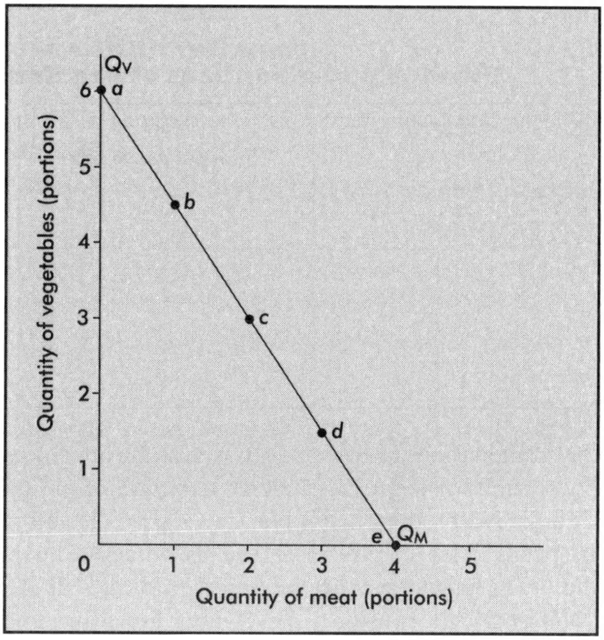

CONSUMER EQUILIBRIUM

A graphical approach

The axes in Figure 3-5 are the same as those in Figure 3-3. We can therefore superimpose the budget line from Figure 3-5 on the indifference map from Figure 3-3 – this is done in Figure 3-6. In principle the indifference map contains an infinite number of indifference curves, but to explain equilibrium we show only three curves, as in Figure 3-3. Our consumer (Jan Burger) can choose any point along the budget line (Q_VQ_M). Any position above and to the right of the budget line is unaffordable and any point below and to the left of the budget line can be ignored, since we assume that Jan Burger spends the full R12 that he has available.

The consumer (Jan Burger) will be in equilibrium when he obtains the maximum satisfaction for the amount he spends. This is indicated by point B in Figure 3-6, which is the same as point B in Figure 3-2. At B the budget line just touches the indifference curve U_2 without intersecting it. This is the highest indifference curve (ie the highest level of satisfaction or total utility) that Jan can reach, given the amount of money that he has available to spend. At equilibrium (point B) the slope of the indifference curve is equal to the slope of the budget line.

Figure 3-6

Consumer equilibrium

The consumer is in equilibrium (ie obtains the highest affordable level of satisfaction) where the highest indifference curve just touches the budget line. This point of tangency is indicated by B on indifference curve U_2. Points on U_1 are attainable (ie affordable) but yield less satisfaction than points on U_2. Points on U_3 yield greater satisfaction but are unattainable (ie not affordable).

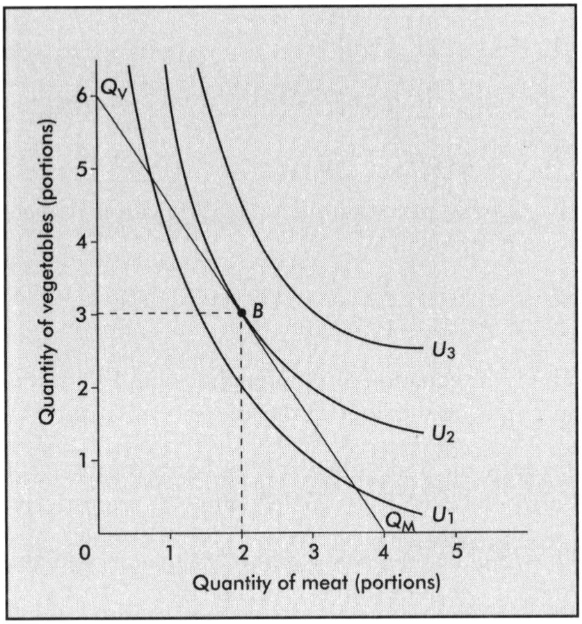

Any indifference curve which intersects the budget line, such as U_1 in Figure 3-6, represents a lower level of satisfaction than U_2. On the other hand, any indifference curve which does not touch or intersect the budget line, such as U_3 in Figure 3-6, is beyond the consumer's means.

An algebraic approach

The consumer's equilibrium position, illustrated in Figure 3-6, can also be derived using symbols and equations. Consider the position of a consumer who spends his or her available income (I) during a certain period on two goods, good x and good y. Let Q_x be the quantity of x and let Q_y be the quantity of y that the consumer purchases in this period. The prices of x and y are P_x and P_y respectively.

We know that the budget line indicates the different combinations of the two goods the consumer can afford to purchase, given his or her income and the prices of the goods. The budget line states that the income (I) is equal to the amount spent on the two goods, ie

Income = (price of y multiplied by the quantity of y) PLUS
(price of x multiplied by the quantity of x)

OR

$I = (P_yQ_y) + (P_xQ_x)$

Dividing both sides of this equation by P_y, we obtain

$I/P_y = Q_y + (P_xQ_x)/P_y$

Subtracting the term $(P_xQ_x)/P_y$ from both sides yields:

$I/P_y - (P_xQ_x)/P_y = Q_y$

By switching the two sides of the equation (which represents the budget line), we can rewrite it as

$$Q_y = \frac{I}{P_y} - \frac{P_x}{P_y}Q_x$$

This is the equation of a straight line with I/P_y as the intercept on the vertical axis and P_x/P_y as the slope of the line.

To draw the budget line, we need only the intercepts on the vertical axis and the horizontal axis. These are I/P_y and I/P_x respectively, as shown in Figure 3-7(a).

Drawing the budget line is simply a matter of joining these two intercepts with a straight line. The slope of this line is

$$\frac{\text{vertical difference}}{\text{horizontal difference}} = \frac{I}{P_y} \div \frac{I}{P_x}$$

$$= I/P_y \times P_x/I$$

$$= P_x/P_y$$

Figure 3-7

Intercepts of the budget line and slope of indifference curves

In (a) we indicate how the two intercepts are obtained. In (b) we show how the slope of an indifference curve can be measured between two points.

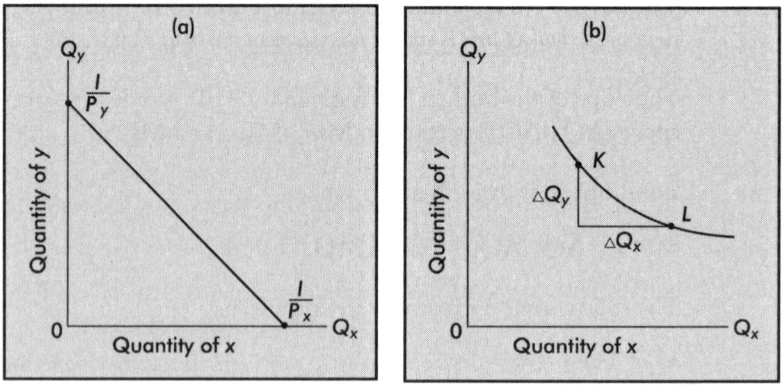

This is a restatement of our previous result that the slope of the budget line is equal to the ratio of the price of good x (ie P_x) to the price of good y (ie P_y).

The same type of approach can be applied to indifference curves. All the points on an indifference curve indicate the same level of consumer satisfaction or total utility. Hence, total utility is unchanged as a consumer moves from one point on an indifference curve to another point, for example from point K to point L in Figure 3-7(b). Total utility will only remain unchanged if the utility that the consumer sacrifices by consuming less of y is exactly compensated for by the additional utility derived from consuming more of x. This means that the following condition must be met:

$$\Delta Q_y \times MU_y = \Delta Q_x \times MU_x \qquad (3\text{-}1)$$

where ΔQ_y = the change in the quantity of y
MU_y = the marginal utility of y
ΔQ_x = the change in the quantity of x
MU_x = the marginal utility of x

We can rearrange Equation 3-1 to obtain:

$$\Delta Q_y/\Delta Q_x = MU_x/MU_y \qquad (3\text{-}2)$$

The term $\Delta Q_y/\Delta Q_x$ is the slope of an indifference curve. From Equation 3-2 we see that this is equal to the ratio between the marginal utilities of the two goods, MU_x/MU_y. We have already seen that the slope of an indifference curve is also equal to the marginal rate of substitution (MRS) between the two goods. It follows, therefore, that

$\Delta Q_y/\Delta Q_x = MU_x/MU_y = MRS$

We are now in a position to reconsider the equilibrium position illustrated in Figure 3-6. Maximum satisfaction (or consumer equilibrium) is attained at the point where the budget line is tangent to (ie just touches) the highest possible indifference curve, indicated by B in Figure 3-6. Moreover, at equilibrium the *slope of the budget line is equal to the slope of the indifference curve.*

The slope of the budget line is given by P_x/P_y while the slope of the indifference curve ($\Delta Q_y/\Delta Q_x$) is equal to MU_x/MU_y and MRS.

Equilibrium is thus obtained where

$$MRS = \Delta Q_y/\Delta Q_x = MU_x/MU_y = P_x/P_y \qquad (3\text{-}3)$$

The following observations are important:

- The marginal rate of substitution (or the slope of the indifference curve) is none other than the ratio of the marginal utility of the one good to the marginal utility of the other good, that is

  $MRS = MU_x/MU_y$

- If the consumer is in equilibrium, the marginal rate of substitution (MRS) is exactly equal to the ratio of the prices of the two goods concerned (P_x/P_y).

- At equilibrium the ratio of the marginal utilities of the two goods is equal to the ratio of their prices, that is

  $$MU_x/MU_y = P_x/P_y \qquad (3\text{-}4)$$

Multiplying both sides of Equation 3-4 with MU_y/P_x we obtain $MU_x/P_x = MU_y/P_y$. In other words, at equilibrium the marginal utilities and prices of the consumer goods must be in proportion to one another. This result is known as the law of equalising the weighted marginal utilities, which means that the consumer is only in equilibrium when he or she derives the same marginal utility from the last rand spent on good x as from the last rand spent on good y. This equation can be expanded to any number of goods, so that consumer equilibrium may be defined as

$$MU_x/P_x = MU_y/P_y = MU_z/P_z = \ldots = MU_n/P_n \qquad (3\text{-}5)$$

As long as the ratios of marginal utility to price are not equal for all goods, the consumer can attain a higher level of total utility by adjusting his or her purchasing pattern. Should the marginal utility per rand spent, derived from the last unit of good y purchased, be greater than that derived from the last unit of good x purchased, then the consumer can increase his or her total utility by buying more of good y and less of good x. When the ratios are equal, however, total utility cannot increase further and consumer equilibrium has been reached.

The consumer's valuation and the market valuation

At equilibrium the consumer's subjective valuation of the relative value of different consumer goods (indicated by the ratio of their marginal utilities) is the same as the objective valuation of the relative value of the goods in the market (indicated by the ratio of their market prices). This is essentially what the equilibrium position is all about. As long as there is a difference between the consumer's subjective valuation and the market's objective valuation of the relative importance of the goods, the consumer can improve his or her position by exchanging goods, but when the valuations coincide, no further improvement is possible and equilibrium is reached.

CHANGES IN EQUILIBRIUM

In this section we investigate how the equilibrium position changes if the consumer's income or the price of one of the goods changes.

A change in income

If the consumer's income changes while prices remain constant, a new table of consumption possibilities, similar to Table 3-2, can be determined. For example, if the consumer's income increases from I_1 to I_2, then he or she can choose to purchase more of one or both goods. The budget line shifts to the right, as indicated in Figure 3-8. Since the price ratio P_x/P_y remains unchanged, the new budget line has the same slope as the original one (ie the two budget lines are parallel). The intercepts increase from I_1/P_x and I_1/P_y to I_2/P_x and I_1/P_y respectively. The new budget line will be tangent to a higher indifference curve than before. In Figure 3-8 the equilibrium shifts from B to B′. If we join points such as B and B′ we obtain an *income-consumption curve*, which indicates the effect of changing income on the consumer's consumption of the *two* goods.

Income-consumption curve

If the consumer's income decreases, *ceteris paribus*, exactly the opposite will happen. The budget line will shift parallel to the left (ie closer to the origin). The original indifference curve will no longer be attainable. The consumer's total utility will be reduced as a result of the decrease in income.

Normal and inferior goods

When the consumer's income changes, the equilibrium quantities of the goods concerned will not always change in the same direction. If an increase in income results in an increase in the quantity demanded of a good, the product is called a *normal good.* If an increase in income causes a decrease in the quantity demanded, the good is called an *inferior good.* Later we will see that whether a consumer regards a good as inferior or normal is a very personal matter.

Figure 3-8
The effect of an increase in income

The original equilibrium is at B. If the consumer's income increases, the budget line shifts parallel to the right and a new equilibrium B′ is obtained on a higher indifference curve U_2. By joining B and B′ we obtain an income-consumption curve.

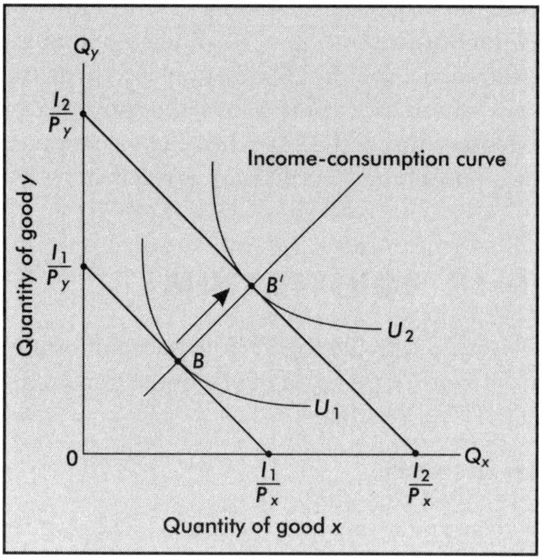

When a consumer's income increases, there are three possible outcomes, as shown in Figure 3-9. In the figure we show the original budget line (HJ), indifference curve (U_1) and equilibrium point (E_0).

The new budget line after the increase in income is represented by KL. We do not show all the possible new indifference curves. We only show three possible new equilibrium points (ie points where the new budget line is tangent to higher indifference curves).

- If the budget line KL just touches the highest attainable indifference curve at point A, then both x and y are normal goods. After an increase in income more of both x and y is consumed.
- If consumer equilibrium occurs at point B, then y is a normal good and x is an inferior good. After an increase in income more of y but less of x is consumed than before.
- If consumer equilibrium occurs at point C, then y is an inferior good and x is a normal good. After an increase in income less of y but more of x is consumed than before.

Figure 3-9

Normal and inferior goods

The consumer is originally in equilibrium at E_0. When the consumer's income increases, the budget line shifts parallel to KL. The new equilibrium point may fall in three ranges, denoted by the broken lines through the original equilibrium point E_0. If equilibrium occurs at a point such as A, then x and y are both normal goods. If the new equilibrium is at a point such as B, then x is an inferior good; if it is at a point such as C, then y is an inferior good.

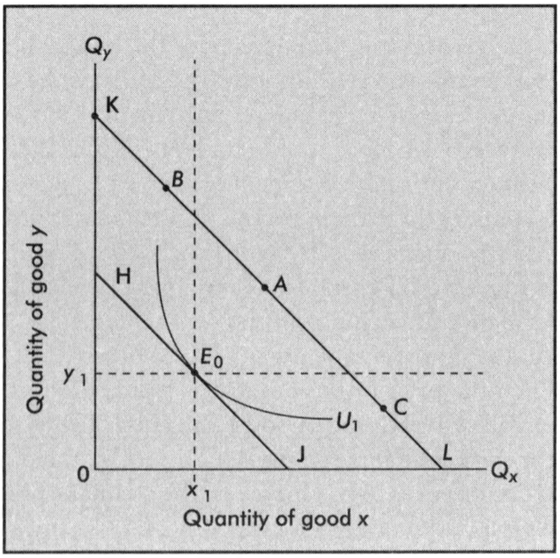

We will return to the impact of changes in income when we analyse the effect of a price change.

A change in price, the price-consumption curve and the demand curve of an individual consumer

What is the reaction of consumers to a change in the relative price of a commodity? In general we can say that as the price of a good declines (ie it becomes relatively cheaper than other goods) the quantity demanded will increase; likewise, if the price of a product increases (ie it becomes relatively more expensive) the quantity demanded will decrease. This relationship can be explained by using indifference curve analysis.

For the purpose of the analysis the price of product y (ie P_y) and the income (I) of a typical consumer are kept constant, while the price of product x (ie P_x) decreases. This is illustrated in Figure 3-10 where the indifference map of the consumer is depicted. We have already seen that the budget line can be drawn if we have its intercepts on the vertical and horizontal axis respectively. (The intercepts we get by asking how much of a commodity could be purchased at the existing price levels if none of the other commodity were purchased.) Consider the horizontal axis. When the price of x is P_x, the amount that can be purchased (if the consumer buys only x) is determined by dividing P_x into total money income I, which gives I/P_x. This is indicated at B in Figure 3-10. When the price of x falls to P'_x, the maximum amount of x that can be purchased expands to B′; and it expands to B″ when the price falls further to P''_x. Thus, even though the money income of the consumer does not change, the amount of x that can be purchased with his income increases with each fall in price.

On the vertical axis the intercept of the budget line is I/P_y and because the price of y does not change, this intercept remains the same (see point A). With each price decrease of x the budget line changes – from the original AB to AB′ and then to AB″. Each time the budget line changes there will be a new point of consumer optimum. At first it is at point E, then point E′, and then point E″. If we connect these three points, we obtain a *price-consumption curve*. The price-consumption curve is defined as the locus of optimum combinations of x and y that result from a change in relative prices, holding money income constant. The course of a price-consumption curve depends on the consumer's indifference map, therefore it is not always shaped exactly like the illustration in Figure 3-10. (When the price of the product is increasing instead of decreasing, the budget line will swivel in the opposite direction. Let us start at point E″ in Figure 3-10 – for successive increases in the price of x, the budget line AB″ will change to AB′ and then to AB. However, the resultant price-consumption curve will be the same and will go through points E″, E′ and E.)

Price-consumption curve

The information depicted by the price-consumption curve in Figure 3-10 forms the basis for the derivation of the price-demand curve (or demand curve, for short) of the particular individual. In the analysis nominal income (I), the price of product y (ie P_y) and the consumer's tastes are held constant. Realising this, we plot the points representing the quantities (x_1, x_2 and x_3) of x demanded at the equilibrium points and the associated prices (P_x, P'_x and P''_x). This gives us three points from which to construct the individual's demand curve shown in Figure 3-10(b). The demand curve shows the quantities of *one* specific good (good x in this instance) that will be demanded at various prices. The price of the good appears on the one axis and the quantity demanded on the other. The shape of the demand curve (falling from left to right) is important and is also a graphic representation of the law of demand, which was introduced in Chapter 2. This shape of the demand curve is regarded as the normal shape and has often been proved to be correct by empirical research. (Note that the demand curve differs from the price-consumption curve. The price-consumption curve relates to the quantities of *both* goods; the demand curve refers to *one* good whose price changes. The price-consumption curve also does not explicitly show the price of the good.)

By horizontally adding all the demand curves of the individuals who buy the particular product, the market demand curve is derived. This has already been explained in Chapter 2.

Income and substitution effects of a price change

Why is there a change in the quantity demanded of a good when the price of the good increases or decreases? To answer this question we have to distinguish between the two separate effects of a price change on a consumer, namely the *income* and the *substitution effect.* One of the major advantages of the indifference approach is that it allows us to point out these two effects.

Income effect

To explain the income and substitution effects, we consider a *decrease* in the price of a good. When the price of a good falls, while the prices of all other goods remain the same, consumers who buy that product experience an increase in their real incomes, even if their nominal incomes are unchanged; consumers can therefore buy more goods with the same income. In terms of indifference curve analysis, an increase in real income means that the consumer is able to reach a higher level of satisfaction by moving to a higher indifference curve. The effect of a change in real income on the consumer's purchases of a certain good is called the *income effect.* This is similar to the effect of a change in real income as a result of a change in nominal income with prices unchanged. We have seen before (Fig 3-9) that a rise in real income leads to an increase in the consumption of a normal good, but causes a decrease in the consumption of an inferior good. With a normal good, therefore, the income effect is positive, but with an inferior good it is negative. Since inferior goods are the exception, we start off by analysing a normal good. Once we have done this, we shall study what happens with inferior goods.

Substitution effect

Quite apart from the income effect, a decrease in the price of a good also means that the good becomes cheaper relative to all other goods, if their prices have remained constant. Therefore it becomes an attractive option to purchase more of the good whose price has fallen. If our consumer buys only meat and vegetables, and the price of meat falls while the price of vegetables stays the same, then there will be a tendency for the consumer to buy more meat, *but less vegetables.* This is known as the *substitution effect*, because the consumer substitutes the good that has become relatively cheaper for the one that has become relatively more expensive.

The income and substitution effects in a normal good can be analysed graphically as in Figure 3-11. If Q_VQ_M is the initial budget line, then the consumer is in equilibrium at point A. Here, the consumer purchases m_1 portions of meat. If the price of meat falls, while the price of vegetables and the consumer's money income remain constant, the position of the budget line will change, to $Q_VQ'_M$. The new point of consumer equilibrium is at B, where m_2 units of meat are

Figure 3–10
The impact of a price change and the derivation of a demand curve

The impact of an increase in the price of product x is illustrated in (a). The original budget line is AB and the original equilibrium point is E on indifference curve U_1. When the price of product x decreases, the budget line swivels to AB′ and a new equilibrium E′ is reached on a higher indifference curve U_2. A further price decrease will have the budget line AB″ with the equilibrium point E″ on indifference curve U_3 as a result. By joining points E, E′ and E″ we obtain a price–consumption curve. The decrease in the price of product x leads to an increase in the quantity demanded of x. This relationship, which is illustrated in (b), is the familiar demand curve of an individual consumer.

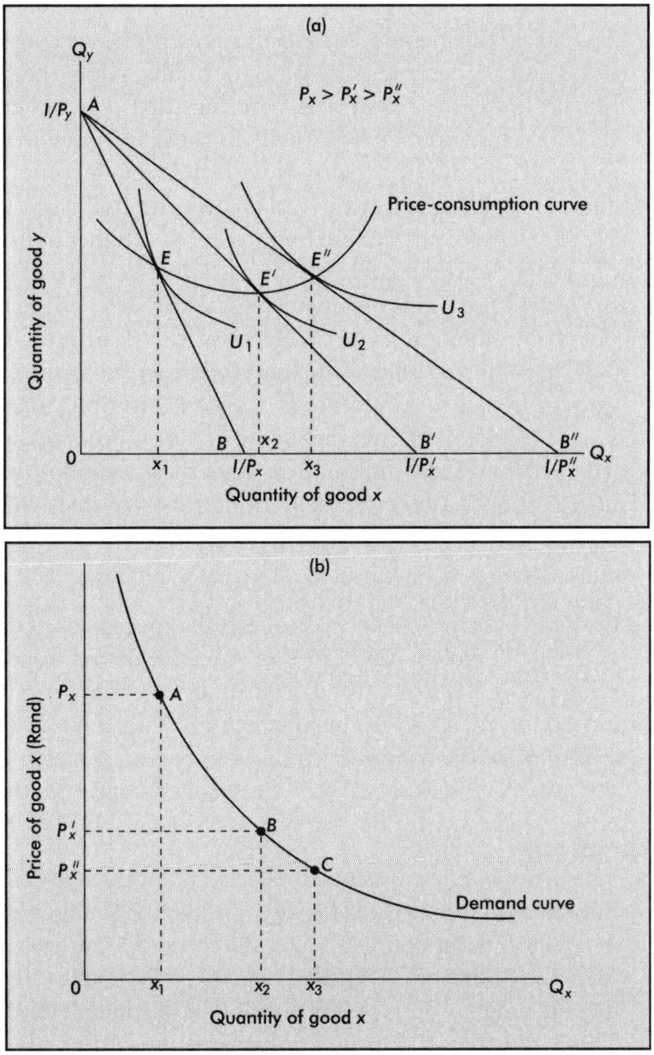

purchased. This increase in the consumption of meat, also depicted by the movement from A to B, is called the price effect and is the combined impact of the income and substitution effects. We now analyse the separate contribution of each effect to this increase in consumption.

We draw an auxiliary line, ZZ, parallel to the new budget line ($Q_V Q'_M$), which therefore has the same slope and indicates the same price ratio as $Q_V Q'_M$. Line ZZ is tangent to the original indifference curve U_1 at point C. That a fall in the price of meat has increased the consumer's real income is reflected in the movement from indifference curve U_1 to U_2. The movement from C to B can be ascribed solely to the *income effect*. Any possibility that the movement could be due to the substitution effect is eliminated because lines $Q_V Q'_M$ and ZZ are parallel, and as such indicate the same price ratio.

What about the movement from A to C? At A, the original price ratio applied, whereas at C the new price ratio applies. Because meat has become relatively cheaper, the consumer purchases more meat but less vegetables – that is to say, the consumer substitutes meat for vegetables, which is shown in the movement from A to C. The movement from A to C can therefore be attributed to the *substitution effect*. Note that the movement from A to C takes place on the same indifference curve, which means that the consumer's real income is kept unchanged. Any possibility of income being even partly responsible for the movement from A to C is thereby eliminated.

Price effect

It is clear that the movement from A to B, termed the *price effect*, indeed comprises two separate effects, namely the *substitution effect* (A to C) and the *income effect* (C to B). In a normal good both the income and substitution effects are in the same direction and reinforce one another. If we draw the demand curve for this normal good, it will have the standard shape of a demand curve, such as the one in Figure 3-10(b). For the sake of completeness the demand curve is also shown in Figure 3-11. The price-quantity combination represented by point A is also reflected by point A′ in the lower half of the figure. The price-quantity combination represented by point B (the decrease in the price of meat had a greater quantity demanded as a result) is also reflected by point B′ in the lower half of the figure. The demand curve therefore has the typical shape, namely sloping downwards from left to right.

Inferior goods

The analysis in Figure 3-11 applies to normal goods, that is goods for which the income effect is positive. But the income effect can also be negative, that is, the quantity demanded may move in the opposite direction to the change in real income caused by the price change. When this happens, the goods are called *inferior goods*. Whether a consumer regards a good as inferior or not is a personal

Figure 3–11

The income and substitution effects of a price change

The original budget line is Q_VQ_M. When the price of meat falls, the budget line swivels to $Q_VQ'_M$. Equilibrium shifts from A on indifference curve U_1 to B on indifference curve U_2. The movement from A to B (or from m_1 portions of meat to m_2 portions of meat) is the *price effect.* By means of the auxiliary line ZZ the price effect can be divided into a *substitution effect* A to C (or from m_1 to m_3) and an *income effect* C to B (or from m_3 to m_2). In a normal product these two effects are in the same direction and the demand curve has a normal course.

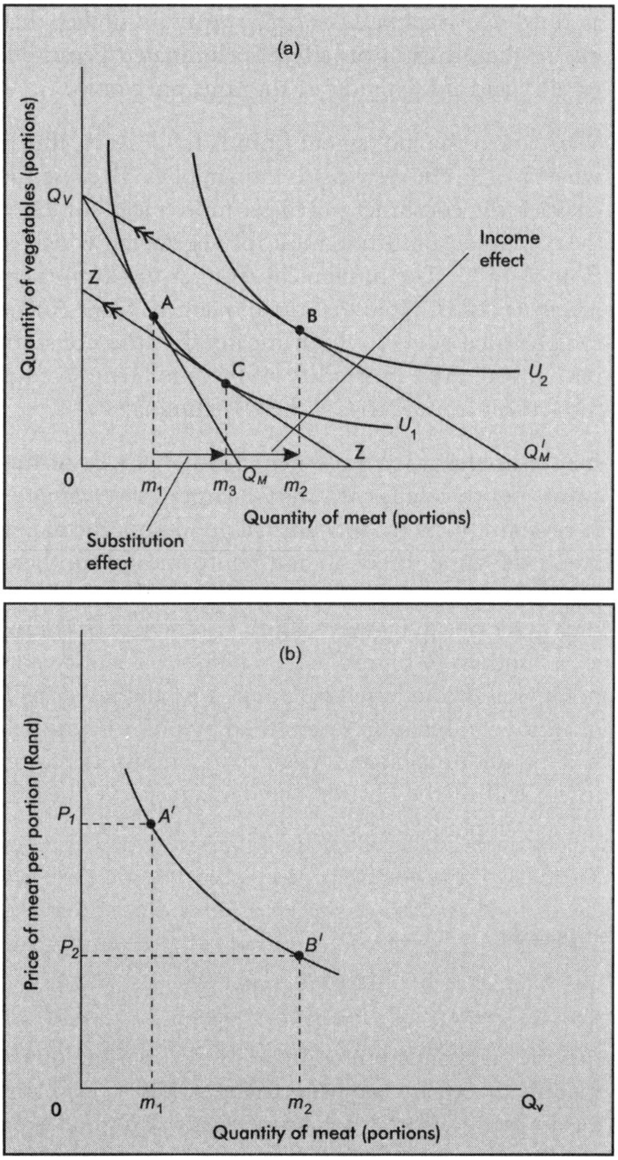

matter and does not necessarily refer to the quality of the product. One consumer may regard bread as an inferior good – if his real income increases he will purchase less bread (and perhaps more meat). Another consumer may regard paraffin as an inferior good – if his real income increases he will rather use electricity for household purposes. Other consumers may have different views on this. Nevertheless, in inferior goods the income effect of a price change is in the opposite direction to the substitution effect. This is shown in Figure 3-12.

In the figure we have two goods, x and y. The original budget line is Q_yQ_x. When the price of x (an inferior good) falls, the budget line swivels to $Q_yQ'_x$. Equilibrium shifts from A on indifference curve U_1 to B on indifference curve U_2. The movement from A to B (or from x_1 to x_2 units of x) is the price effect. This can be divided into a substitution effect A to C (from x_1 to x_3) and an income effect C to B (from x_3 to x_2). ZZ is an auxiliary line parallel to the new budget line ($Q_yQ'_x$) which enables us to isolate the substitution effect from the income effect. The only difference between this figure and Figure 3-11 is that the income effect is negative (because x is an inferior good) and is now in the opposite direction to the substitution effect. However, the substitution effect is stronger than the income effect and the price effect is therefore still normal. The demand curve for an inferior good will also slope downwards from left to right (see the bottom half of Fig 3-12) and there is still an inverse relationship between the price of the good and the quantity demanded. However, the demand curve of an inferior good will be less elastic than that of a normal good because the negative income effect results in the quantity demanded of an inferior good being less sensitive to price changes.

Giffen goods

It is theoretically possible (but unlikely to happen) that the negative income effect from a decrease in the price of an inferior good can be stronger than the substitution effect. If this is so, we will have the peculiar situation where a price decrease of such a product will result in less (instead of more) of the good being demanded. Similarly, a price increase will be accompanied by an increase in the quantity demanded of the good. This is contradictory to the law of demand. This possibility is called the *Giffen case* (or Giffen paradox) after Sir Robert Giffen, who reputedly observed in the nineteenth century that the demand curve for bread among poor English households was positively sloped – an increase in the price of bread resulted in an increase in the demand for bread by the households. However, it is doubtful whether such Giffen goods really existed and even if they do exist they will be extremely rare. The theoretical possibility is nevertheless illustrated in Figure 3-13.

Giffen paradox

In Figure 3-13 we again have two goods, x and y. The original budget line is Q_yQ_x. When the price of x (a Giffen good) decreases, the budget line swivels

Figure 3–12

The income and substitution effects in an inferior good

The original budget line is Q_yQ_x. When the price of x (an inferior good) falls, the budget line swivels to $Q_yQ'_x$. Equilibrium shifts from A on indifference curve U_1 to B on indifference curve U_2. The movement from A to B (or from x_1 to x_2 units of x) is the price effect. This can be divided into a substitution effect A to C (from x_1 to x_3) and an income effect C to B (from x_3 to x_2). ZZ is an auxiliary line parallel to the new budget line ($Q_yQ'_x$) which enables us to isolate the substitution effect from the income effect. The income effect is now in the opposite direction to the substitution effect. It is, however, smaller than the substitution effect and the price effect is therefore still normal. The demand curve of an inferior good also slopes downwards from left to right, but is less elastic than that of a normal good.

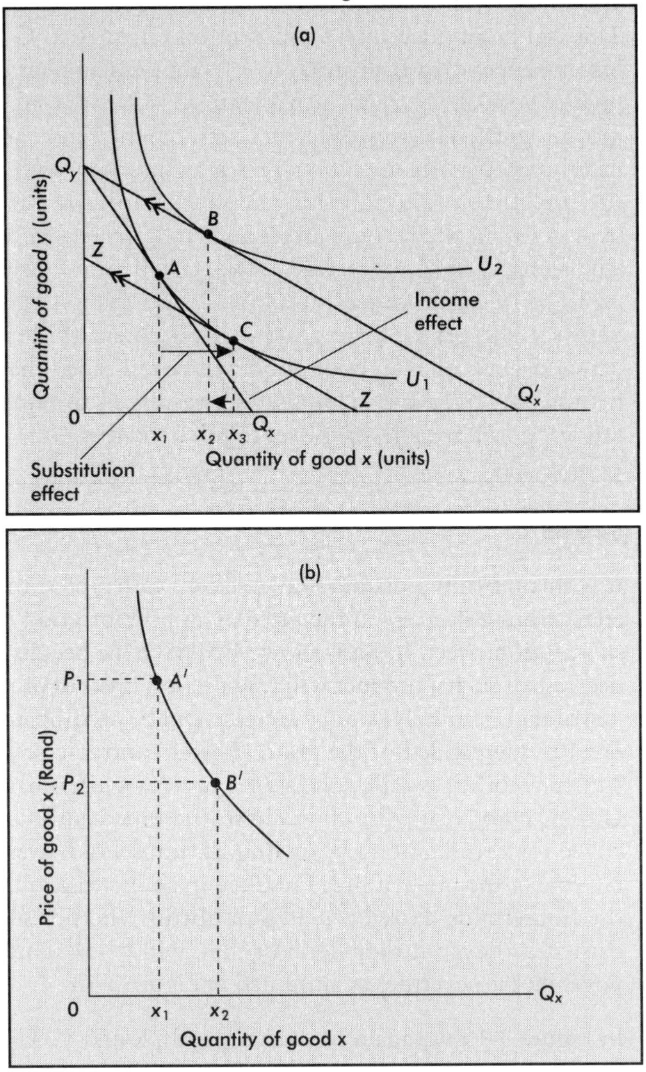

Figure 3–13
The income effect and substitution effect in a Giffen good

The original budget line is Q_yQ_x. When the price of x (a Giffen good) decreases, the budget line swivels to $Q_yQ'_x$. Equilibrium shifts from A on indifference curve U_1 to B on indifference curve U_2. The movement from A to B (or from x_1 to x_2 units of x) is the price effect. With the aid of the auxiliary line ZZ the price effect can be divided into a substitution effect A to C (from x_1 to x_3) and an income effect C to B (from x_3 to x_2). The income effect is not only in the opposite direction, but is also stronger than the substitution effect – therefore the price effect is not normal. The demand curve for a Giffen good slopes upwards from left to right.

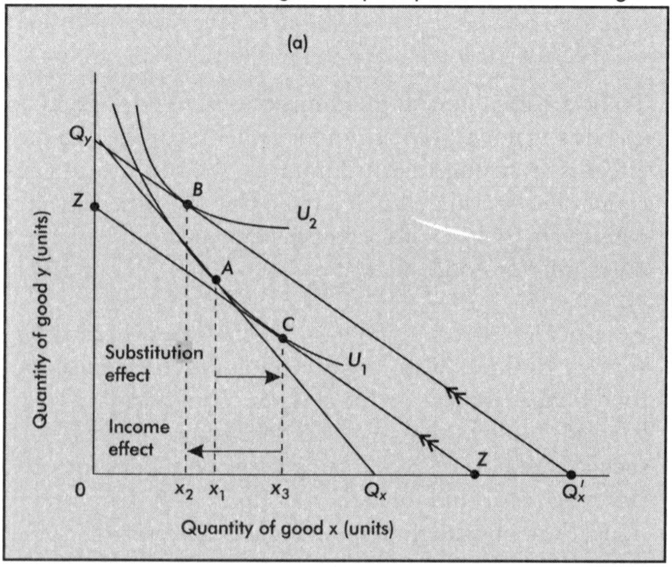

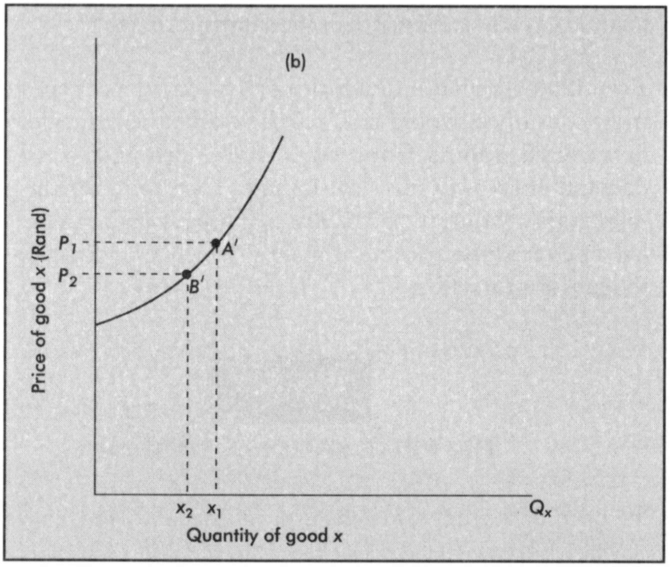

to $Q_yQ'_x$. Equilibrium shifts from A on indifference curve U_1 to B on indifference curve U_2. The movement from A to B (or from x_1 to x_2 units of x) is the price effect. This can be divided into a substitution effect A to C (from x_1 to x_3) and an income effect C to B (from x_3 to x_2). ZZ is an auxiliary line parallel to the new budget line $Q_yQ'_x$ which enables us to isolate the substitution effect from the income effect. Here the income effect is not only in the opposite direction from the substitution effect, but the income effect is also stronger than the substitution effect. The price effect is therefore not normal, because a decrease in the price of good x resulted in a decrease in the quantity demanded of good x (it decreased from x_1 to x_2). The abnormal demand curve which follows from this is depicted in the bottom half of Figure 3-13.

To be a Giffen good a good must be an inferior good on which the consumer spends a major percentage of his or her income, with the result that the income effect is so strong that it dominates the substitution effect. This leads to the conclusion that the Giffen paradox, if it exists, may apply only to very poor consumers (only a poor consumer would spend a large proportion of income on an inferior good).

Consider an extremely poor individual whose limited budget is devoted almost entirely to food. With the exception of a little meat, most of this consumer's food budget is spent on the cheapest form of nutrition available – we assume it is bread. Now assume that the price of bread increases. Since bread comprises such a large portion of the budget, the poor consumer is now even poorer. The price increase could force the consumer to give up meat entirely and buy additional bread instead. In response to the increase in the price of bread, more bread instead of less bread will therefore be consumed – this is because the negative income effect is stronger than the substitution effect.

Even if a particular individual were to regard a certain good as a Giffen good, most consumers would not, and the market demand curve for the good will be downward sloping from left to right, although one consumer's individual demand curve was upward sloping. Therefore, for the purpose of predicting market behaviour, the possibility of Giffen goods can be ignored. It is nevertheless an interesting theoretical analysis which also illustrates the income effect and the substitution effect.

Box 3-2

THE PRICE EFFECT: A SUMMARY

When the price of a product increases or decreases it leads to a reaction by the consumer which is known as the price effect. The price effect consists of an income effect as well as a substitution effect and there is no a priori reason to expect these two effects to work in the same direction.

Price effect = Income effect + Substitution effect

Following a fall in price of one of the goods, the *substitution effect* will always induce an individual to purchase more of the cheaper good.

The *income effect*, however, may work in two entirely opposite directions. If the good is a normal good, then more of the good whose price fell will be purchased. If the good is an inferior good, then less of the good will be purchased.

The price effect can therefore manifest itself in three different ways, depending on the good in question. In the following table the three possible cases following a fall in the price of a product are summarised. The convention is followed that if more of the good is desired we refer to the effect as being positive; if less of the good is desired we refer to the effect as being negative.

	Substitution effect	**Income effect**	**Price effect**
Normal good	+	+	+
Inferior good	+	–	+
Giffen good	+	–	–

In a *normal good* both the substitution effect and the income effect are in the same direction and the price effect is therefore positive. The demand curve has a normal slope, namely downwards from left to right. In an *inferior good* the price effect is also positive because the positive substitution effect is stronger than the negative income effect. The demand curve still has a normal slope. In a *Giffen good* the price effect is negative because the negative income effect is stronger than the positive substitution effect. The demand curve of the individual consumer at issue will be abnormal – it will slope upwards from left to right.

THE INDIFFERENCE TECHNIQUE APPLIED TO LABOUR

Trade-off between work and leisure

It has already been said that indifference curves are used not only to analyse consumers' behaviour, but also to analyse the production factor market. For example, an interesting application of the indifference curve technique is found in the labour market. When individuals offer their labour in the market, they are offering something that they themselves can also use, because the time that they do not work can be used for leisure activities. The extent to which an individual is willing to trade off leisure for work depends on the shape and position of his or her indifference curves.

In Chapter 2 we have seen that supply curves of goods normally slope upwards from left to right, which means that higher prices usually lead to an increase in the quantity supplied. An interesting characteristic of an individual's supply curve of labour, however, is that it can bend backwards at some stage. In such a case a further increase in the wage rate (the price of labour) may lead to less of the production factor labour being offered by the individual.

Consider Figure 3-14 where the indifference curves describe how a hypothetical individual feels about the trade-off between leisure and income. The time period we are considering in this analysis is one day, therefore 24 hours are indicated on the horizontal axis as the maximum hours available for leisure. A second horizontal axis in Figure 3-14 measures the number of hours the individual worked during the day. Per definition all time must be spent in either leisure or work – therefore the second horizontal axis starts at 24 (when no time is spent in leisure) and ends at 0 (when 24 hours are spent in leisure). When the two axes are considered together it is obvious that if for example the individual works 14 hours (lower axis), then 10 hours were used for leisure (higher axis); if 6 hours were spent working, then 18 hours were available for leisure, etc.

If the wage rate (rand per hour) is equal to W, then we can easily compute the daily income Y the individual receives for working H hours, since

$$Y = WH$$

This equation is linear and is drawn in Figure 3-14 for five different hourly wages. All of these lines originate at the right end of the horizontal axis, because if leisure equals 24 hours, then work must equal 0 hours, so that Y will also be equal to 0 regardless of the hourly wage rate. For example, if the hourly wage is R1,00, then the straight line depicting the equation Y = WH originates at the right end of the horizontal axis where 0 hours are worked per day, because $Y = 0 \times R1,00 = 0$. The same line will intersect the vertical axis at a daily income of R24,00, since $Y = 24 \times R1,00 = R24,00$. For any number of hours worked between these two extremes, the daily income can be read from this line. If the wage rate is R0,50 per hour and 6 hours per day are worked, we would be at point A in the figure, representing a daily income of R3,00 on the vertical axis. As the hourly wage rate rises, the lines depicting the equation Y = WH intersect at increasingly higher points on the vertical axis (measuring daily income), while the horizontal axis intercept remains the same. Thus, the hourly wage determines the slope of the straight lines, which economists call constraint lines. Each

Figure 3–14

Backward-bending supply curve of labour

The indifference curves show that as the hourly wage rises, the individual is initially willing to work extra hours – see the equilibrium points A, B and C. However, a point is reached where a further increase in the wage rate results in a decrease in the hours worked – see points D and E. This results in a backward-bending supply curve.

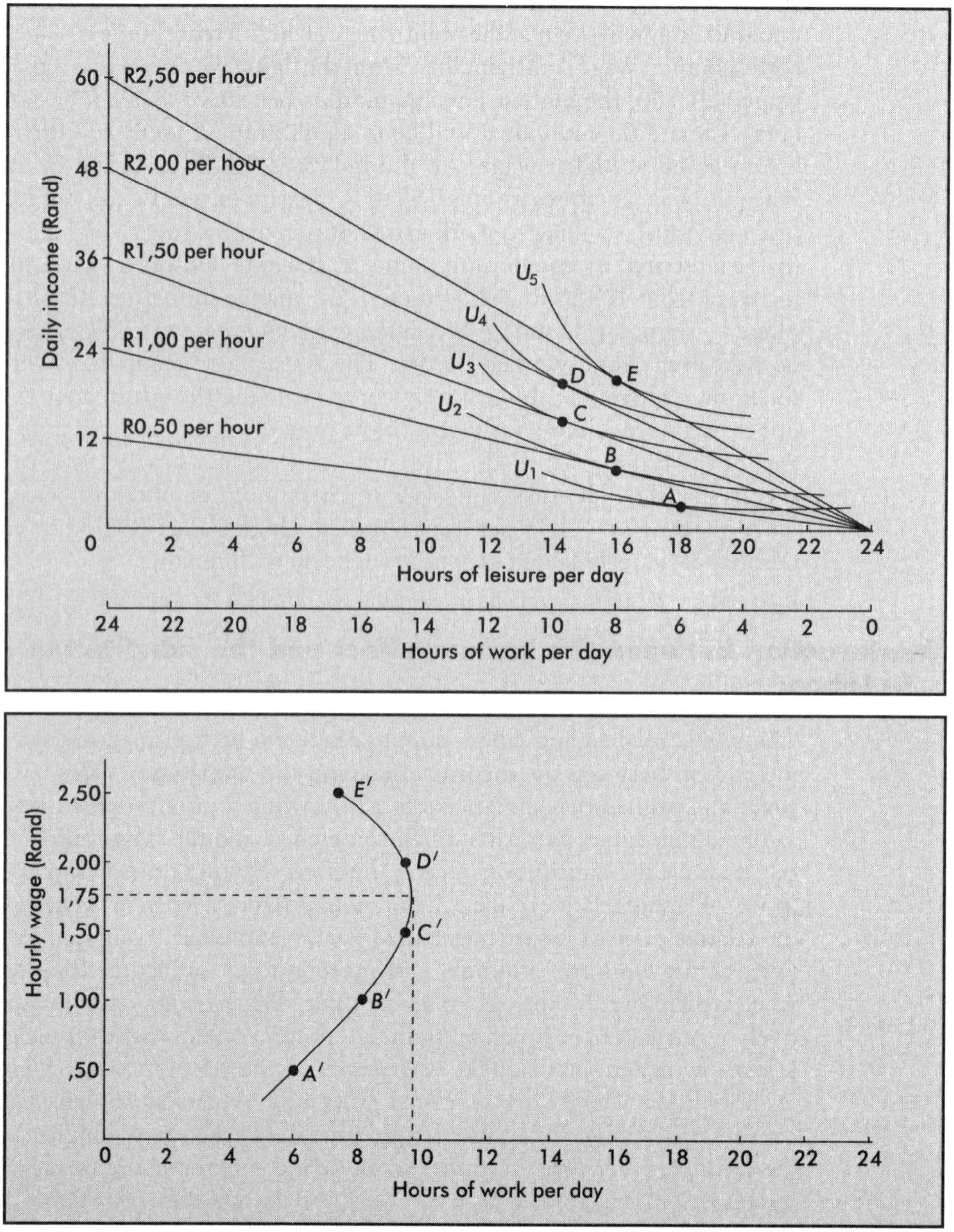

of these lines represents a wage constraint under which the individual must maximise utility.

Backward-bending supply curve of labour

The two 'products' between which the consumer has to choose in the indifference curve diagram are income on one axis and leisure on the other axis. Utility maximisation will occur at the point where an indifference curve is tangent to its corresponding wage constraint line. From the figure we can see that if the hourly wage is R0,50, the highest possible indifference curve that can be reached is curve U_1 and the individual will be in equilibrium at point A. Other equilibrium points at higher wages are also indicated (see B, C, D and E). Initially, when the wage increases from R0,50 to R1,00 and then to R1,50, our hypothetical individual is willing to work extra hours in order to earn a higher income – that is illustrated by equilibrium points A, B and C. However, when the wage increases from R1,50 to R2,00 there is no change in the quantity of labour offered – see points C and D. When the wage increases to R2,50 there is even a decrease in the hours worked per day. This is also illustrated in the lower part of the figure, where the labour supply curve depicting the information from the upper part of the figure, is shown. (Note how the horizontal axis in the lower part of the figure is labelled.) The backward-bending supply curve of labour reveals that the individual will work the maximum number of hours per day when the wage is R1,75 per hour. At wages higher than R1,75 per hour the number of hours of labour supplied will begin to diminish.

Interaction between the income effect and the substitution effect in labour

The backward-bending labour supply curve can be explained in terms of the interaction between the income effect and the substitution effect. We have already explained that the price effect (following a price increase or decrease) can be divided into two parts: the income effect and the substitution effect. In our example the substitution effect is the effect resulting from an increase in the 'price' of leisure relative to the price of other products. When the wage increases, the relative price of leisure increases as well, because each hour spent in leisure (rather than working) will now cost more in terms of income forgone. (The wage is therefore also the cost of leisure time.) When leisure time becomes relatively more expensive it will result in the consumer decreasing the time used for leisure – which means that if the wage increases, the substitution effect will result in more hours being worked. Stated differently: when the wage increases, the consumer is willing to sacrifice leisure time in order to earn a higher income; the consumer therefore substitutes work (ie income) for leisure (ie more work, less play).

In addition to the substitution effect there is an income effect, which in this example is quite different from the income effect in the purchase of most consumer goods. In the first place, the income effect here works in the opposite direction from the income effect in the purchase of the typical consumer product. As we have seen previously, the income effect of a price decrease of a (normal) good is generally to increase the consumption of the good, because the consumer's real income has increased. Similarly, the income effect of a price increase will result in the consumer buying less of the product, because his real income has decreased. However, this is not so here. An increase in the price of his leisure time due to an increase in his wage makes the consumer more affluent and better able to afford the things he wants, including leisure. Thus the income effect of an increase in the price of leisure is likely to be an increase in the demand for leisure.

Figure 3-15

Income effect and substitution effect in labour

The individual is initially in equilibrium at point A. Following an increase in the wage rate, the individual is in equilibrium at point C. The substitution effect is the movement from A to B – an increase in the wage rate (ie the price of leisure time) results in work being substituted for leisure time (ie more work, less play). The income effect is the movement from B to C – an increase in real income results in more time being used for leisure. Leisure time is regarded as a normal 'product'.

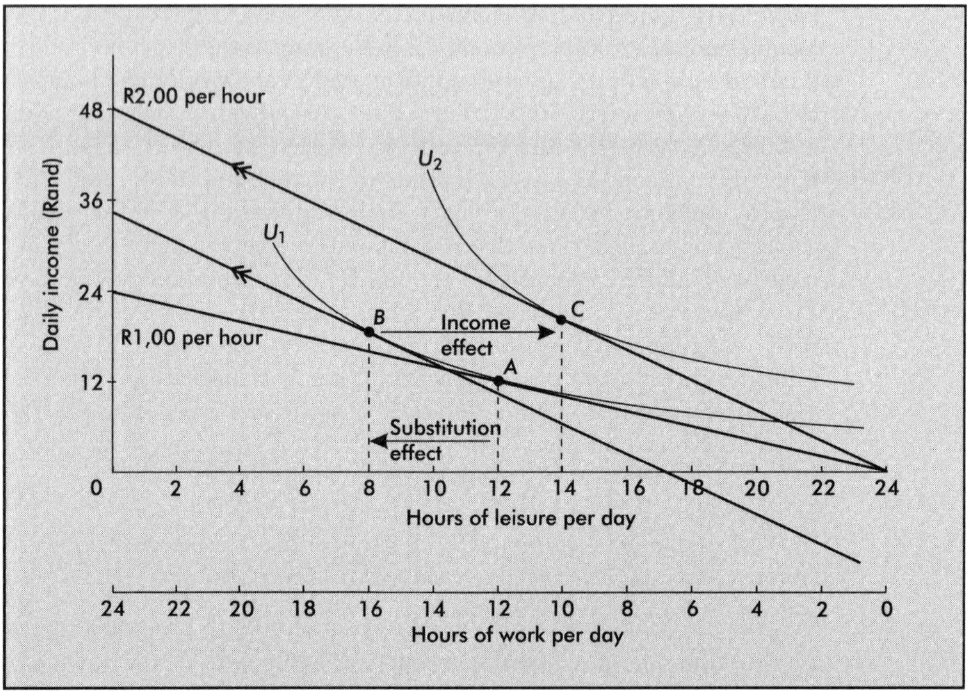

The income effect in this example differs from the income effect for most consumer products in another important respect: it is likely to be much stronger than for most consumer products. In general the consumer spends only a small percentage of his budget on the product in question, with the result than an increase (or decrease) in its price has only a small impact on his real income. However, with leisure, an increase in its price (ie the wage rate) will almost certainly have a great effect on his real income, since most of his income is likely to originate from the sale of his labour. Thus an increase in the price of leisure time is likely to have a great effect on the consumer's income and on his consumption pattern.

The income effect is in the opposite direction from the substitution effect and may offset the latter, with the result that an increase in the wage rate may reduce the supply of labour. Stated differently: an increase in the price of leisure time may increase the quantity demanded of leisure time. (It should be mentioned here that institutional constraints, like the 40-hour week, often prevent workers from choosing their own working hours. It has nevertheless been found that as workers have become more affluent over the years, the average work week has tended to become shorter.)

Graphic representation

Figure 3-15 is a graphic representation of what we have just explained about the income and substitution effects. If the initial wage is R1,00 per hour, the individual at issue will be maximising utility at point A and working 12 hours per day. When the wage is raised to R2,00 per hour, the individual will prefer point C on indifference curve U_2, thereby reducing the amount of work supplied from 12 hours to 10 hours per day. To separate the income and substitution effects, we employ the same techniques that were introduced earlier in the chapter. We construct an auxiliary line that is parallel to the new budget constraint and is tangent to indifference curve U_1 at point B. The substitution effect is the movement from A to B, indicating that when the price of leisure (ie the wage rate) rises, less leisure will be consumed (more work will be done). The income effect is the movement from B to C which indicates that leisure time is a normal good – an increase in real income results in more leisure being consumed. In our example the income effect is stronger than the substitution effect, which shows that the individual wants to work fewer hours per day when the wage rate increases from R1,00 to R2,00 per hour. When the labour supply curve is positively sloped, the substitution effect is stronger than the income effect; when the labour supply curve is negatively sloped (backward-bending) the income effect is stronger than the substitution effect.

It is important to note that it is the labour supply curve of an individual which can become backward-bending at sufficiently high wage rates. The market supply curve for a given occupation or profession cannot be backward-bending, however, because additional workers will be attracted to the market as wages in that market increase relative to wages in other labour markets. Even though the number of hours worked per day, week or month might decline for some workers in that occupation, the total number of hours supplied will increase when wages increase. The *market supply curve* of labour will therefore slope upwards from left to right. This also applies to all variable factors of production.

IMPORTANT CONCEPTS

- Cardinal utility
- Ordinal utility
- Indifference curve
- Indifference map
- Law of substitution
- Marginal rate of substitution
- Budget line
- Consumer equilibrium
- Income-consumption curve
- Price-consumption curve
- Income effect
- Substitution effect
- Price effect
- Normal, inferior and Giffen goods
- Backward-bending supply curve of labour (of an individual)

QUESTIONS

(1) Define each of the following types of consumer goods:
- normal product
- inferior product
- Giffen product (6)

(2) Define an indifference curve. (3)

(3) Explain the three basic assumptions underlying the indifference approach. (6)

(4) Briefly describe the characteristics of indifference curves. (6)

(5) Briefly define the marginal rate of substitution with the aid of an indifference curve diagram. (8)

(6) Briefly define a budget line. Use an indifference diagram to explain consumer equilibrium. (18)

(7) You work for ABC (Pty) Ltd, a firm that sells two products – one that consumers regard as a *normal product*, and the other as an *inferior product*. The Minister of Finance makes a speech in which he emphasises the fact that the economy is doing extremely well at the moment and that the *real income* of the population is going to increase substantially in the next year. One of your colleagues happens to mention that he is unsure how the demand for the firm's two products will change and that he wishes someone could explain it to him scientifically. *Explain in writing in your own words and with the aid of an income-consumption curve, the probable change in demand that the firm can expect in respect of the two products.* (Hint: see the discussion of Figs 3-8 and 3-9.) (12)

(8) Explain in your own words and with the aid of indifference curves, how the demand curve of an inferior product can be derived and how the shape thereof affects the quantity demanded if the price were to decrease. Also explain the operation of the income and substitution effect with the aid of a diagram. (Hint: see the discussion of Fig 3–12.) (20)

(9) Summarise in table form the price effect, the substitution effect and the income effect in respect of a normal, an inferior and a Giffen product. (Follow the convention that if more of a product is required after a decrease in price, the effect can be regarded as positive.) (9)

(10) You work for a production company. During a meeting on wages, the financial manager makes the remark that an individual will always work longer hours if his or her wage rate increases, because according to him 'in all circumstances, the labour supply curve of an *individual* runs upwards from left to right'. *Explain to him that this is not the case, and that sometimes the labour supply curve of an individual may bend backwards. Use indifference curves to illustrate your explanation. Also explain how the income effect and the substitution effect operate in this particular case.* (Hint: see the discussion of Figs 3-14 and 3-15.) (25)

4

PRODUCTION, PRODUCTION FUNCTIONS AND COST CURVES

In the previous chapter the theoretical principles of consumer behaviour were analysed and the demand curve was derived. In this chapter we will start looking at the other side of the market, namely the supply side. The supply side also has a theoretical foundation which is referred to as *production theory*. A number of concepts used in demand theory are applied to analyse production theory.

Production is the process whereby existing factors of production (ie natural resources, labour, capital and entrepreneurship) are used to produce goods and services. Goods, or products, are tangible items such as ballpoint pens, cars or bread; whereas services are intangible, such as the services that a doctor, hairdresser or transport company provides. In this book we will concentrate on the production of tangible items.

The ability and willingness of firms to supply a product on the market depend inter alia on the costs of production. The manufacture of any product involves the use of factors of production which in turn have cost implications. The quantity of a good that a firm would be prepared to supply on the market depends on the price and productivity of the factors of production used, on the one hand, and, on the other hand, on the price that the product will fetch on the market. In this chapter attention will be paid to the general characteristics of production costs. In later chapters product prices will also be considered and the supply decisions of producers will be explained in the light of costs and prices. The price that the producer will fetch for his product is therefore not dealt with in this chapter.

Once you have studied this chapter you should be able to

- describe the various cost and profit concepts
- explain the difference between the short run and the long run
- understand the short-run production function and present it graphically
- use the total product curve to derive the marginal and average product
- understand the long-run production function and the way in which isoquants are used to derive it
- grasp how the different cost curves are derived
- understand the relationship between the different cost curves

THE COST CONCEPT

Opportunity cost

When an economist wishes to determine production costs implicit and explicit costs are both taken into account. What does this entail? *Explicit costs* are the actual expenditures incurred by the firm in order to buy or hire the inputs required in the production process. *Implicit costs,* on the other hand, refer to the value of inputs owned by the firm itself which are also used in the production process. The value of these self-employed inputs must be calculated in terms of what they could have earned in the best alternative use elsewhere.

Implicit costs include the maximum wage or salary which the entrepreneur could have earned in the same position elsewhere (eg as a manager of a similar firm), plus the highest return that the firm could obtain from investing its capital elsewhere and renting out its land and other inputs. The inputs which the firm owns and uses in its own production process cannot be regarded as being free, even if their use is not accompanied by actual (explicit) expenditure.

As has already been mentioned, the costs of using any input by a firm are equal to the highest earnings which the input could be earning elsewhere (outside the firm). This applies to inputs hired by the firm as well as inputs owned by the firm which are used in the production process. If one of the employees of a firm can earn R60 000 in his best alternative occupation (in another firm), the present employer will be obliged to pay that amount. If the employer pays less, the employee concerned will merely terminate his services and go and work for the other firm. The same applies if the entrepreneur can earn more by managing another firm than he is making in his own business – it would be pointless continuing with his own enterprise. (We ignore the high premium that the entrepreneur could place on being his own boss.) Should a firm use any input itself, the costs thereof have to be taken into account by looking at what the input would earn in its best alternative application (outside the firm).

Opportunity costs

Economists' view of costs, known as *opportunity costs,* therefore include explicit and implicit costs. We can say the following:

economic costs of production = explicit costs + implicit costs
= opportunity costs

An example will help highlight the difference between explicit and implicit costs even more. Suppose that Joe Citizen is the sole proprietor of a small estate agency. He owns the building where his office is housed and uses his own labour and capital to operate the business. Although his business does not incur any explicit rental, interest or labour expenses, by implication rent, interest and a salary are paid. By using his own building as an office Joe is forgoing the rental income that he would have earned if he had rented the building out to someone else. In the same way, by using his capital and labour in his own business, Joe is forgoing the highest interest and salary which he could have earned by applying these resources elsewhere. Joe Citizen's total opportunity costs therefore amount to all the explicit costs (electricity, water, property tax, travel expenses, etc) which he may have *plus* the implicit costs (forgone rent, interest and salary).

It is important to remember that when costs are referred to in this book, the economist's view of costs is assumed. Under certain circumstances these costs may differ markedly from the costs which would be calculated by an accountant.

Normal profit, economic profit and accounting profit

Included in implicit costs is a portion which economists call normal profit. This is the minimum earnings that would be necessary to prevent an entrepreneur from applying his talents and factors of production elsewhere. Stated differently: normal profit is the minimum profit that the owner of a firm would accept in order to become involved in a specific activity and to stay with it. If a firm is making normal profit, it means that the entrepreneur is making exactly as much as he would be making in the best alternative occupation with his own self-employed resources elsewhere. If this minimum profit (or normal profit) is not reached, the entrepreneur will withdraw his factors of production and apply them elsewhere, where the prospects look better. Or, alternatively, the individual will stop being an entrepreneur and go and earn a salary.

Accountants have a somewhat different view of costs, which means that their view of profit also differs from that of economists. For the sake of comprehensiveness the following cases need to be differentiated:

Normal profit

- *Normal profit* is the minimum earnings that will prevent an entrepreneur from employing his factors of production elsewhere. It will therefore be exactly equal to the highest net income which the firm's own self-employed factors of production could earn elsewhere.

Economic profit

- *Economic profit* (also known as excess profit) is the difference between the total income derived from the sale of a firm's output and the opportunity costs (ie explicit and implicit costs, where the latter includes normal profit). If a firm is making economic profit it means that the firm is earning more than it could be earning elsewhere. It is therefore the profit over and above normal profit.

Accounting profit

- *Total or accounting profit* is the difference between a firm's total income from the sale of its product and its explicit costs.

Because of accountants' narrower view of costs, accounting profit is also higher than economic profit. The following should clarify this:

Economic profit = total income – total costs (explicit and implicit)

Accounting profit = total income – total explicit costs

In conclusion: if an economist says that a firm is making a *normal profit*, it means that the firm is covering its economic costs (explicit and implicit costs) and that it is making a profit large enough to retain its factors of production in the present enterprise. If a firm is making more than this, it is earning an *economic profit* (also called an excess profit). A firm can of course also be in a situation where the economic costs surpass the total income – then the firm is making an *economic loss*.

Short and long run

The costs which a firm incurs in the production process will depend on the quantities and combinations of the various factors of production being used. The quantities of some of the factors of production can be changed quickly, whereas others need more time. For example, the capacity of a plant, that is to say the size of the factory and the machinery and equipment that it has at its disposal, can only be adapted over a long period of time. In some industries it can even take years to change the capacity. Differences in the amount of time needed to make such changes have resulted in economists differentiating between the short run and the long run.

Short run: plant size remains unchanged

The short run refers to a time period that is so short that the firm cannot change the size of its production plant, but it can adapt the utilisation of the production plant. Although the firm's capacity remains unchanged over the short run, production can be altered by using more labour and raw materials or less. The existing capacity can therefore be used more intensively over the short run or less.

Long run: plant size changes

From the viewpoint of existing firms the long run refers to a time period that is so long that firms are able to change the quantities of *all their factors of production* – this means that the *capacity* of the production plant can also be changed. From the viewpoint of the industry the long run refers to a time period whereby new firms can come into operation and enter or leave the industry. If SA Breweries employees 100 extra workers, this will be a short-run adjustment. If the same SA Breweries builds a new factory plant, or expands the existing plant by building on or installing new equipment, this will be a long-run adjustment.

It is important to note that the difference between the short run and the long run is more a conceptual difference than a reference to a specific time period. A small firm that manufactures T-shirts can increase its productive capacity within a few days by buying a few new tables and sewing machines. On the other hand, it can take an enterprise like Iscor years to build a plant. The long run is a few days for the T-shirt manufacturer, whereas for Iscor it is a few years.

THE SHORT-RUN PRODUCTION FUNCTION

An example

How do the quantities that a firm produces change as more and more factors of production are used? The answer lies in the production function, which shows the relationship between the quantity of inputs and the outputs that are obtained from the inputs. The production function can be depicted by means of a table, an algebraic equation or a graph.

To illustrate we will look at the most simple case, namely the short-run production function, where it is assumed that at least one factor of production remains unchanged. We assume that we are concerned with the production of maize, where there is only one variable factor of production (labour) which is combined with a fixed quantity of land (say one hectare) in order to produce maize. We also assume that the state of technology remains unchanged. More and more labourers, all of the same quality, are combined with the fixed quantity of land and the maximum total production (TP) per time period (eg bags of maize per month) is recorded. This information appears in Columns (1) to (3) of Table 4-1. The average product (AP) appears in Column (4) which is the total product divided by the number of labourers; the marginal product (MP), which shows the change in TP if labour increases by one unit, appears in Column (5). The same information can also be depicted graphically, as is done in Figure 4-1.

If total product (or output) is represented by TP and L represents labour units, the production function can be written as

$$TP = f(L) \qquad (1)$$

which merely means that the total product is a function of labour inputs.

Table 4–1
Total, average and marginal product
(one variable factor of production)

(1) Land	(2) Labour	(3) TP	(4) AP_L	(5) MP_L
1	0	0	0	–
1	1	3	3	3
1	2	8	4	5
1	3	12	4	4
1	4	15	3,8	3
1	5	17	3,4	2
1	6	17	2,8	0
1	7	16	2,3	–1
1	8	13	1,6	–3

Law of diminishing returns

A closer observation of Table 4–1 and Figure 4–1 shows that total, average and marginal product initially increase, reach a maximum and then decrease. This phenomenon is known as the *law of diminishing returns*. Formally this law can be stated as follows: *if the quantity of a variable factor of production used in the production process increases while the other factors of production remain constant, levels of production will be reached where first the marginal product, then the average product and finally the total product will begin to decrease over time.*

This is a general phenomenon found amongst production functions and does not only apply to the production function which was used here. It originates from the idea that when the variable factor of production (labour) increases, it will initially be very beneficial for production, but the original benefit will eventually become exhausted. In the example in Table 4–1 the use of the second unit of labour contributed significantly to the total product (Column (5) shows that the marginal product was 5), but after that the contribution by additional labour units to the total product starts to decline, until by the seventh unit of labour the contribution becomes negative, as can be seen in the last column. This phenomenon originates from the fact that for a given state of technology it is not always beneficial to employ more of the variable factor of production (labour). A stage is reached where additional workers start to get in the way of and irritate other workers, which means that total production will not increase. It may even decrease as in Table 4-1, Column (3).

It is interesting and somewhat amusing to note that if it were not for the law of diminishing returns, enough maize could be produced for the entire world population on a small piece of land. What is not so funny is that a tragic mis-

Figure 4–1

The relationship between total, average and marginal product

The total product curve appears in the top panel. The point of inflection is at point B where the marginal product changes from increasing to decreasing. At point C the marginal product is equal to the average product, as is shown on the bottom panel at $Q_{C'}$. Beyond point C the average product begins to decrease. At point D the total product reaches a maximum; the marginal product is equal to zero at point D and thereafter becomes negative. Phases I, II and III of the production process are shown in the top panel. Phase II is the economic phase of production.

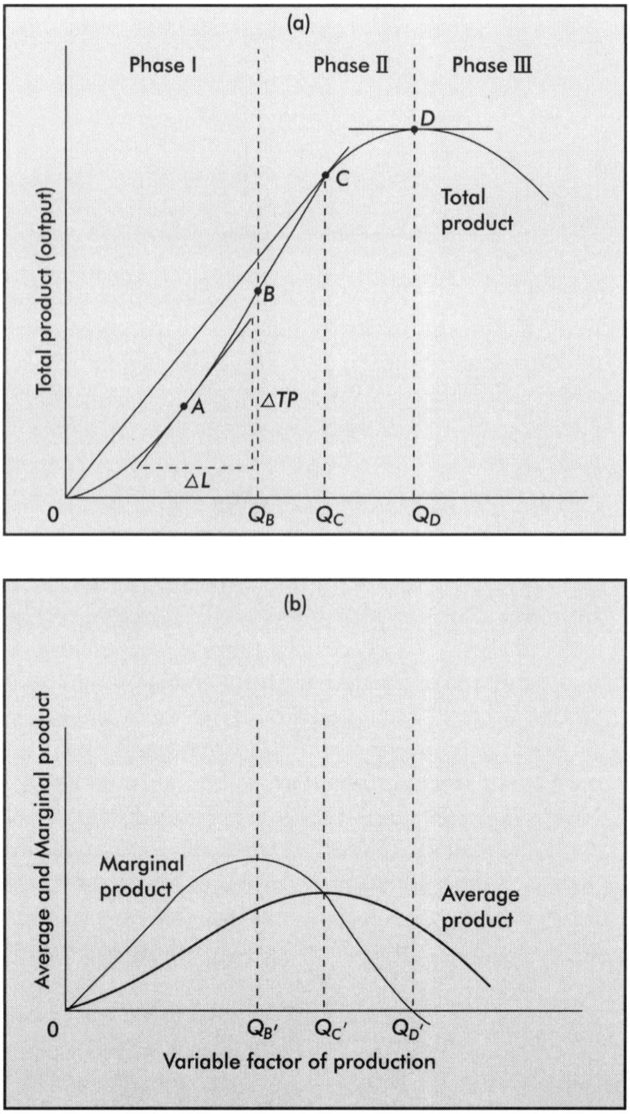

conception as recently as 40 years ago led to the death of millions of people. Read about this in Box 4-1.

Box 4–1

MAO ZEDONG'S MISCONCEPTION

Mao Zedong was elected president of the People's Republic of China in 1949. Shortly thereafter he formulated an eight-point plan to reform agriculture in his country. The most important part of his plan was to plough deep, plant close together and exterminate pests. Mao conceived that it was logical that if 100 rice plants per square metre produced 100 kilograms of rice, then 10 000 plants (the variable factor of production) would produce 10 000 kilograms on the same piece of land. Naturally, the grain died and people starved on a massive scale.

Until as recently as 1980, after many Chinese had died of starvation, numerous small farmers continued to overcultivate – probably as a result of the continuous propaganda from the authorities. Photographs of grain growing so high and so lush that children could sit on top of it often appeared in the press. A photographer later revealed that the children were actually sitting on a bench.

It is obvious that Mao Zedong and his advisors did not know much about agriculture and they most probably had never heard of the law of diminishing returns.

Source: Mao het 30m Chinese laat sterf, *Insig,* March 1997.

Graphic presentation of the short-run production function

Figure 4-1(a) is a graphic presentation of the law of diminishing returns, whereas Figure 4-1(b) is useful for explaining the relationship between total, average and marginal product. The graph is not an exact representation of the figures that appear in Table 4-1 but, what is more important, it reflects the typical course of the curves. By drawing the curves it is assumed that fractions of labour units can be employed, consequently the curves run smoothly. Note that the total product goes through three phases: initially it rises at an increasing rate up to point B, thereafter it continues increasing, but at a decreasing rate up to point D, finally it reaches a maximum at point D, whereafter it begins decreasing. Point B, where the rate of change in the total product curve alters, is known as the point of inflection. As can be seen in the bottom section of Figure 4-1, point B (the point of inflection) can be described as the point where the marginal product changes from increasing to decreasing.

If the total product is known, it is possible to determine the average and marginal products graphically. The technique for this is used repeatedly later in the chapter and must therefore be understood thoroughly.

Marginal product

The *marginal product* (MP) is defined as the change in total product (ΔTP) which occurs if the variable factor of production, labour, increases by one unit (ie $\Delta L = 1$). We can also state it as follows: the marginal product measures the rate of change in the total product (ΔTP) which occurs with each additional labourer (ΔL) – ie $MP_L = \Delta TP/\Delta L$. It is therefore geometrically equal to the slope of the tangent at any point along the total product curve. If at point A in Figure 4-1 the slope of the tangent is $\Delta TP/\Delta L = 3/1 = 3$, then the value of the marginal product at that point is 3. By drawing more tangents, such as the one at point A along the total product curve, the marginal product can be determined, as is done in Column (5) of Table 4-1. (For mathematically minded students, note that the derivative of the function can also be used.)

The three phases through which the total product passes are also reflected by the marginal product. Refer to Figure 4-1: where total product increases at an increasing rate (up to the point of inflection), the marginal product also increases, that is to say, the extra labourers are making increasing contributions to the total product. Where the total product is increasing at a decreasing rate (after the inflection point) the marginal product is positive, but it is decreasing – every additional labourer is actually making a positive contribution, but is adding less to the total product than the previous labourer did. When the total product reaches a maximum the marginal product is equal to zero, that is to say, the last labourer employed contributes nothing to the total product. When the total product starts to decrease the marginal product is negative – the last labourer employed thus causes the total product to decrease rather than increase.

Average product

The *average product* (AP) is defined as the total product (TP) divided by the number of units of labour (L) used in the production process, that is to say $AP_L = TP/L$. The average product is determined geometrically by calculating the slope of a ray from the origin to a point on the total product curve. If at point C in Figure 4-1 a total of 8 bags of maize are produced ($CQ_C = 8$) and 2 units of labour are used in the process ($0Q_C = 2$), then the slope of the ray from the origin to point C will be equal to $CQ_C/0Q_C$, or $8/2 = 4$; this will reflect the value of the average product at point C. Once again points like point C, with rays from the origin, would put us in a position to calculate the average product in Column (4) in Table 4-1.

The average product reflects the same 'increasing-maximum-decreasing' relationship between variable labour inputs and total output as the marginal product. A definite technical relationship exists between the marginal product and the average product (see Fig 4-1(b)): where the marginal product is greater than the average product, the latter increases; where the marginal product is less than the average product, the latter decreases. Hence it follows that the marginal product curve intersects the average product curve at its maximum. This relationship is a mathematical one. In terms of our production example it can be stated as follows: as long as the contribution by each additional worker to the total product is greater than the average product of all the workers who are already employed, then the average product will increase. However, if an additional worker's contribution to the total product is less than the average product at that stage, that worker will cause the average product to decrease.

The law of diminishing marginal output is reflected by the shape of all three curves, in other words by the total product, the average product and the marginal product. Economists, however, are most concerned with the marginal product. In Figure 4-1 the three stages of production, which have already been referred to, are therefore differentiated, namely the stages of increasing, decreasing and negative marginal product (or output) – they are reflected as Phases I, II and III. If we look at Columns (2) and (5) of Table 4-1, we will see increasing marginal output for the first two workers, decreasing marginal output for workers 3 to 6 and negative marginal output for workers 7 and 8. A producer will not want to be in Phase III, because there additional labourers (and therefore costs) lead to a decrease in total product (because marginal product is negative). Up to Phase II additional labour leads to an increase in the total product (because the marginal product is positive) – a producer would therefore prefer to be in Phase II, but will not want to move on to Phase III from there.

THE LONG-RUN PRODUCTION FUNCTION

In the previous section the short-run production function was investigated in which one factor of production remained constant and the other one was variable. In this section the situation is observed where a firm uses two factors of production, namely labour (L) and capital (K) and both factors of production are variable. As long as all factors of production are variable, we are concerned with the long-run production function, which is written as follows:

$$Q = f(L,K) \tag{2}$$

where Q represents the quantity produced.

The technique used in the previous section to analyse the production function with one variable factor of production is somewhat clumsy if there are two variable inputs. We therefore use a new technique which makes use of isoquants. The isoquant concept corresponds with that of indifference curves in many respects.

Definition of isoquants

An isoquant shows the different combinations of labour (L) and capital (K) with which a firm can produce a specific output. A higher isoquant (further from the origin) represents a higher output and a lower isoquant a smaller output.

Properties of isoquants

As has already been mentioned, isoquants have many similarities to indifference curves, which were dealt with in Chapter 3. There are, however, also important differences between isoquants and indifference curves which must be taken into account.

As is already clear from the definition, isoquants show all the combinations of two inputs (factors of production) which, given the production function, produce a specific output. Three isoquants which show how capital and labour are combined to produce three different quantities of output appear in Figure 4-2 – these are only three of an infinite number of isoquants which we could have drawn. The isoquants in the diagram are depicted as Q = 20, Q = 30 and Q = 40 respectively, which refer to the output Q which each one represents. For example, the isoquant Q = 20 shows all the possible combinations of capital and labour which, according to the production function, will produce 20 units of output. In so doing 10 units of capital combined with 2 units of labour (point a in Fig 4-2), or 6 units of capital combined with 4 units of labour (point b in Fig 4-2) will produce an output of 20 units each time. An important difference between indifference curves and isoquants now comes to the fore – the production which an isoquant indicates can be quantified, that is to say it can be depicted in quantifiable units, whereas the level of satisfaction depicted by an indifference curve cannot be quantified.

Isoquants (just like indifference curves) can *never intersect or touch* each other. If two isoquants were to intersect each other, then the same quantity of capital and labour would produce two different levels of output at the point of intersection. This is impossible, seeing that the production function shows the *maximum* output that can be achieved with any combination of inputs. The isoquant which represents the smaller output therefore cannot exist at the intersection. The same argument holds for a point of tangency.

In order to produce a constant level of output, the technical aspect of production requires that if less capital is used in the production process, it must be replaced with labour. This requirement of *technical substitution* has resulted in isoquants having a negative slope, that is to say the relevant part of an isoquant slopes downwards from left to right. The reason for this will become clear in the next paragraph. (Why we talk about the *relevant* part will become clear under the heading 'Ridge lines' on page 100.)

Figure 4–2

An isoquant map

Over the long run both capital and labour can vary in the production process. An isoquant shows different combinations of capital and labour with which a specific output will be produced. Isoquants further away from the origin represent a larger output.

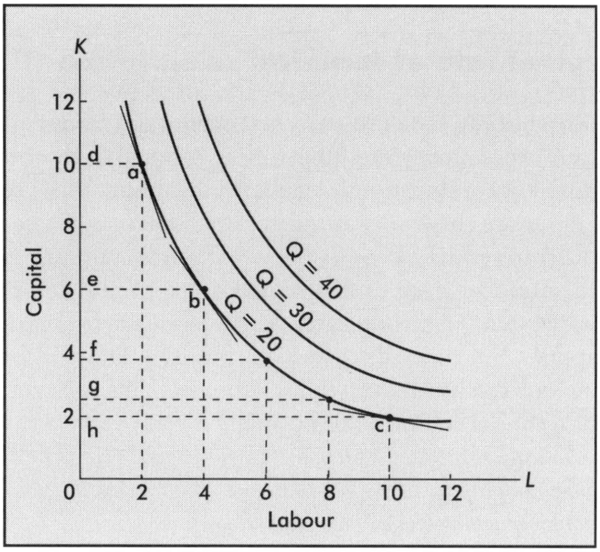

Isoquants are *convex* when viewed from the origin of a graph, that is to say the curves form a 'bulge' which points towards the origin. This property arises because although technical substitution can take place between capital and labour, the substitution is not perfect. This means that if the firm reduces the amount of capital by equal amounts in the production process, the amount of labour that would be required to keep output constant would become more and more. This is also illustrated in Figure 4–2. If the amount of capital required to produce 20 units is decreased from 10 to 6 units, the amount of labour must increase from 2 to 4 units (compare points a and b). A reduction of 4 units of capital thus means that 2 more units of labour need to be used to continue producing an output of 20. If we now move from point b to point c in the diagram, we see that a further decrease of 4 units of capital will result in labour having to be increased by 6 units to keep output constant. To move from point b to point c the firm therefore has to substitute more labour per unit of capital than when moving from point a to b. (The same principle applied to indifference curves.)

Another (reverse) method of explaining the same result is as follows: for a constant level of output the quantity of capital which is replaced by an additional amount of labour will decrease as more and more substitution takes place. This is obvious because in our example the relation of the change in labour to the change in capital

($\Delta L/\Delta K$) was originally 2:4 (ie 1:2) and thereafter changed to 6:4 (ie 1:2/3). Between a and b 1 unit of labour could replace 2 units of capital, but between b and c 1 unit of labour could only replace 2/3 units of capital. This property of the production process is called the principle of the *diminishing marginal rate of technical substitution*. It will be discussed more formally in the next section.

The marginal rate of technical substitution

It has already been proved that if capital and labour are combined in the production process over the long run, it is possible to obtain the same output with different combinations of capital and labour. These combinations of capital and labour are shown by means of an isoquant. We have also mentioned that in order to produce a constant level of production, the technical side of production requires that if less capital is used in the production process, it must be replaced by labour. (The opposite, where labour is replaced by capital, of course also applies, but is not discussed specifically.) The relationship whereby capital can be replaced by labour while output remains constant is called the marginal rate of technical substitution. Formally it can be stated as follows: the *marginal rate of technical substitution of labour (L) for capital (K) (or rather $MRTS_{LK}$) refers to the amount of capital that a firm can give up by increasing the amount of labour by one unit, while remaining on the same isoquant.*

The value of the *marginal rate of technical substitution* of labour for capital at any point along an isoquant is also shown by the absolute value of the *slope* ($\Delta K/\Delta L$) at that point (the negative sign in front of the slope is ignored here and in the rest of the chapter). If we observe points a, b, and c in Figure 4-2, we notice that the absolute value of the slope of the isoquant Q = 20 decreases as we move from point a to b to c. This tendency will continue as we move downwards along an isoquant and we therefore say that the *marginal rate of technical substitution of labour for capital ($MRTS_{LK}$)* decreases. As has already been explained, one unit of labour will be able to replace fewer and fewer units of capital as there is a movement down along the isoquant. (Also study Box 4-2.) It can also be seen in the fact that in Figure 4-2 for *equal increases* in labour on the horizontal axis, the amount of capital replaced on the vertical axis gets *smaller* – compare the decreasing distances between points d, e, f, g and h.

The marginal rate of technical substitution can also be expressed in terms of the marginal product (ie marginal output). The total production, when moving along an isoquant, can only remain unchanged because the production that the producer is 'giving up' by using less capital ($\Delta K \times MP_K$) is exactly cancelled out by the production that the producer 'gains' by using more labour ($\Delta L \times MP_L$). This means that the following condition must be upheld (once more we ignore the signs):

$$\Delta K \times MP_K = \Delta L \times MP_L \qquad (3)$$

where ΔK = the change in the quantity of capital
MP_K = the marginal product of capital
ΔL = the change in the quantity of labour
MP_L = the marginal product of labour

Equation (3) can be rearranged to arrive at the following:

$$\frac{\Delta K}{\Delta L} = \frac{MP_L}{MP_K} \qquad (4)$$

The term $\Delta K/\Delta L$ is the slope of an isoquant. From equation (4) we can therefore determine that the slope of an isoquant is equal to the relation between the marginal products of the two factors of production. We already know that the slope of an isoquant is also equal to the marginal rate of technical substitution (MRTS) between two factors of production. It therefore follows that:

$$\frac{\Delta K}{\Delta L} = \frac{MP_L}{MP_K} = MRTS_{LK} \qquad (4)$$

The marginal rate of technical substitution between labour and capital is therefore also equal to the ratio of the marginal product of labour to the marginal product of capital (in other words $MRTS_{LK} = MP_L/MP_K$). This result is important and will be used again later.

Box 4–2

SUMMARY: THE SLOPE OF AN ISOQUANT

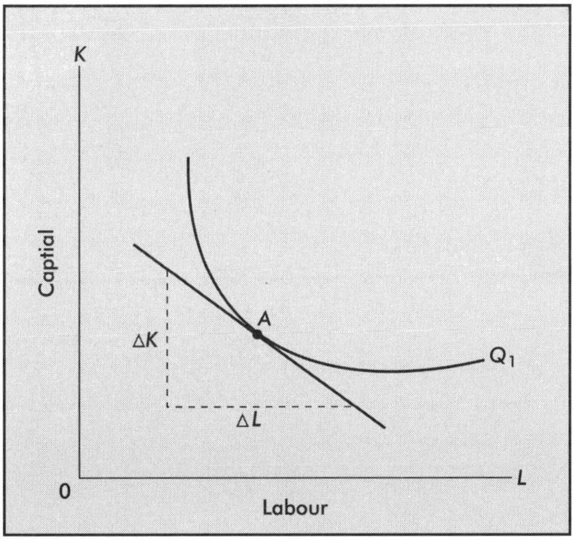

The slope of an isoquant shows the ratio $\Delta K/\Delta L$, which is the ratio whereby capital is replaced by labour while output remains constant. It is known as the marginal rate of technical substitution. At point A the following applies: $MRTS_{LK} = \Delta K/\Delta L = MP_L/MP_k$.

Ridge lines

An isoquant can also have sections with a positive slope, in other words that rise from left to right, like the parts AB and GH in Figure 4-3. A firm, however, will not produce at these points on an isoquant, because the same output can be produced by using less of both labour and capital. For example, at point A in Figure 4-3 more labour and more capital is being used than at point B – the same output can therefore be produced more cheaply at point B than at point A. The same argument holds for points G and H in Figure 4-3. Lines through such points which separate the relevant sections (ie with negative slopes) from the irrelevant sections (ie with positive slopes) of isoquants are called *ridge lines*. In Figure 4-3 0Y and 0X are examples of ridge lines. The area between the ridge lines is called the *technically efficient area* and is the part of the isoquants along which the firm would want to produce.

Figure 4-3
Ridge lines

0Y and 0X are ridge lines. The area between the ridge lines is the technically efficient area where a firm will produce.

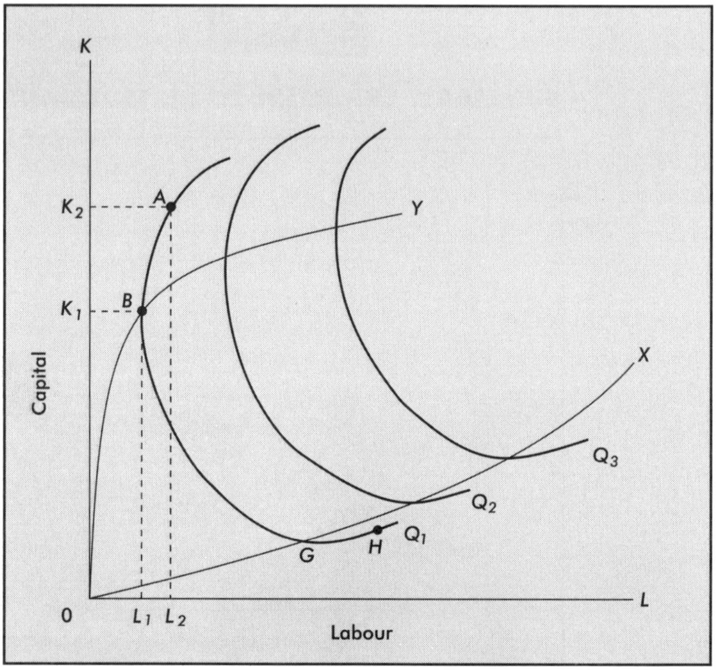

Economies and diseconomies of scale

Economics of scale

Diseconomies of scale

The isoquant concept makes it possible to explain at this stage an economic concept which comes under discussion later in the chapter. In practice it is a general phenomenon that the unit costs of production will decrease as a firm expands by building a bigger plant and increasing production volumes. This is known as internal *economies of scale* and occurs because mass production gives rise to the possibility of lower unit costs of production as a result of factors such as specialisation and the use of better technology. A firm can, however, get too big and reach a stage where additional expansion will lead to greater unit costs – this is known as *diseconomies of scale.*

The concepts of economies and diseconomies of scale are illustrated with the aid of isoquants in Figure 4-4. In each of the diagrams a ray with a 45° angle is drawn. The axes have the same scale, and if there is a movement along the ray the factors of production will increase proportionately. To illustrate we allow the quantity of capital and labour to increase by 100% in each case (from 10 to 20 units) and see what happens to production volumes as a result. The isoquants which appear in each of the diagrams present exactly the same production volumes (100, 200 and 300 units).

Constant returns to scale. In diagram (a) the distance between the three isoquants is constant. If the quantity of capital and labour increases by 100% in this instance, then the output also increases by 100% (from 100 to 200 units). The increase in the output is therefore exactly the same as the increase in the factors of production (in percentage terms). This is known as constant returns to scale and in this case the firm experiences neither economies nor diseconomies of scale.

Increasing returns to scale. In diagram (b) the successive distances between the isoquants become smaller. An increase of 100% in the quantity of capital and labour leads to an increase in output of 200% (from 100 to 300 units) in this case. The output therefore increases by more, in percentage terms, than the factors of production. This is known as increasing returns to scale and in such a case a firm will experience *economies of scale* if it expands. Economies of scale give rise to lower unit costs.

Decreasing returns to scale. In diagram (c) the successive distances between the isoquants become larger. An increase of 100% in the quantity of capital and labour in this case results in a below 100% increase in the quantity of output (from 100 to 180 units). The output therefore increases by a smaller amount, in percentage terms, that the factors of production do. This situation is known as decreasing returns to scale and in such a case the firm experiences *diseconomies of scale* if it expands. Diseconomies of scale lead to higher unit costs.

It is possible that a production function could give rise to increasing, decreasing or constant returns to scale. In reality all three possibilities would probably occur at different stages of production. Initially, when production volumes are small, it can be expected that a firm which expands will experience increasing returns to scale. Thereafter it will most probably experience constant returns to scale. Finally, with high production volumes, decreasing returns to scale will be experienced. As will be seen later, this phenomenon has an influence on the shape of the long-run cost curves.

Figure 4–4

Constant, increasing and decreasing returns to scale

Figure (a) illustrates constant returns to scale, whereas Figure (b) illustrates increasing and Figure (c) decreasing returns to scale.

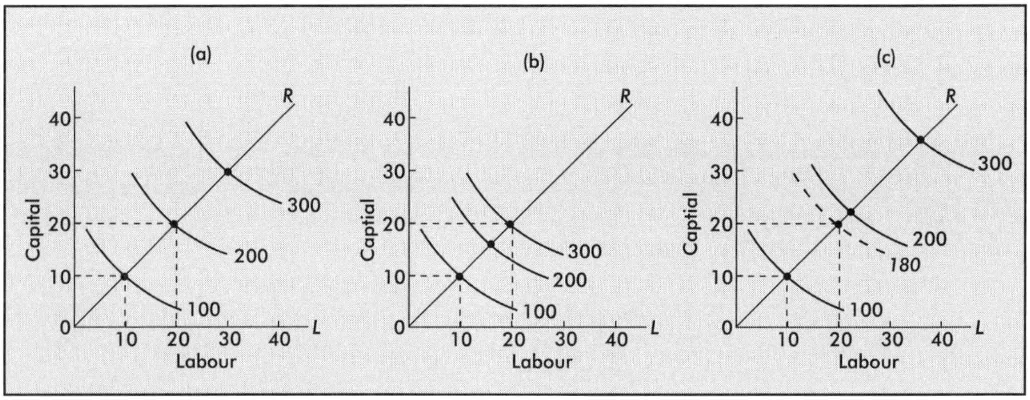

OPTIMAL INPUT COMBINATIONS

In the previous section we saw that if two inputs are used in the production process, the firm will produce in the technically efficient area of an isoquant. This information, however, is not sufficient to determine the exact combination of inputs which the firm will employ in order to deliver a given output, the reason being that an infinite number of possible input combinations exist within the technically efficient region of any isoquant. To show exactly how a firm decides on an input combination, production and cost theory must be combined. To do this it is assumed that in order to produce any given input the firm will choose the combination of inputs that will minimise costs of production; such an input combination is known as an *optimal input combination*. Before proceeding any further with the optimal input combination, we must first introduce a new concept, namely isocost curves. This is a concept which concurs with the budget line which we came across in Chapter 3.

Isocost curves

An isocost curve (also referred to as an isocost line) shows the different combinations of labour and capital that a firm can buy, given the amount of money (also called the total outlay) that the firm has available and the current prices of the factors of production.

Observe a firm that has a total amount of R1 000 to spend on labour and capital and that the price of labour (P_L) and the price of capital (P_K) are both R10 per unit. (We could have used bigger, more realistic amounts, but the principles remain the same.) Table 4-2 shows some ways in which the firm could have spent R1 000.

Table 4-2

Combinations of capital and labour

(R1 000 is available. P_K = R10 per unit, P_L = R10 per unit)

Combination	Capital (K) (units)	Labour (L) (units)	Total costs (R)
a	100	0	1 000
b	80	20	1 000
c	60	40	1 000
d	40	60	1 000
e	20	80	1 000
f	0	100	1 000

Isocost curve

The combinations in Table 4-2 (as well as the combinations in between, such as 70 units of capital and 30 units of labour) are illustrated graphically in Figure 4-5 by means of the straight line which is drawn from point a to point f. At a the firm buys only capital and no labour, whereas at point f only labour and no capital is purchased. This line is known as an *isocost curve* (or equal cost curve) because it shows the combinations of capital and labour that the firm can acquire for a given outlay.

In reality the intercepts on the axes are all that are necessary to draw the isocost curve, that is to say the maximum number of units of each factor of production that the firm can afford if the available amount of money is spent in its entirety on that factor of production. If the firm spends its entire outlay (TO) on capital, it can buy TO/P_K units of capital – in the example that is R1 000/R10 = 100 units. In the same manner the firm, if it only buys labour, can purchase TO/P_L units, which also works out as R1 000/R10 = 100. By joining these two points on the axes we get the isocost curve of the firm. As has already been said, the firm can purchase any combination of labour and capital along the isocost curve. Every isocost curve represents a given outlay, in other words, what is available to spend on labour and capital. In the example the total outlay is R1 000. If it were to increase to, say, R2 000 while the prices of labour and capital remained the same, a new isocost curve, further from the origin, would be obtained.

The *slope of the isocost curve* is as follows:

$$\frac{TO/P_K}{TO/P_L} = \frac{TO}{P_K} \cdot \frac{P_L}{TO} = \frac{P_L}{P_K} \qquad (6)$$

The slope of the isocost curve is equal to the relation of the price of labour to the price of capital, that is to say P_L/P_K. In the example which we are using $P_L = P_K$ = R10 and TO = R1 000. This means that the isocost curve in Figure 4-5 has a slope of 1. The slope is calculated as follows: P_L/P_K = R10/R10 = 1.

Figure 4-5

Isocost curves

They show the combinations of capital and labour that a firm can buy for a given outlay. If the intercepts on the axes (TO/P_K and TO/P_L) are calculated, the isocost curves can be drawn. The slope of the isocost curve is P_L/P_K.

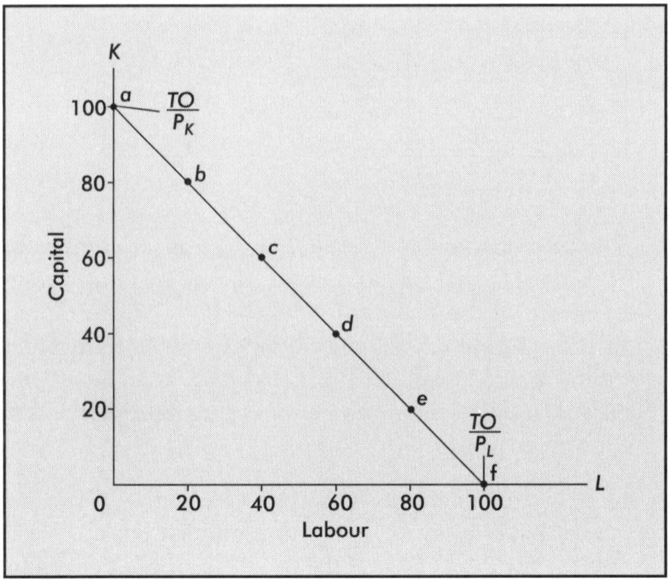

Choice of input combination

We can now determine how a firm will choose the optimal input combination, that is the combination of inputs that will minimise production costs, or – which amounts to the same thing – we can look at how a firm chooses its input combination in order to produce the maximum output for a given cost. To do this a diagram which depicts the isocost curve and the isoquants of a producer is used.

Equilibrium

A producer will be in *equilibrium* if he produces a maximum output with a given cost outlay. Another way of putting this is that a producer is in equilibrium if, with a given isocost curve, he reaches the highest possible isoquant. This happens when the isocost curve just touches an isoquant, in other words forms a tangent to the isoquant. This is illustrated in Figure 4-6, where isoquant Q_2 is the highest isoquant which can be reached by the isocost curve concerned – the producer is therefore in equilibrium at point M. Isoquant Q_3 cannot be reached with the given isocost curve and if the firm produces on isoquant Q_1 it will not maximise output.

At the point of tangency M on Figure 4-6 the slope of the isoquant ($MRTS_{LK}$) is equal to the slope of the isocost curve (P_L/P_K). It therefore applies that in equilibrium $MRTS_{LK} = P_L/P_K$. From Equation (5) it is also known that $MRTS_{LK} = MP_L/MP_K$ and it therefore applies that for a *producer to be in equilibrium*

$$\frac{MP_L}{MP_K} = \frac{P_L}{P_K} \quad \text{or} \quad \frac{MP_L}{P_L} = \frac{MP_K}{P_K} \qquad (7)$$

This is an important result – it means that the *producer is in equilibrium* if the marginal product (MP) of the last rand spent on labour is exactly the same as the marginal product (MP) of the last rand spent on capital. If the firm uses more than two factors of production, the same will apply (in the equilibrium situation) for the other factors of production.

If the relationship between the marginal product and the price (eg MP_L/P_L) is not the same for all factors of production, the producer can reach a higher level of production by changing the combination of the factors of production. If the marginal product (or marginal output) which the producer obtains from the last rand spent on labour is greater than the marginal product that he obtains from the last rand spent on capital, he can increase total production by spending more on labour and less on capital. If, on the other hand, the relationship between the marginal product and the price is the same for both factors of production, then production cannot be increased further and production equilibrium (ie maximum production) is reached. That is the best that the producer, given his cost constraint, can do.

The expansion path

Earlier in the chapter it was said that the long run of the firm is under consideration if all the factors of production, capital included, are variable. An implication of this is that in order to produce a certain output the firm can expand and can build the plant size that will minimise costs. If it is assumed that the firm uses two factors of production, labour and capital, and that their prices remain constant if the firm expands its production activities, we can determine how the firm will act if it increases production over the long run.

In Figure 4-7 the production function of the firm is presented by means of four isoquants Q_1, Q_2, Q_3 and Q_4. Four isocost curves, C_1 to C_4, are also drawn on the diagram. These isocost curves are equally spaced and all have the same slope because the relationship of the price of labour to the price of capital (ie P_L/P_K) remains constant. The further away the isocost curve lies from the origin, the larger the output it represents. The isocost curves are drawn in such a way that they form tangents to the isoquants at points H, I, J and K – each of these points also represents a point of equilibrium for the firm, in other words the maximum output that can be produced with the costs concerned. By joining these equilibrium points a curve is obtained which shows how the input combinations which minimise costs change for increasing levels of production. Stated differently: this curve, which is called the *expansion path* of the firm, shows the *lowest possible input costs (combinations of K and L) at which different levels of production can be produced.* The benefit of this information will become clear in the next section. (The similarity between the expansion path and the income-consumption curve which was explained in Chapter 3 should already be clear at this stage.)

Expansion path

Figure 4-6

Production equilibrium

The firm is in equilibrium at point M on isoquant Q_2. That is the highest isoquant that can be reached by the isocost curve. At M the following applies: $MRTS_{LK} = P_L/P_K = MP_L/MP_K$.

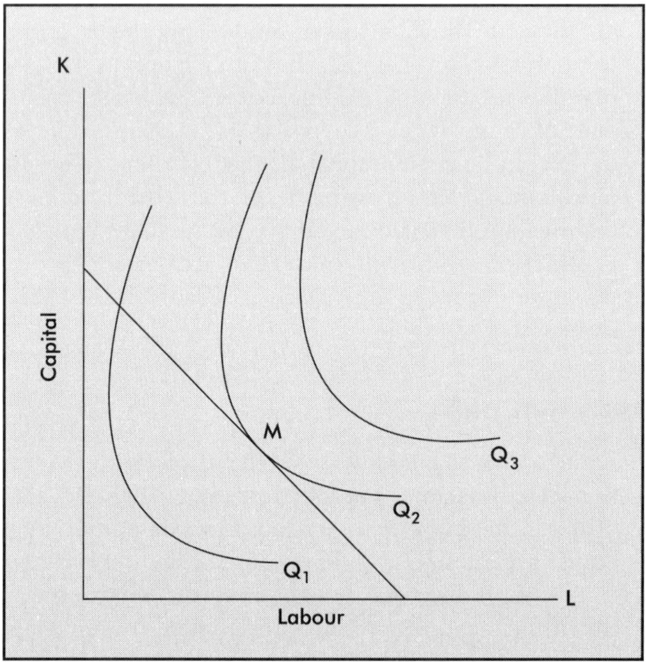

Figure 4–7

The expansion path of the firm

The curve shows the lowest possible input costs (combinations of K and L) at which different output levels can be produced.

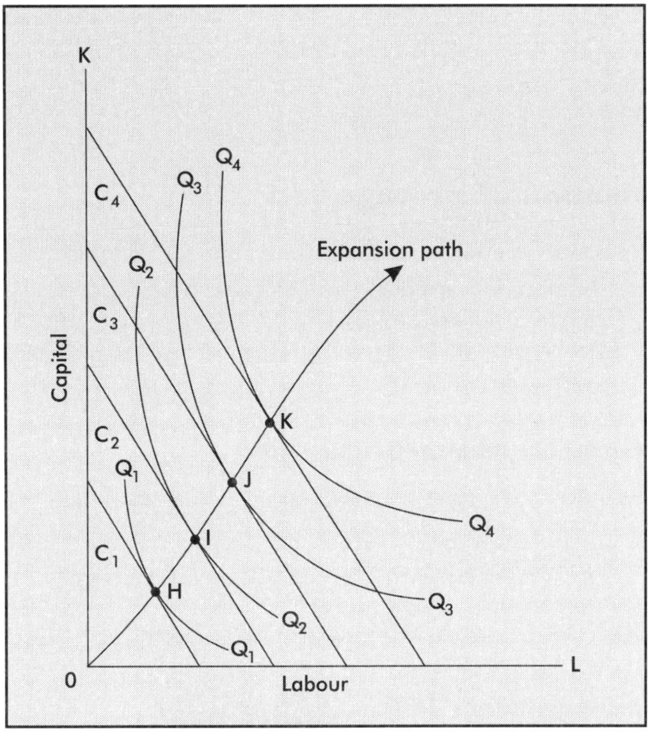

Box 4–3

COST CURVES: A SUMMARY

In the rest of the chapter the various cost curves of the firm are derived. The following is a summary of all the cost curves. You will probably only understand it fully once you have studied the rest of the chapter, but it will be of benefit to you to work through this section beforehand. Once you have studied the chapter it will serve as a good summary.

No fewer than ten different cost curves are derived below. For many a student this is an intimidating thought. Note, however, that as soon as the total cost curves (for both the long and the short run) are determined, the average and marginal cost curves easily result from them.That leaves only four cost curves that need to be studied. Of the latter, the constant cost curve should pose the fewest difficulties; to derive the average constant cost curve from it is easy. All that remains to be studied is the variable cost (total and average). Seen in this light, the determination of cost curves is not such a big task.

The derivation of the cost curves of a firm can be carried out graphically by constructing a *total cost curve* (for the long or the short run) as a point of departure; this is done with the aid of an isoquant map and an expansion path. If the total cost curve is known, the *average cost curve* and the *marginal cost curve* (for both the short and the long run) can easily be determined. The following is a handy principle to remember:

Derivation of average cost

An average cost curve is graphically derived by calculating the *slope of the rays* from the origin of the graph to points along the total cost curve. See, for example, the derivation of the LAC, ACC, AVC and SAC curves with the aid of the LTC, TCC, TVC and STC curves respectively.

Derivation of marginal costs

A marginal cost curve is derived graphically by calculating the *slope of the tangents to points along the total cost curve.* See, for example, the derivation of the LMC and the SMC curves with the aid of the LTC and STC curves respectively.

The following cost curves are explained in the chapter:

Long-run total cost (LTC)

- It is illustrated graphically by using the information about costs and production volumes (output) which is reflected by the expansion path (Figs 4-7 and 4-8(a)).
- Total cost includes explicit cost plus implicit cost (the latter includes normal profit).

Long-run average cost (LAC)

- LAC = LTC/Q
- It is graphically determined by calculating the slope of rays that are drawn from the origin to points along the LTC curve (Figs 4-8(a) and 4-8(b)).

Long-run marginal cost (LMC)

- LMC = ΔLTC/ΔQ
- Definition: the LMC is the addition to long-run total costs (ΔLTC) if one additional unit of output (ΔQ) is produced.
- It is graphically determined by calculating the slope of tangents to points along the LTC (Figs 4-8(a) and 4-8(b)).

Short-run total cost (STC)

- It is illustrated graphically by using the information in terms of the costs and quantities of production reflected by the expansion path (Figs 4–10 and 4–11).
- Short-run total cost consists of total constant cost plus total variable cost: STC = TCC + TVC.

Total constant cost (TCC)

- Also known as total fixed cost.
- Even if nothing is produced, total cost must be paid.
- It forms the constant component of STC.
- Examples: rent and interest.
- It is presented graphically by means of a horizontal line which represents the total of constant cost such as interest, rent, etc (Fig 4–12).

Total variable cost (TVC)

- TVC changes if output increases/decreases.
- TVC = STC – TCC
- It is graphically determined by subtracting TCC from STC (Fig 4–12).
- Examples: labour cost, cost of materials, fuel, electricity.

Average constant cost (ACC)

- ACC = TCC/Q
- ACC decreases as long as output increases.
- It is graphically determined by calculating the slope of the rays which are drawn from the origin to points along the TCC (Figs 4–13(a) and 4–13(b)).

Average variable cost (AVC)

- AVC = TVC/Q
- It is graphically determined by calculating the slopes of the rays that are drawn from the origin to points along the TVC curve (Figs 4–14(a) and 4–14(b)).

Short-run average cost (SAC)

- SAC = STC/Q
- It is graphically determined by calculating the slopes of rays that are drawn from the origin to points along the STC curve (Figs 4–14(a) and 4–14(b)).

Short-run marginal costs (SMC)

- $SMC = \Delta STC/\Delta Q$ or
- $SMC = \Delta TVC/\Delta Q$
- Definition: the SMC is the addition to short-run total costs (ΔSTC) if one additional unit of output (ΔQ) is produced.
- Alternative definition: the SMC is the addition to total variable cost (ΔTVC) if one additional unit of output (ΔQ) is produced.
- The SMC is graphically determined by calculating the slopes of tangents to the STC curve or TVC curve (Figs 4-14(a) and 4-14(b)).

COSTS

The expansion path which was derived in Figure 4-7 reflects information that can be used to derive the cost curves of a firm. If the cost curves of a firm are available, it can be seen how firms decide how much they are going to produce and supply to the market under various market conditions (this is done in later chapters). The determination of the cost curves of a firm is a relatively technical process and is sometimes repetitive in nature. At the end of the chapter practical methods which are used to determine cost curves are also discussed. Before we do this we must study the underlying principles of the various cost curves. This can be done in two ways. First, use can be made of numerical tables which show what the relationship between the various costs is and how they are calculated. Second, the manner in which the various costs are derived and how they are related to one another can be explained graphically. The latter method is followed in the rest of this chapter (it is probably the easier method).

When studying the rest of the chapter it is advisable to continuously refer to the summary in Box 4-3.

Long-run total cost (LTC)

Seeing that the expansion path shows the lowest possible costs at which various output levels can be produced when all factors of production are variable, it can be used to construct the long-run total cost curve (LTC); this is done by plotting the costs and the corresponding quantities of production on a graph. This is done in Figure 4-8, where point H′ provides the same information as point H in Figure 4-7. Point H in Figure 4-7 shows that C_1 is the lowest cost at which Q_1 can be produced. In Figure 4-8 H′ shows exactly the same thing, that is to say Q_1 and C_1 are used as coordinates to plot H′. (In both Fig 4-7 and Fig 4-8 Q_1 for example will indicate 100 000 tins of beer and C_1 a total cost of R250 000.) In the same manner points I′, J′ and K′ in Figure 4-8 are plotted by using the output and total cost represented by points I, J and K in Figure 4-7 respectively. The curve which is drawn from the origin through points H′, I′, J′ and K′ in Figure 4-8 is the long-run total cost curve (LTC).

Figure 4–8

Derivation of the long-run total cost, long-run marginal cost and long-run average cost

The expansion path is used to calculate the long-run total cost curve. This curve enables us to determine the LMC and LAC.

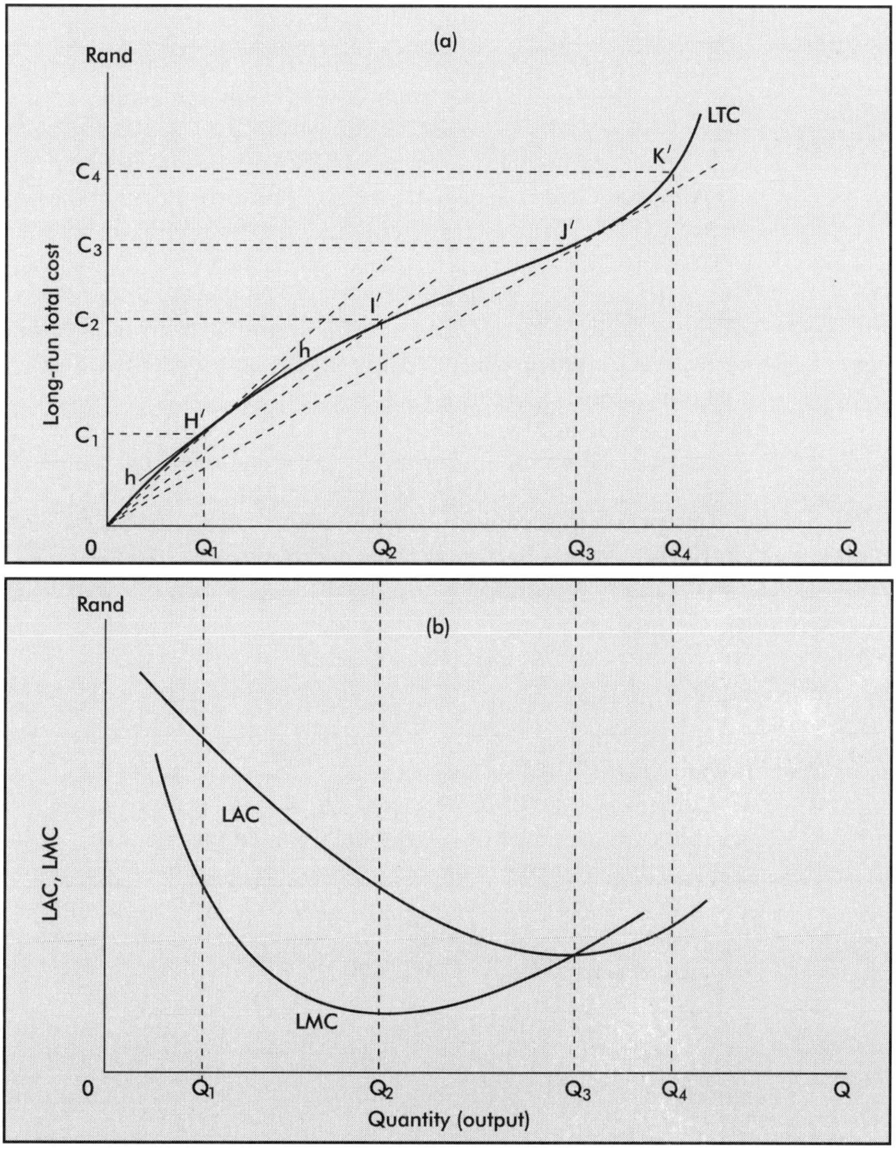

Long-run average cost (LAC) and long-run marginal cost (LMC)

Once the long-run total cost curve has been determined it can be used to calculate the long-run average cost as well as the long-run marginal cost. The method used to do this is the same as that used earlier in the chapter to derive the marginal product and the average product curve from the total product curve.

The long-run average cost (LAC) is the long-run total cost (LTC) which is necessary to produce a given output divided by that output, that is to say

$$LAC = LTC/Q \qquad (8)$$

If we draw a ray from the origin in Figure 4-8 to a point along the LTC curve, the slope of the curve, by definition, will be the long-run average cost at that point. For example, the slope of ray 0H′ is C_1/Q_1 (or Q_1H'/Q_1), which is the same as the LAC (ie LTC/Q) at point H′. Rays are also drawn to points I′ and J′ in Figure 4-8. Given the path of the LAC curve, the slopes of the rays which pass through H′, I′ and J′ decrease respectively. The ray 0J′ forms a tangent to the LTC curve and rays which are drawn from the origin to points to the right of J′ (eg to K′) will be steeper than 0J′. This means that the slope of the rays from the origin to the LTC curve reaches a minimum at J′. In other words, the LAC decreases as output increases until output Q_3 is reached, thereafter LAC increases. This is illustrated in Figure 4-8(b), where the LAC curve which is derived from the LTC curve in Figure 4-8(a) appears. It is clear that the LAC curve initially decreases, reaches a minimum at output Q_3 and then begins increasing.

A concept which accompanies the long-run average cost is the *long-run marginal cost* (LMC), which is defined as the addition to total cost (ΔLTC) if one additional unit of output (ΔQ) is produced and all inputs are variable, that is to say

$$LMC = \Delta LTC/\Delta Q \qquad (9)$$

On a graph the long-run marginal cost is obtained at any point along the LTC curve by calculating the slope of a tangent at that point. For example, the line hh in Figure 4-8(a) forms a tangent to the LTC curve at point H′ and the slope of line hh indicates the LMC at output Q_1. Besides, if we compare the slope of the line hh with the slope of the ray 0H′, we see that the slope of 0H′ is greater (steeper) than the slope of hh – this means that at output Q_1 the long run average cost is greater then the long-run marginal cost. This is also shown in Figure 4-8 (b) where the LAC and LMC curves are drawn – at an output level of Q_1 the LAC curve lies above the LMC curve.

If we move towards the right along the LTC curve, the slopes of the tangents to the LTC curve will decrease, until point I′ in Figure 4-8 (a) is reached – you already know that a point such as this is called a point of inflection. (The slope of the LTC curve changes at the point of inflection from increasing at a decreasing rate to increasing at an increasing rate.) After point I′ the slopes of the tangents once more become steeper (not shown in the diagram) and the LMC therefore increases, which results in the LMC curve reaching a minimum at Q_2, that is to say at that output which corresponds with the point of inflection. This is clearly shown in the diagram. Seeing that the slope of ray 0I′ is still greater than the slope of a tangent to the LTC at I′, it follows that at an output level of Q_2 the LAC is still greater than the LMC. At J′, as we have already discussed, the LAC reaches a minimum value. Because the slope of ray 0J′ is the same as the slope of a tangent at point J′ would be, it follows that for an output level of Q_3 LMC = LAC. Therefore the LMC curve (which is increasing) intersects the LAC curve from below at the latter's minimum point, as is shown in Figure 4-8(b). To the right of point J′ LMC is greater than LAC because the slopes of the tangents to the LTC curve will be greater than the slopes of the rays from the origin to the same points.

Economies and diseconomies of scale and the shape of the long-run average cost curve

Economies and dis-economies of scale

The long-run average cost curve in Figure 4-8(b) displays the typical U shape found in theoretical discussions. Initially the curve decreases from left to right, reaches a minimum point and then increases again from left to right. If the LAC curve decreases, it is said that *economies of scale* exist; if the LAC curve increases, it is said that *diseconomies of scale* exist. This is a concept which was illustrated with the aid of isoquants earlier in the chapter.

Economies of scale occur in the first place when a firm expands and division of labour and specialisation take place. Workers can specialise in smaller tasks, which enables them to be more productive. Second, economies of scale occur because, when a firm expands, more and better technology is usually used in the production process. This all results in the average cost of producing an article decreasing.

Diseconomies of scale are usually ascribed to the fact that when a firm expands the effectiveness of management eventually decreases. A distance between management and the actual production process develops, authority is delegated and the decision-making process becomes longer and more complicated. All these factors contribute to the effectiveness of management being reduced and if the scale of production is increased any more the average cost of production increases.

Modern theory claims that instead of LAC curves being U-shaped, they are often more L-shaped or saucer-shaped. The LAC curve also initially decreases, but instead of increasing beyond the minimum point, it runs almost horizontally and may even drop a little more; if the LAC curve decreases, it means that economies of scale can be reached up to very high production volumes. If the LAC curve does indeed begin to rise at even greater production volumes, it will have a saucer-shaped path. Such a curve is shown in Figure 4-9.

Figure 4-9

Economies of scale and the shape of the LAC curve

Modern theory claims that LAC curves are often L-shaped instead of U-shaped. Sometimes the LAC curve only begins increasing at very high production volumes, in which case it is saucer-shaped.

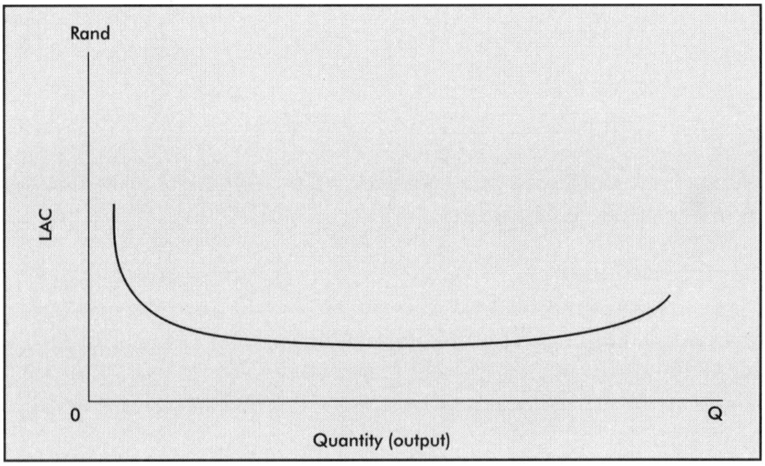

Short-run total costs (STC)

It has already been shown how the long-run expansion path of the firm is derived with the aid of isoquants and isocost curves and how the long-run expansion path is used to determine the long-run total cost curve. The short-run total cost curve (STC) curve can also be derived with the aid of isoquants and isocost curves.

In Figure 4-10 the production function of a firm is illustrated and the expansion path shows the route along which the firm will expand over the long run. The question now is how can the figure be used to acquire information about costs over the short run? It is already known that over the short run one or more of the factors of production is constant – if we therefore assume labour to be variable and keep capital constant at KK on Figure 4-10, the total costs over the short run at various levels of production can be determined. For example, if the firm wishes to produce the quantity depicted by isoquant Q^*, point B will be the lowest cost at which production can take place. Because B lies on KK (remember that the latter indicates that capital is constant), point B shows the lowest cost at which Q^* can be produced over the *short run*. The quantity produced and the cost at point B can be used to plot one point along the short-run total cost curve, namely point D in Figure 4-11. (Point B also lies on the long-run expansion path and at the same time provides a point along the long-run cost curve; it can therefore be seen in Figure 4-11 that point D is common to both STC and LTC.)

More points like point B can be determined, which can then be used to plot other points along the STC curve. If the firm for example wants to produce Q_0, it will produce at point A′ in Figure 4-10 in the short run. Over the long run the firm would prefer to produce at point A, but because capital is constant over the short run, the firm must (over the short run) produce at A′ which lies along KK. If we draw an isocost curve through A′, it will show higher costs than the one which is drawn through A. Therefore because A′ lies to the right of the isocost which forms a tangent to Q_0 at A, it means that the total cost to produce Q_0 over the short run is higher than the cost of producing Q_0 over the long run; this is clear in Figure 4-11. In the same way, if the firm wants to produce Q_2 it will produce at point C in Figure 4-11 over the long run, but at point C′ over the short run. Because C′ lies to the right of the isocost which forms a tangent to Q_2 at C, the total cost to produce Q_2 in the short run is higher than the total cost to produce Q_2 over the long run (also see Figure 4-11). If a sufficiently large number of isoquants and isocost curves are drawn in Figure 4-10 and more points like A′, B and C′ are obtained, a continuous STC curve can be drawn, as is done in Figure 4-11.

Just as the long-run total cost curve is used to derive the long-run average and marginal cost, so too the *short-run total cost curve* can be used to derive the *short-run average* and *marginal* cost. This is done later in the chapter.

Total constant cost (TCC) and total variable cost (TVC)

The short-run total cost of a firm can be divided into two parts, namely total constant cost and total variable cost. This can also be written as follows: STC = TCC + TVC. This division is especially important for the management of any enterprise, as will be explained.

Even if a firm produces nothing, there are costs which must be incurred over the short run. This cost is called *total fixed cost or total constant cost* (TCC) – it forms the constant component of STC and is also the reason that the STC curve in Figure 4-11 intersects the vertical axis at a positive value. Total constant cost does not change as the firm's output varies and even if nothing is being produced, expenditures such as rent, interest, depreciation, insurance and salaries for the management must be paid. Because constant cost does not change, the TCC curve (see Fig 4-12) is a horizontal line, irrespective of the output.

Figure 4–10

Short-run production

By keeping capital constant along KK, the short-run total cost can be determined at various output levels. The information can be used to determine the STC curve.

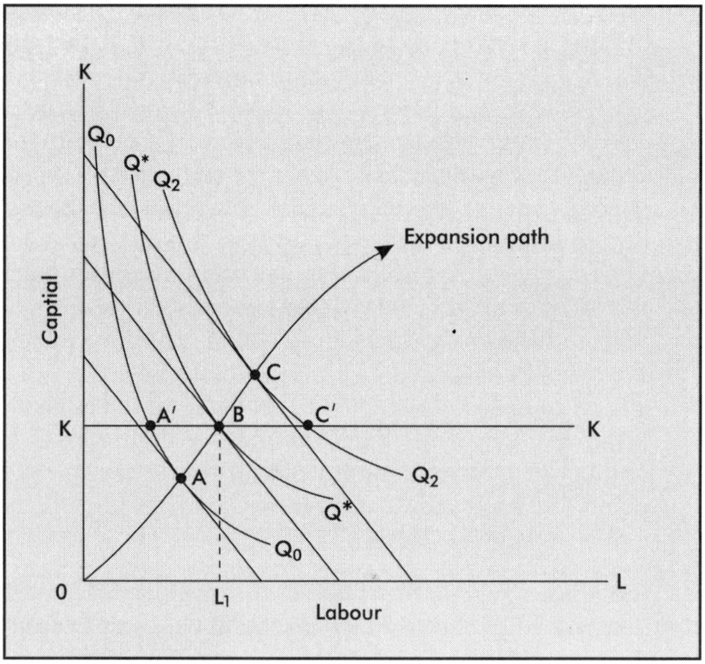

Total variable cost, as the name indicates, is that cost which changes as output varies. Cost items such as labour, cost of materials, fuel, electricity and transport costs are included. If the TCC and the STC curves are known (see the previous section), we are in a position to determine the *total variable cost* (TVC): that is the difference between short-run total cost (STC) and total constant cost (TCC). The TVC is determined graphically by simply subtracting the total constant cost (TCC) from the short-run total cost (STC), as is shown in Figure 4-12.

Differentiating between constant and variable costs is particularly important for the management of any enterprise, the reason being that management can control or vary variable cost over the short run by changing the level of production (the importance of this is discussed again in Chapter 5). On the other hand, constant cost is beyond the control of management over the short run – it must be paid irrespective of the level of production. Constant cost is sometimes referred to as unavoidable cost, fixed cost, overhead cost or indirect cost.

Figure 4–11

Comparison of the long-run total cost curve with the short-run total cost curve

The STC curve lies above the LTC curve. The STC curve does not start at the origin because of the constant cost component which applies over the short run.

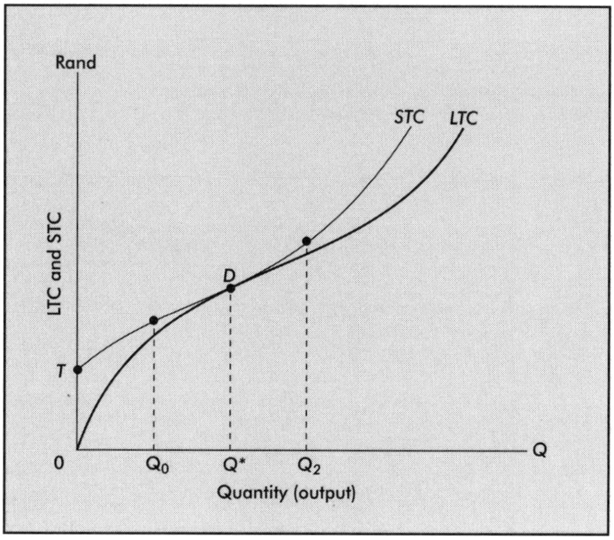

Figure 4–12

The total constant cost curve and the total variable cost curve

TCC does not change if the firm's output varies and the curve therefore runs horizontally. The TVC curve is determined graphically by subtracting TCC from the STC.

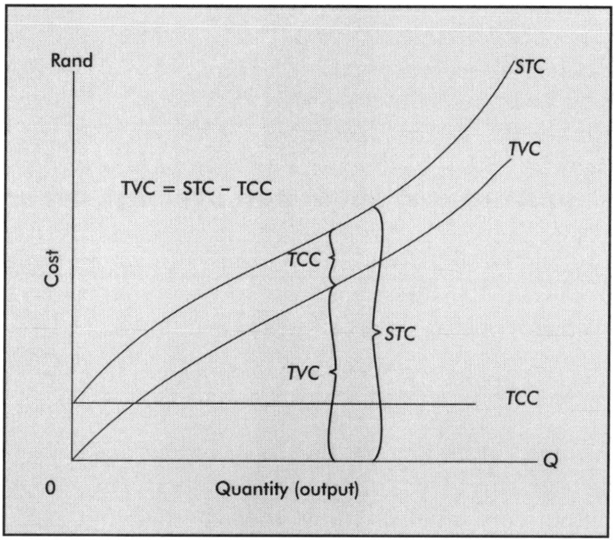

Figure 4–13

The average constant cost curve

The slope of the rays from the origin to points such as A, B and C on the TCC curve shows the average constant cost.

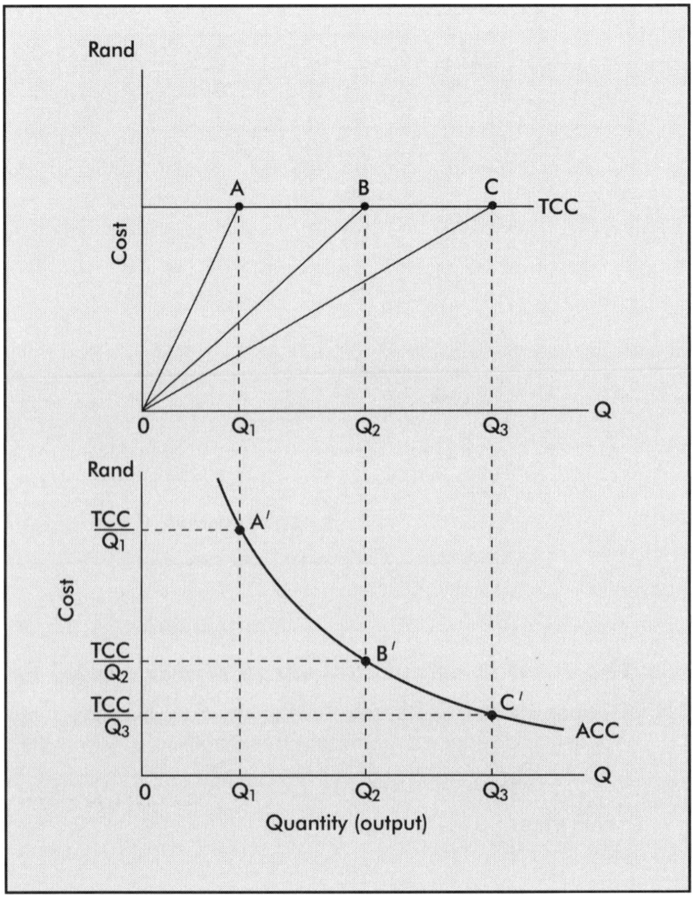

Average constant cost (ACC) and average variable cost (AVC)

Although *total* constant cost remains constant per definition and is independent of output, the *average* constant cost will decrease as long as output increases. Average constant cost is calculated as follows:

$$ACC = TCC/Q \tag{10}$$

Assume, for illustration, that total constant cost amounts to R1 000. As output increases, the given constant cost will be spread over an increasing output. If the output only involves 1 unit, total constant cost and average constant cost are both R1 000 (ie ACC = TCC/Q = 1 000/1). If output increases to 2 units, total constant cost is still R1 000, but ACC then becomes R500 (ie ACC = 1 000/2) per unit produced; then R333,3 if R1 000 is spread over 3 production units; R250 if R1 000 is spread over 4 production units, etc. Business people refer to this as the 'spreading of overhead costs'.

The graphic derivation of ACC is presented in Figure 4–13. Rays are drawn from the origin to points A, B and C on the TCC curve. The slopes of these rays amount to the ACC – for example at point A the slope is $AQ_1/0Q_1$ which amounts to TCC/Q_1 at point A, which is by definition ACC. The same happens at points B and C. In the bottom part of Figure 4–13 the ACC, which is calculated in this way, is plotted at points A′, B′ and C′. Once more note that the average constant cost curve (ACC) decreases as production expands.

The attention now shifts to the *average variable cost curve*. The principle for deriving the curve is the same as that used previously to derive an average cost curve from a total cost curve (see for example the derivation of the LAC). The curve which shows *total variable cost*, was already derived in the previous section and it appears again in Figure 4–14. If the curve is known it can be used to calculate the *average variable cost*. Average variable costs are defined as

$$AVC = TVC/Q \qquad (11)$$

If rays are drawn from the origin to intersect the TVC curve at points such as A, C and D in Figure 4–14(a), the slopes of the rays will give the AVC at the levels of production that correspond with the points of intersection. For example, the slope of ray 0L at point A is equal to $AQ_1/0Q_1$ which is also equal to TVC/Q_1 and therefore indicates the average variable cost at A, which is also reflected by A′ in Figure 4-14(b). At point C the slope of the ray is smaller than at A and therefore the AVC is lower at C′ than at A′; in the same way the AVC at D′ is lower than it is at C′. It can also be seen from the figure that if the AVC is calculated at D, it will indicate the minimum point of AVC; if more rays are drawn from the origin to points to the right of D on the TVC curve, their slopes will increase and therefore AVC increases to the right of D′.

Short-run average cost (SAC) and short-run marginal cost (SMC)

The STC curve which was associated with the production function in Figure 4-10 and was shown in Figure 4-11 also appears in Figure 4-14(a). Earlier in the chapter we showed how the long-run average and long-run marginal cost curves could be derived with the aid of the long-run total cost curve. In exactly the same way the *short-run average cost* and the *short-run marginal cost* can be derived from the *short-run total cost curve*. (The method to derive the SAC is also exactly the same as that used in the previous section to derive the average variable cost from the total variable cost curve.)

The short-run average cost is defined as

$$SAC = STC/Q \tag{12}$$

To determine the SAC graphically we can once more refer to Figure 4–14(a). Rays are drawn from the origin to points such as B and E on the STC curve; the slopes of these rays are equal to the SAC at the corresponding output levels. This enables us to draw the SAC curve in the bottom part of the figure; the curve reaches a minimum at E′ because the slope of the ray to the STC curve reaches a minimum at E in Figure 4–14 (a).

The short-run marginal costs of a firm can be defined as the increase in short-run total costs (ΔSTC) if one additional unit of output (ΔQ) is produced. Mathematically this can be stated as follows:

$$SMC = \Delta STC/\Delta Q \tag{13}$$

Alternatively short-run marginal costs can be defined as the increase in total variable costs (ΔTVC) if one additional unit of output (ΔQ) is produced, that is to say

$$SMC = \Delta TVC/\Delta Q \tag{14}$$

Both definitions of short-run marginal costs are correct because, as we have already seen, the difference between STC and TVC is a constant, namely total constant cost (TCC). Diagrammatically the paths of the STC and the TVC curves are therefore the same with a constant difference between them – as can be seen in Figure 4–14(a). To determine the SMC at any output, we merely draw a tangent to the STC or the TVC curve at the output level under consideration. The slope of any of the tangents represents the SMC. In Figure 4–14(a) it can be seen that the slopes of the tangents at A and F are the same, giving the SMC at output Q_1 – in the bottom part of the diagram the SMC is represented by A″. In the same way points such as B″ and the rest of the SMC curve can be determined. At B the slope of a tangent to the SMC curve (and therefore the value of SMC) reaches a minimum, as is reflected by B″.

Note that in Figure 4–14(a) the tangents at points D and E are also rays 0N and 0M from the origin. Therefore SMC is equal to SAC at output Q_5 (see point E′) and SMC is equal to AVC at output Q_4 (see point D′). This is not merely a coincidence, but a mathematical fact which results from the path of the STC and TVC curves.

Figure 4–14(b) is an important diagram. It shows all the short-run curves which were derived and their relation to each other. The SAC and the AVC curves are U-shaped. The SAC curve always, at any output level, lies above the AVC curve and reaches a minimum at a higher level of production. The SMC curve is also U-shaped and reaches a minimum value at an output level which

Figure 4–14

The average variable cost curve

The slopes of the rays from the origin to points such as A, C and D on the TVC curve in Figure 4–14(a) show the average variable cost at these points; this is shown at A′, C′ and D′ respectively in Figure 4–14(b). The SAC and SMC curves also appear in Figure 4–14(b).

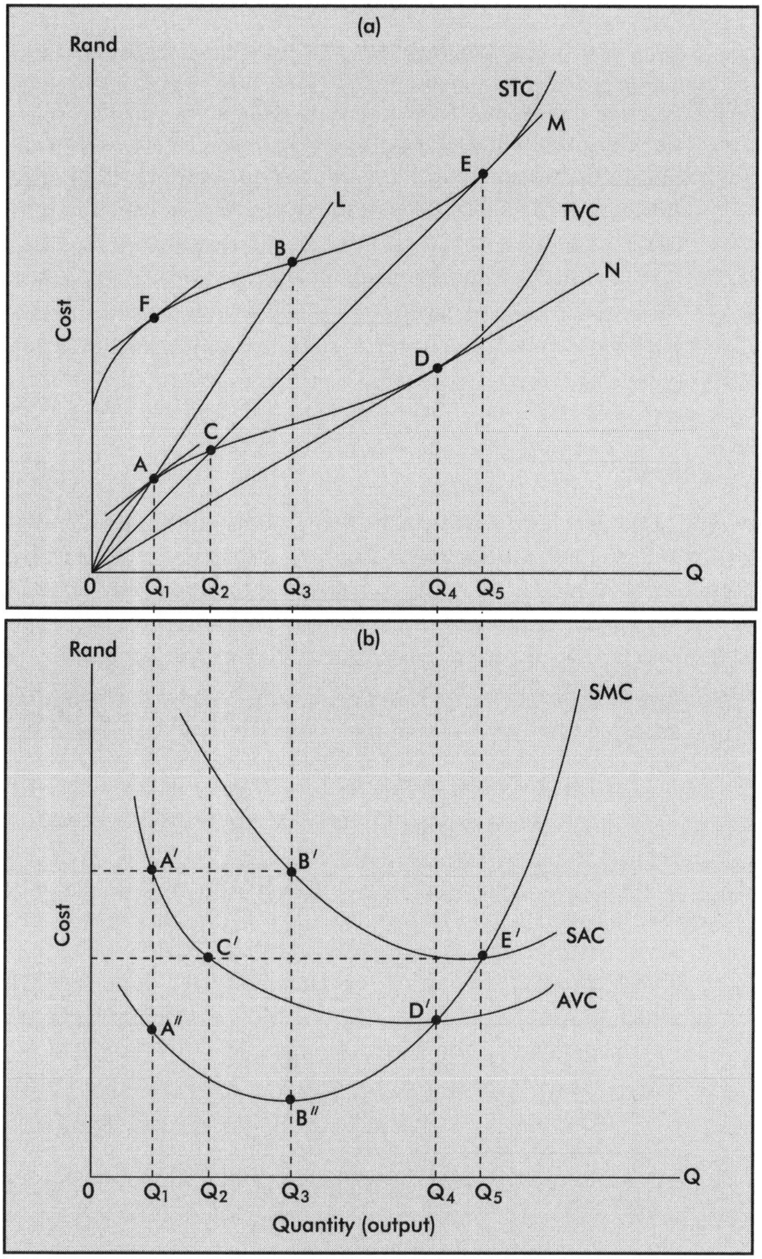

corresponds with the point of inflection on either the STC or the TVC curve. The SMC curve intersects the AVC and the SAC curves from the bottom at their minimum values.

Relationship between short-run and long-run costs

An important decision which a firm must take is how big the production plant should be. Assume that the firm is unsure about future demand for its product and that it considers three alternative plant sizes. In Figure 4-15 STC_1 represents the short-run total cost curve of a small plant which is designed to produce output Q_1, whereas STC_2 represents the medium-sized plant which is designed to produce Q_2. It is clear that Q_2 is a lot bigger than Q_1. The total constant cost of the medium-sized plant is also greater than that of the small plant, TCC therefore lies further from the origin for the medium-sized plant. STC_3 represents the short-run total cost curve of a plant which is even bigger and is designed to produce output Q_3. The TCC of this plant lies furthest away from the origin.

We have explained how the LAC curve is derived by means of the LTC curve. Suppose now that the firm initially experiences economies of scale when a larger plant is built, but subsequently experiences diseconomies of scale as the plant becomes too big. The firm's LTC curve appears in Figure 4-15; the LAC curve which is derived from the LTC curve will exhibit the typical U-shape as in Figure 4-16. In Figure 4-16 SAC_1, SAC_2 and SAC_3 which are derived from the short-run total cost curves STC_1, STC_2 and STC_3 in Figure 4-15 are shown. (The purpose of SAC' in Figure 4-16 will become clear in the next paragraph.) Figure 4-16 illustrates the typical case where various plant sizes are shown for a firm which first experiences economies and then diseconomies of scale. In this example average cost is at its lowest for a medium-sized plant which is represented by SAC_2.

To explain the relationship between the short- and long-run cost curves, we suppose that the firm wants to produce an output of Q_1. If the firm uses the small plant which is represented by the short-run average cost curve SAC_1, it means that the average cost to produce Q_1 is Q_1R_1. In order to produce Q_1 the small plant is better than a bigger plant such as SAC', because the latter will produce Q_1 at an average cost of Q_1R_2. Because Q_1R_1 shows the lowest average cost at which Q_1 can be produced, R_1 will be a point along the LAC curve. Should the firm produce Q_2, the situation changes: with the small plant represented by SAC_1, the average cost of Q_2 will be Q_2M_1. A bigger plant such as SAC' can produce Q_2 at a lower average cost of Q_2R'. Once again, because it is impossible to produce Q_2 at a lower average cost than Q_2R', point R' will lie on the LAC curve. By carrying out an analysis for an infinite number of SAC curves (like SAC_1 and SAC') an infinite number of points such as R_1 and R' will be obtained, which will enable us to plot the LAC curve. (It should already be clear

Figure 4–15

The long-run total cost curve and the short-run total cost curve

Three different plant sizes are represented by STC_1, STC_2 and STC_3. LTC represents the long-run total cost curve of the firm throughout.

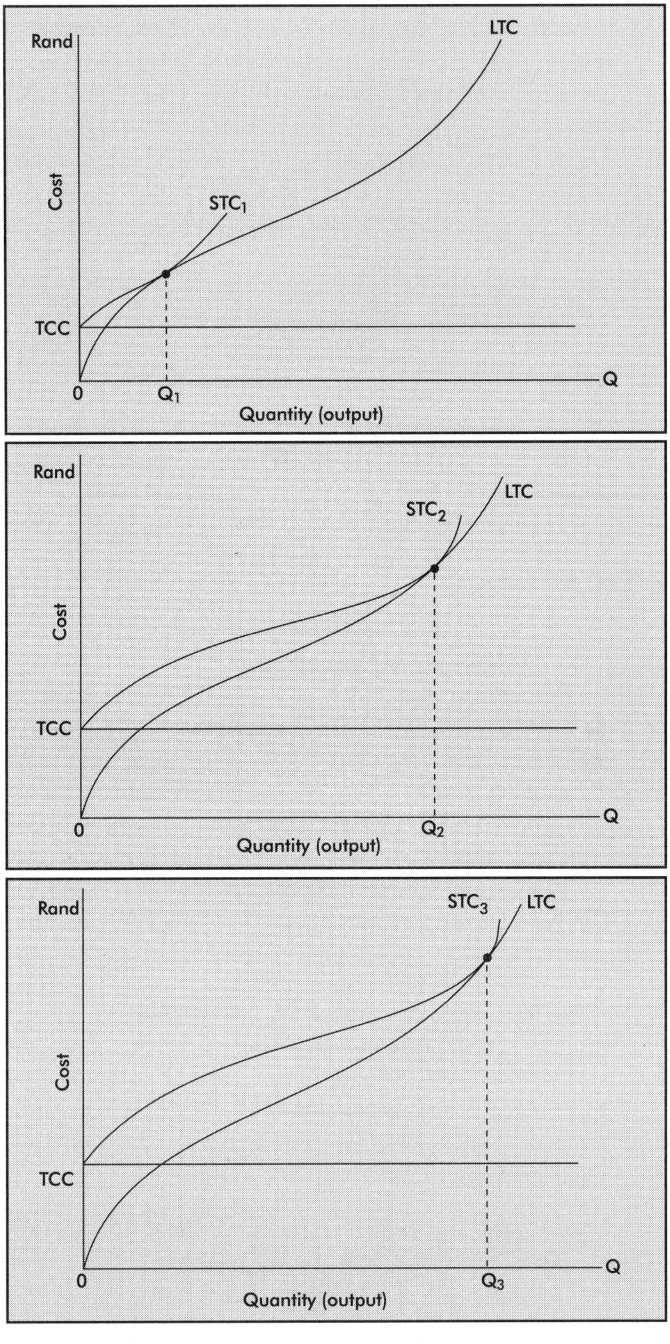

by now that this method also provides an alternative way of deriving the LAC curve. This comes under discussion again later.) At this stage it is easy to see why the LAC curve is also called the envelope curve – it envelops or surrounds the SAC curves in a manner of speaking.

It seems that even if the small plant (SAC_1) produces the quantity Q_2 at the plant's lowest average cost at M_1, this is not the best option for the entrepreneur over the long run, because the bigger plant (SAC') can produce the quantity Q_2 at a lower average cost. It is therefore of benefit to the entrepreneur to build a bigger plant and in so doing to enjoy increasing returns to scale by producing at a lower average cost. The argument applies to the falling part of the LAC curve. The economies of scale which larger plants offer naturally cannot continue indefinitely. (It means that average costs will eventually amount to zero, which is impossible.) An entrepreneur who does good cost predictions however, will not build a plant which is bigger than SAC_2 in Figure 4-16, because beyond that diseconomies of scale will come into operation and the LAC curve increases, as is shown to the right of point E. Point E therefore represents the lowest average cost at which the firm can produce over the long run. If the firm wants to produce at E, it must obviously build a plant which is as big as the one which is represented by SAC_2 in Figure 4-16.

APPLICATIONS

Production functions in practice

Many researches have investigated the nature of production functions in practice and a number of techniques for estimating these functions have been developed. Researchers, for example, have analysed data over a long period of time in order to show which and how many inputs were used in each period under investigation and what the output was. It would be possible to gather information about the quantity of labour and capital which was used by the clothing industry over the time period 1970 to 1995. The researcher would then have 26 observations which could be used to predict the relationship between inputs and output.

Alternatively statistical data for a large number of firms or for various sectors of an industry can be analysed at a specific time. For example, information can be collected about the quantity of capital and labour used by firms in the tyre industry in 1997. The number of observations will be equal to the number of firms on which data was obtained. Such data can also be used to determine the relationship between inputs and output.

Statisticians and economists who collect data in order to predict production functions are faced with many problems. It is often difficult to measure the capital input at a specific time, because the capital stock consists of equipment which is not identical, nor is it the same age, nor is it equally productive. Even the labour input is difficult to measure because labour quality in a firm can vary considerably. To discuss all the problems concerning the calculation of production functions can take up volumes, but there is no need to go deeper here.

Figure 4–16

Economies and diseconomies of scale and the shape of the LAC curve

Along the falling part of the LAC larger plants, as a result of economies of scale, will lead to lower average costs. If the plant becomes too big, diseconomies of scale come into operation and the LAC curve rises, as it does to the right of E.

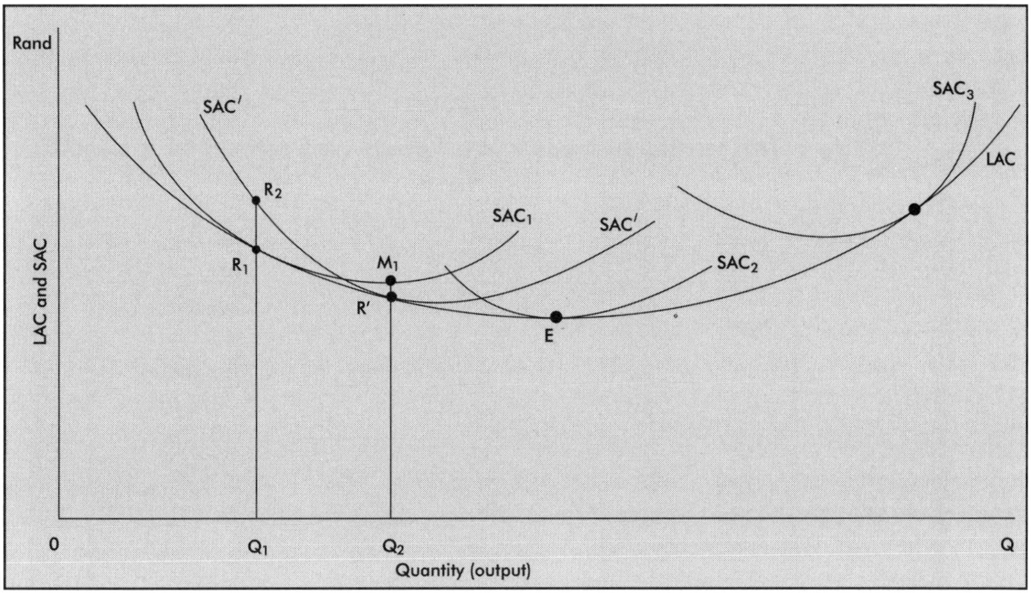

Cobb-Douglas

The production function which appears at the beginning of the chapter (equation (2)) is very general, but for this type of research the exact mathematical form of the production function must be chosen. Researchers in this area often assume that the production function is of the so-called Cobb-Douglas type, which is named after two researchers who worked extensively in this field. The Cobb-Douglas production function is as follows:

$$Q = AL^{\alpha}K^{\beta} \tag{15}$$

where Q = output
L = labour input
K = capital input

The parameters A,α and β differ from one firm to the next and also from one industry to the next.

The labour coefficient α in the Cobb-Douglas production function is the percentage increase in output which results from a 1% increase in labour, while the quantity of capital is held constant. Accordingly β is the percentage increase in output which will occur as a result of an increase of 1% in capital, when the labour input remains constant. Research of this nature, for example, would make it possible to predict for the sugar industry that if $\alpha = 0{,}59$, then an increase of 1% in the labour input would lead to a 0,59% increase in output. Accordingly, if $\beta = 0{,}33$, then an increase of 1% in the capital input will result in sugar production increasing by 0,33%. It is therefore possible to compare various industries and determine where changes in capital or labour will make the greatest changes to output.

Figure 4–17

The relationship between total costs and output of a specific firm

The levels of output of a firm are plotted against the total costs over a number of years. This gives a rough approximation of the firm's cost function.

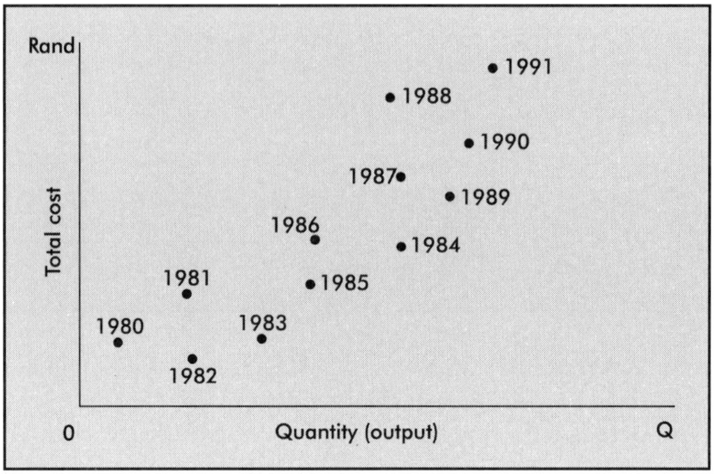

Estimation of costs

Businesses which expand (or become smaller) are usually interested in how costs will change if output varies. Estimations in terms of future costs can be obtained by calculating a cost function which shows the relationship between costs of production and the level of output (and possibly the relationship between costs and other variables which the firm can control). As with production functions, economists have carried out many studies to calculate cost functions (or cost curves, as they are often called) for firms and industries. These studies are usually also based on the statistical analysis of historical data given on costs and output. (It should be clear that this type of information goes hand in hand with what was discussed in the previous section – there the relationship between inputs and output was studied, here it is the relationship between total costs and output.)

As has been mentioned, typical studies of this nature are based on historical time series data. An example of this appears in Figure 4–17, where the output levels of an imaginary firm are plotted against the total costs over a number of years. In order to predict costs relatively accurately, it is necessary to calculate the underlying relationship between costs and output. This is done with the aid of statistical methods, whereby the long-run total cost curve is estimated with the available data. If a firm wants to increase production, the accompanying costs can be predicted. This can therefore be an important aid in decision making.

Figure 4–18

The construction of the LAC curve with the aid of SAC curves

The fact that the LAC curve envelopes the SAC curves provides a method of determining whether economies of scale exist.

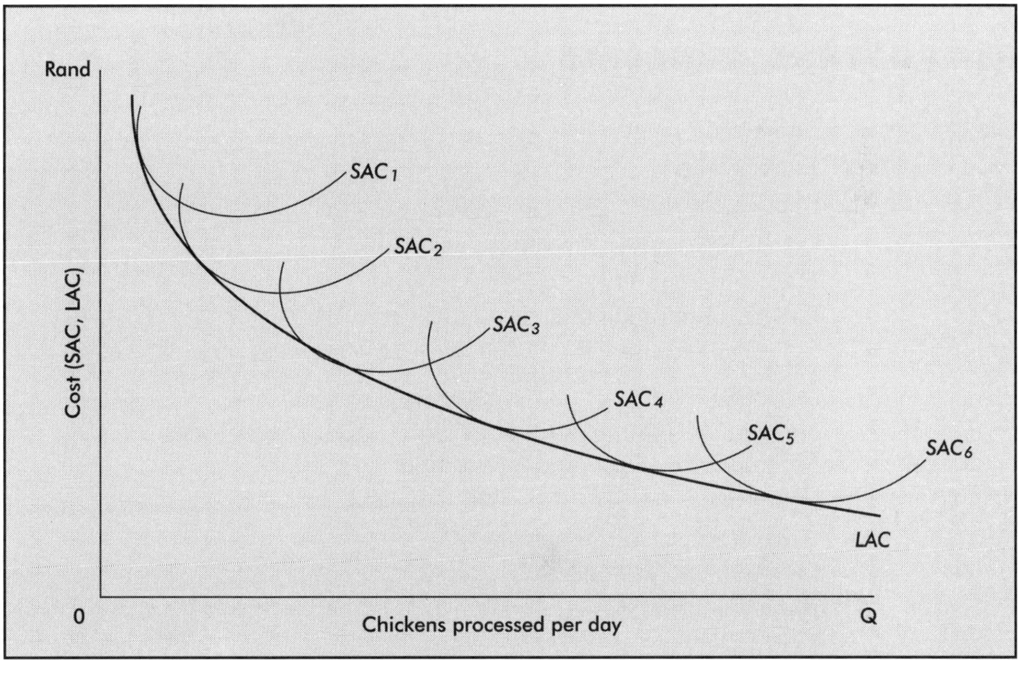

Construction of LAC curves

Envelope curve

Earlier in the chapter the long-run total cost curve was used to derive the long-run average cost curve (see Fig 4–8). We also saw that if the SAC curves for different plant sizes of a firm are available, the LAC curve forms an envelope around them (see Fig 4–16). This is not only of academic interest – the phenomenon of an envelope curve allows economists to calculate the LAC curve in an alternative manner, which in practice is often the easiest way of determining whether economies of scale can be achieved.

For example, a few decades ago it became obvious that the price of chicken broilers could be decreased by increasing the size of the plants where the chickens were slaughtered and processed. In one such research project the short-run average cost curves of a number of plant sizes were determined – they varied from plants that processed a few hundred chickens per day to plants that processed thousands. Figure 4–18 provides an indication of how the SAC curves are used to determine the LAC curve (or envelope curve). It is obvious that if the SAC curves are known it is not difficult to draw the LAC curve. In conclusion it can be noted that the LAC curve in Figure 4–18 corresponds with what was said previously, namely that modern theory on LAC curves claims that the curves are L-shaped (instead of being U-shaped). This indicates that economies of scale can be achieved up to very high levels of output.

IMPORTANT CONCEPTS

- Opportunity costs
- Explicit costs
- Implicit costs
- Normal, economic and accounting profit
- Short and long run
- Law of diminishing returns
- Marginal output
- Average product
- Isoquants (definition, properties)
- Marginal rate of technical substitution
- Ridge lines
- Area of technical efficiency
- Isocosts (definition, slope)
- Production equilibrium
- Expansion path
- Long-run total cost (derivation)
- Long-run average cost (definition, derivation)

- Long-run marginal cost (definition, derivation)
- Economies and diseconomies of scale
- Short-run total cost (derivation)
- Total constant cost
- Total variable cost (definition, derivation)
- Average constant cost (definition, derivation)
- Average variable cost (definition, derivation)
- Short-run average cost (definition, derivation)
- Short-run marginal cost (definition, derivation)
- Relationship between short-run and long-run cost

QUESTIONS

(1) Explain fully the concept of opportunity cost. (5)

(2) Explain what is meant by normal profit and economic profit. (6)

(3) Explain why accounting profit is greater than economic profit. (5)

(4) Explain the difference between short run and long run. (6)

(5) Explain the meaning of the law of diminishing returns. Use a diagram to illustrate your explanations. (10)

(6) Define an isoquant. (3)

(7) Define the concept of technical substitution; also explain why one speaks of the diminishing marginal rate of technical substitution. Use a diagram to illustrate your explanation. (10)

(8) Explain fully (on an isoquant map) the meaning of the technically efficient region of production. Use a diagram to illustrate your explanation. (10)

(9) Explain what an isocost curve is. Draw an isocost curve (by calculating the intercepts on the axes) if total outlay is R2 000 and the price of capital (P_K) equals R20 per unit and the price of labour (P_L) equals R10 per unit. Draw another isocost curve (in the same fig) if the total outlay increases to R3 000, but the prices of labour and capital remain the same. (12)

(10) Explain how a firm will choose the optimal input combination. Use a diagram with isoquants and isocost curves to illustrate your explanation. Also explain how the equation for production equilibrium, $MP_L/P_L = MP_K/P_K$, is derived and the meaning thereof. (15)

(11) Explain how the long-run expansion path of a firm is derived with the aid of isoquants and isocost curves. Use a diagram to illustrate your explanation. (12)

(12) Explain in your own words (with the aid of a diagram) how isoquants, isocost curves and an expansion path can be used to derive the LTC curve for a firm. Draw the LMC and LAC curves that correspond with the LTC curve. (15)

(13) Use a diagram representing an LTC curve and explain how this curve can be used to derive the LMC and LAC curves (you must also draw the last-mentioned two). (10)

(14) Define the concepts of economies and diseconomies of scale. Also explain how they influence the shape of the LAC curve. (8)

(15) Draw a diagram representing the STC and TCC curves. Then explain how the figure can be used to derive the TVC curve. (You must also draw the TVC curve.) (5)

(16) Explain how the so-called 'envelope' curve can be derived if (say) three SAC curves of different size plants are available. Use a diagram to illustrate your explanation. (8)

5

PERFECT COMPETITION

In the preceding chapters the emphasis was on the derivation and discussion of important theoretical principles which explain the behaviour of consumers and firms. In this chapter, these principles are used to analyse perfect competition. In Chapter 2 reference was made to perfect competition, and in practice this assumption has applied throughout – in this chapter, however, it will be discussed in greater detail.

We shall start this chapter by first briefly discussing the conditions for or assumptions of perfect competition. Although these assumptions may appear somewhat far-fetched, perfect competition serves as a norm that firms should strive for and as a measure against which other market forms can be measured. Some of the concepts encountered in the previous chapter such as marginal cost and average cost will be used in this chapter, together with concepts such as marginal revenue to determine at what level of output the firm will maximise profit, as well as to derive the firm's supply curve and determine the firm's equilibrium. Initially, the analysis focuses on the short run, where the firm may make normal profit, economic profit or even a loss. This is followed by an analysis of the firm's long-run situation. It will be become apparent that in the long run, where all the production factors are variable, the firm will set up a plant size that will result in normal profit so that there will be no reason to leave or enter the industry. Finally, the long-run supply curve of the industry is derived for constant, increasing and decreasing cost industries.

On completion of this chapter, you should be able to

- define the conditions for perfect competition
- explain the conditions for profit maximisation
- derive the short-run supply curve of the individual firm
- explain long-run profit maximisation and long-run equilibrium
- derive the long-run industrial supply curve for constant, increasing and decreasing cost industries

MARKET STRUCTURE

In the preceding chapters the behaviour of consumers and firms was discussed. In the following three chapters the focus will be on the price and production decisions of firms. Two key questions in microeconomics are: What determines the price of the product? and What determines the quantity to be produced? These questions will be answered for different market conditions in the following chapters.

Economists distinguish between four different types of markets, namely perfect competition, monopoly, monopolistic competition and oligopoly. The distinction between the groups is based on

- the number of firms in the market
- the nature of the product – that is, whether it is homogeneous or differentiated
- accessibility of the market
- the control that an individual firm has over prices

The table below will help to distinguish the different market forms and their unique characteristics.

Table 5-1
Characteristics of the four main market models

Characteristic	Perfect competition	Monopolistic competition	Oligopoly	Monopoly
Number of firms	Very large number	Very large number	Few	Only one
Type of product	Homogeneous (identical)	Differentiated	Homogeneous or differentiated	Unique without close substitutes
Control over prices	None	Limited	Determined by interdependence	Considerable
Access to the market	Free. No restriction	Free	There may be restrictions	Limited
Nonprice competition	None	Much emphasis on advertising and trademarks	A great deal, especially in price differentiation	Mostly public relations

Although Table 5-1 indicates four market forms, often only two broad groups are distinguished, namely perfect and imperfect competition. In such a case, perfect competition is contrasted with all the other market forms and imperfect competition is regarded as the collective name for monopolistic competition, oligopoly and monopoly.

The characteristics of the different market forms are such that price and production decisions of firms are taken according to circumstances which may differ from one market form to the next. This obviously has significant implications for the behaviour of firms and forms the subject matter to be studied in this and the next two chapters.

PERFECT COMPETITION

The first market form used to study the behaviour of firms is that of perfect competition. In preceding chapters, it appeared that the market consisted of all the buyers (the demand side) and sellers (the supply side) of the specific good or service. There was competition on both sides of the market. In the goods market, buyers compete to obtain the product, while sellers compete to sell the product to buyers.

What does the market form of perfect competition involve? An economist will define perfect competition as a theoretical market form of such a nature that no individual participant (buyer or seller) in the economic process can have any influence on the market price because his or her contribution is too small compared with the market as a whole. The market price is determined by the interaction between demand and supply and all the participants must accept the market price. In a perfectly competitive market, all the participants are price takers – they have to accept the price as given and can only decide what quantities they will offer or request at that price.

An important characteristic of perfect competition is its impersonal nature in terms of which individual participants act completely independently of one another. For example, under perfect competition the individual firm, in its pursuit of maximum profit, will only take into consideration the market price and its own cost structure to determine its output quantity and take no notice whatsoever of the actions of its competitors or be influenced by them in any way. As strange as this may sound, perfect competition is therefore a market form characterised by a total lack of competition between individual firms – not in respect of price, quality, packaging or any other aspect. The meaning of perfect competition, as it is used in economic theory, is exactly the opposite of what it means in conversational speech. In the business world, people use the word 'competition' as a synonym for the word 'rivalry' where each firm is aware of its competitors and all sorts of methods (eg advertising) are used to entice clients away from competitors. In the theoretical world of perfect competition, this does not exist. Because there are so many firms in the industry, and individual firms can supply only a small portion of the market demand, no firm regards another firm as a threat. Selling its products is also no problem for a producer.

Characteristics of perfect competition

Perfect competition exists if the following conditions are met:

- There must be so many buyers and sellers of the product that each market participant is insignificantly small in relation to the market. Thus no individual buyer or seller can influence the market price.

- All the goods sold in the specific market are homogeneous, that is, identical. It makes no difference to the buyer from whom or where he or she buys the product.

- All production factors are completely mobile – in other words, labour, capital and all other production factors can move freely from one market to another.

- All the buyers and sellers have complete knowledge of all market conditions. For example, if one firm increases its price above the market price, all the buyers will immediately know about it and buy from those firms that still ask a lower price. The firm that asks for higher prices will then sell no products. (No firm will allow its price to drop below the market price, because it can sell as much as it likes at the market price.)

- There is total freedom of entry and exit – in other words, buyers and sellers are free to enter or leave the market. There should be no constraints on entry in the form of legal, financial, technological or other obstacles that restrict the freedom of movement of buyers and sellers.

- There is no government intervention to influence buyers and sellers.

- There is no collusion between sellers. Each seller acts independently.

With such strict conditions, it is not surprising that there are so few examples of perfect competition. The individual farmer is often regarded as a prime example of a perfect competitor. Sophisticated markets such as the stock exchange, an international grain exchange or a market for foreign currency, in which the equilibrium price is determined by the interaction between buyers and sellers, can also come close to being classified as a perfectly competitive market. In these markets there are thousands (even millions) of buyers and sellers; entry to and exit from markets are fairly easy; the products are homogeneous; participants are usually well informed about the market conditions; and as a rule large quantities of the product are bought and sold at the prevailing price. No individual has any noticeable power – everyone is a price taker.

Applicability

Because it is difficult to find an example of perfect competition in practice, this leads one to ask the following question: Why is it necessary to study the market form in the first place? The following remarks should clear up any doubts you may have:

- It was pointed out in Chapter 1 that a model can be useful, even if some of the assumptions appear somewhat unrealistic. The model of perfect competition leads to conclusions which are valuable in explaining practical events in the economy and making predictions about what may happen in the future.
- The model serves as a frame of reference or norm for studying and comparing markets. In the agricultural sector in particular, or other markets, where almost all the conditions for perfect competition are satisfied, the model has numerous applications when the operation of the markets is analysed.
- Perfect competition is a good point of departure for any analysis of the determination of prices and output.

Perfect competition, like all other models, has to be handled with caution. However, it is always a useful analytical tool. In conclusion, note that the adjective 'perfect' in perfect competition does not mean that it is necessarily the most acceptable form of competition – it merely indicates that it is the purest or highest form of competition.

The demand for the product of the perfectly competitive firm

In a perfectly competitive market, the market price is determined by the interaction between market demand and market supply. Since the perfectly competitive firm forms only a fraction of the market supply, it can have no influence on the market price and the firm must accept this price as given. The firm can also offer any quantity on the market and sell it at the prevailing market price. The implication is that the demand curve for the product of the perfectly competitive firm runs horizontal to the market price – in other words, it is perfectly elastic.

Horizontal demand curve

This situation is illustrated in Figures 5-1(a) and (b). The market demand and supply curves determine the market price P_1. At this price, the firm can sell as much of its product as it wishes, as shown by the perfectly elastic demand curve in Figure 5-1(b).

Under perfect competition, the firm receives the same price (the market price) per unit for all the units it sells. The firm's average revenue (AR) is therefore equal to the market price, that is OP_1, and the demand curve therefore also represents the average revenue curve. At the same time, the revenue from any additional unit that the firm sells – that is, the marginal revenue (MR) – is also equal to the market price OP_1 and the demand curve therefore also represents the marginal revenue curve. Hence under perfect competition: Price = AR = MR.

P=AR=MR

Figure 5-1(a)
The market price
Market demand and market supply curves determine the market price P_1 and the quantity Q_1 which will be offered on the market.

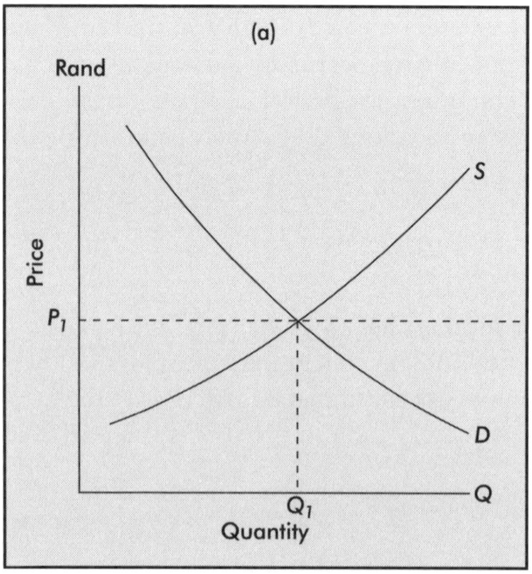

Figure 5-1(b)
The firm's demand curve
The curve is perfectly elastic and is determined by the market price P_1.

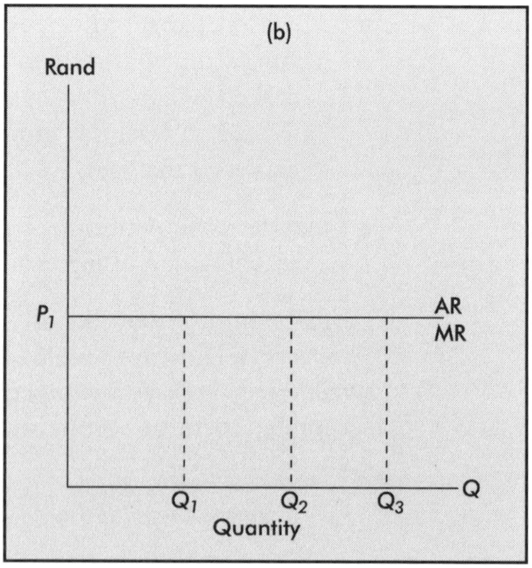

Total revenue, average revenue and marginal revenue

The average revenue and the marginal revenue of the perfectly competitive firm were briefly discussed in the previous section. Here they are stated more formally.

As mentioned earlier, the perfectly competitive firm is a price taker and the price of its product is given (P_1 in Fig 5-2). The firm's total revenue (TR) will therefore increase by a constant amount for each additional unit sold. The total revenue for the firm from the sale of its product is the quantity sold multiplied by the price: that is, $TR = P \times Q$. The total revenue curve is a straight line from the origin, which indicates that the price is constant.

Average revenue (revenue per unit) equals the total revenue divided by the quantity:

Figure 5-2

Total revenue, average revenue and marginal revenue

The firm's total revenue is indicated by TR. The slope of TR is equal to the price. The individual firm's AR and MR will be the same as the market price P_1.

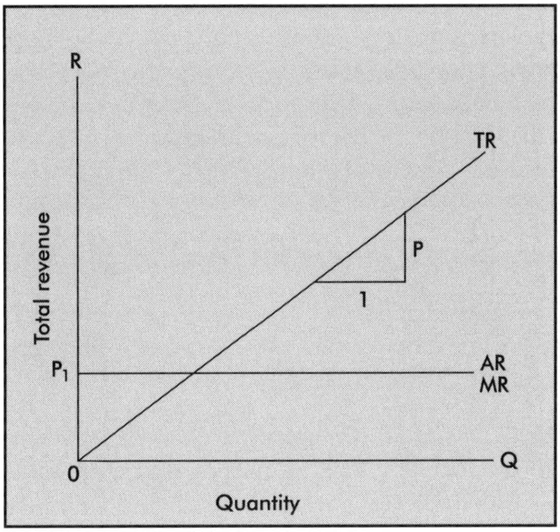

$$AR = \frac{TR}{Q}$$

$$= \frac{PQ}{Q}$$

$$= P$$

This result is the same as what was stated in the previous section, namely that the price at which the firm sells the product and its average revenue is the same (AR = P).

Marginal revenue (MR), which is the increase in the total revenue from the sale of an additional unit of the product, will also be equal to the price of the product. This is evident from the following:

$$MR = \frac{\Delta TR}{\Delta Q}$$

$$= \frac{\Delta(PQ)}{\Delta Q}$$

$$= P$$

The end result is also the same as that in the previous section, namely that under perfect competition Price = AR = MR applies.

SHORT-RUN EQUILIBRIUM

To determine the equilibrium of a perfectly competitive industry it is necessary to derive the market supply. This requires determining the supply of individual firms, since the market supply is the sum of the supply of all the individual firms in the industry. What follows below is an analysis of the supply of a typical firm under perfect competition.

Equilibrium (profit maximisation) of the firm in the short run

We assume that a firm's behaviour is determined mainly by its pursuit of profit. Any other motives depend on or are at best achieved if the firm's pursuit of maximum profit succeeds.

A firm that produces under perfect competition and wishes to maximise profit will produce that level of output where the difference between total revenue (TR) and total cost (TC) is the greatest. Profit is defined as

Profit = TR – TC

It is important to note once again that economists regard normal profit as part of production costs. In Chapter 4 it was explained that normal profit is a part of implicit cost, which in turn forms part of total cost. When total revenue is exactly equal to total cost, normal profit is made. When total revenue is greater than total cost, economic profit is made.

Equilibrium

If the firm produces the output that maximises the difference between total revenue and total cost (ie maximises profit), it will be in equilibrium. The equilibrium position of the firm can be represented graphically in two ways: by using the TR and TC curves, or by using the marginal revenue curve (MR) and marginal cost curve (MC). These curves were all discussed earlier.

Equilibrium according to the total approach (total revenue and total cost)

Figure 5-3(a) represents the total revenue curve (TR) and short-run total cost curve (STC) for a perfectly competitive firm. As shown earlier in this chapter, the TR curve is a straight line through the origin of the graph which indicates that price is constant for all levels of output. The firm is a price taker and can sell any quantity at the market price; hence the TR curve will rise in proportion to its sales. The slope of the TR curve indicates marginal revenue (MR), which is

Figure 5-3

Short-run profit maximisation

The firm will produce the output where the positive difference between TR and TC is the greatest. This will be at Q_2, where MR = SMC, that is, point e in part (c) of the figure.

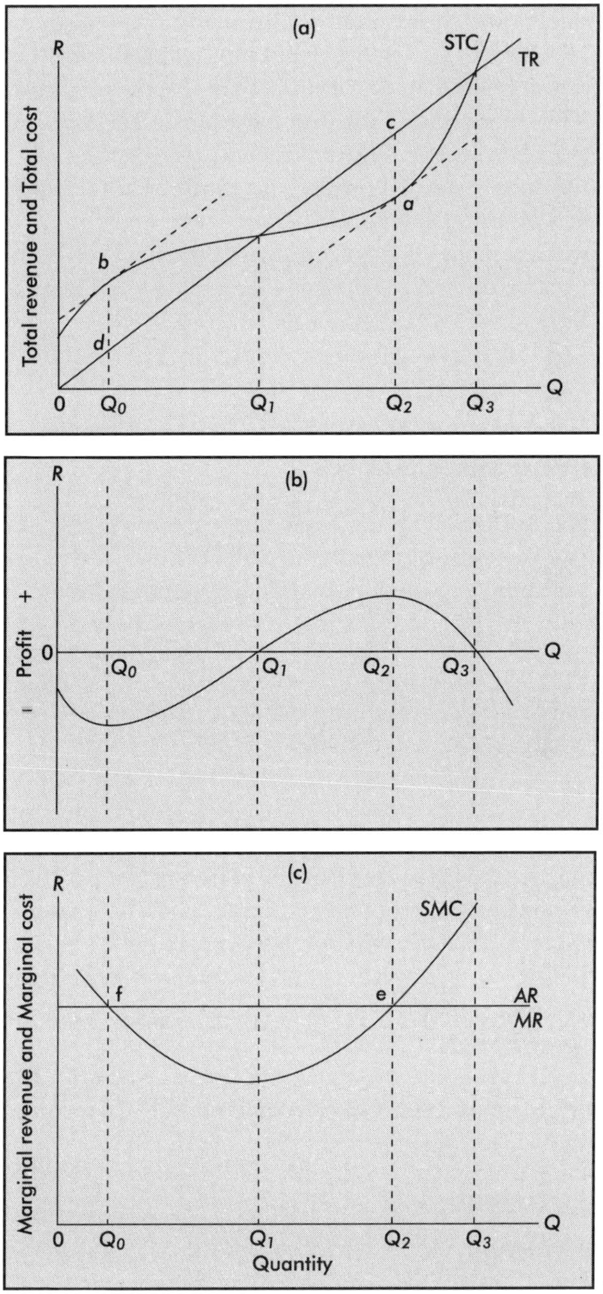

constant and equal to the prevailing market price. The slope of the STC curve indicates the short-run marginal cost (SMC).

The firm will maximise profit at a level of production of Q_2 where the difference between the TR and STC for a given level of production is the greatest (see points a and c). At smaller or greater levels of production, the difference between TR and STC is smaller than at Q_2 and total profit is not maximised. In fact, if output is less than Q_1 or more than Q_3, the total cost is more than total revenue (STC runs above TR), and the firm suffers losses. At a production level of Q_1 and Q_3 respectively, total revenue is exactly equal to total cost and the firm makes only normal profit. This profit position is also reflected in Figure 5-3(b). At a production level of Q_2, profit is a maximum, while at Q_1 and Q_3 normal profit is made. If Q_0 is produced, the firm suffers maximum loss, because the negative difference between TR and STC is the greatest there (see points b and d).

Equilibrium according to the marginal approach (marginal revenue and marginal cost)

The total-revenue-total-cost approach is somewhat clumsy to use when firms have to be added together in order to study the industry as a whole. An alternative approach based on marginal revenue and marginal cost uses price expressly as a variable and leads to a rule that firms must follow in order to maximise profit.

Figure 5-3(c) contains the short-run marginal cost curve (SMC) which is derived from the STC curve in Figure 5-3(a). The SMC is U-shaped, which reflects the law of diminishing returns which applies in the short run. The demand curve of the perfectly competitive firm also appears in Figure 5-3(c). It was indicated earlier that the demand curve also represents the average revenue curve and the marginal revenue curve of the perfectly competitive firm. The firm is in equilibrium (maximises profit) at the output level that is determined by the point of intersection of the MC and MR curves, that is at point e in Figure 5-3(c). Why? To the left of e, profit is not yet maximised because each unit to the left of Q_2 ensures a revenue for the firm that is greater than the marginal cost (MR lies above SMC). To the right of e, the production cost of each additional unit is greater than the revenue it can earn if it is sold (SMC lies above MR), which means that a loss is made on such units, and total profit is reduced. To sum up:

- When $MC < MR$, total profit is not maximised and the firm will benefit by expanding.
- When $MC > MR$, total profit is reduced, and the firm will benefit by producing less.

- If MR = MC, short-run profit is maximised and the firm is in equilibrium.

The first condition for the firm to be in equilibrium is therefore that marginal cost should be equal to marginal revenue. This is a necessary condition for equilibrium but it is not sufficient because it is possible to satisfy the condition without the firm being in equilibrium. Figure 5-3(c) seems to show that the condition MR = MC can also be satisfied at point f. However, closer examination shows that the firm cannot be in equilibrium at f. In fact, as shown in Figures 5-3(a) and 5-3(b), Q_0 is a production level where a *maximum* loss is made. What is the important difference between points e and f? The difference is that the second condition for equilibrium (or profit maximisation) for the firm requires the MC curve to have a positive slope at the point where it intersects the MR curve, as at e. This means that the MC curve must intersect the MR curve from below. The second condition for equilibrium can therefore be added to the first, namely, profit is maximised if MR = MC and the marginal cost curve has a positive slope – in other words, it intersects the MR curve from below. In Figure 5-3(c), both of these conditions are satisfied at point e.

Thus far it has been assumed that the firm will make a profit, and reference has been made only to the maximisation of that profit. However, although a firm is in short-run equilibrium this does not always mean that it makes economic profit. This is dealt with in the next section.

Three possibilities for the firm: normal profit, economic profit or a loss

In the short run there are various profit and loss possibilities for a perfectly competitive firm. Whether a firm makes normal profit, economic profit or even a loss depends on the position of the short-run average cost curve (SAC) in respect of the market price when the firm is in equilibrium. (Remember here that the SAC curve represents the average *total* cost in the short run – in other words, the total of constant cost – also known as fixed cost – plus variable cost.)

Normal profit

In Figure 5-4(a) the minimum point of the SAC is at the same level as the market price P_1. The firm is in short-run equilibrium at point e_1 where MR = SMC and the firm will produce the quantity Q_1 at the market price P_1. At this point, total cost and total revenue will be exactly equal – total revenue is represented by $0P_1 \times 0Q_1$ and total cost by $0Q_1 \times Q_1e_1$, which amount to same thing. Given its cost structure, at e_1 the firm makes the maximum profit possible at price P_1 (because MR = SMC), although only normal profit is made.

Economic profit

In Figure 5-4(b), the minimum point of the SAC is lower than the market price P_2. The firm is in equilibrium at point e_2 where MR = SMC and the firm will produce quantity Q_2 at market price P_2. At this point, total revenue will exceed total cost – total revenue is represented by $0P_2 \times 0Q_2$, and total cost by $0S \times$

Figure 5–4
Price determination in the short run

Depending on the price, the firm can make normal profit, economic profit or a loss in the short run.

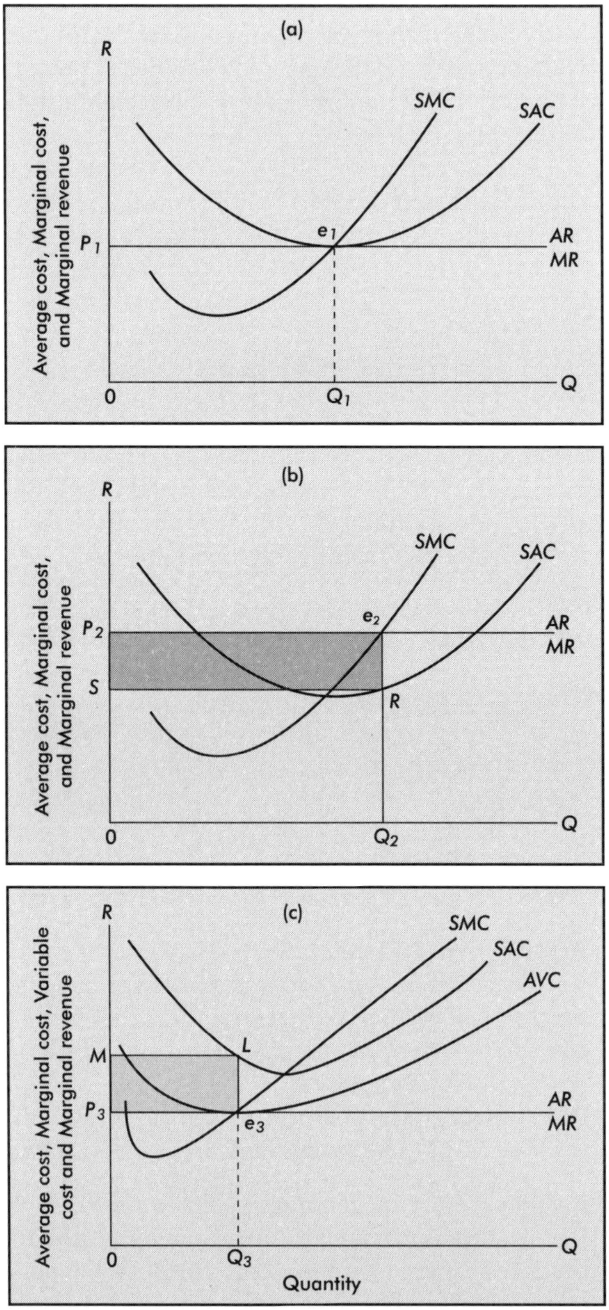

$0Q_2$. Given its cost structure, the firm makes economic profit at e_2 which is represented by the area P_2e_2RS.

Loss

In Figure 5-4(c) the minimum point of the SAC is higher than the market price P_3. The firm is in equilibrium (in this case the loss is minimised) at point e_3, where MR = SMC, and the firm will produce the quantity Q_3 at the market price P_3. At this point total cost will exceed total revenue – total cost is represented by $0M \times 0Q_3$ and total revenue by $0P_3 \times 0Q_3$. Given its cost structure, at e_3 the firm makes a loss which is represented by P_3MLe_3. At e_3 the firm covers its variable cost of $0Q_3 \times Q_3e_3$, but the fixed cost of $P_3e_3 \times e_3L$ (which represents the loss) is not covered. Because fixed cost has to be paid regardless of whether the firm produces, at a market price P_3 the firm can choose whether or not to cease production – in both cases the loss is the same (equal to fixed cost). If the price falls below P_3 (ie below the AVC curve), the firm will not even cover its variable cost, and production will stop. In this case the firm will minimise its loss by stopping production, because then variable cost does not have to be paid (besides fixed cost).

Closing-down point

The point at which the firm just covers its variable cost, such as e_3 in Figure 5-4(c), is referred to as the closing-down point. As explained above, if the price goes below the closing-down point, the firm does not cover its variable cost, and it would be better to close its doors. This also works the other way round: if the price is lower than the closing-down point and then starts to rise, at this point the firm will consider starting to produce.

Figure 5-5

Derivation of the firm's short-run supply curve

To maximise profit, the firm will produce at each price where MR = MC. If the price falls below the AVC curve, the firm will offer nothing. As price increases, larger quantities are offered.

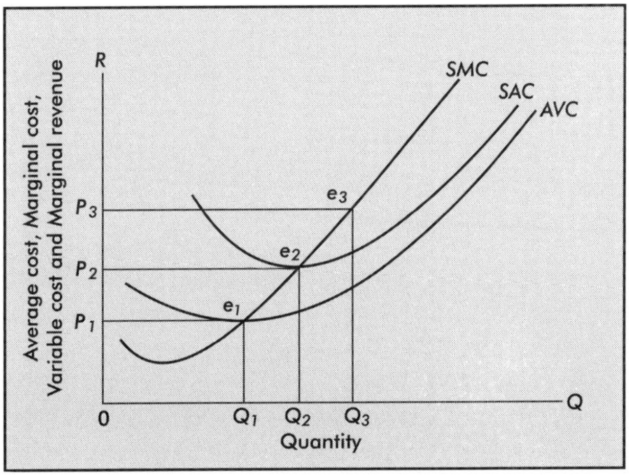

The firm's short-run supply curve

In the previous section it appeared that to remain in equilibrium, regardless of the price, the firm will always produce that quantity where MR = MC. Because the (horizontal) demand curve of the firm under perfect competition also represents the marginal revenue (MR), the firm will produce that quantity where the demand curve intersects the MC curve. This information is important in the analysis to follow.

The supply curve of the firm under perfect competition can now be derived by taking different market prices and seeing how much the firm will produce at each price. Assume that the market price increases slowly – in Figure 5-5 this is indicated as an increase from P_1 to P_2 to P_3. This means that the horizontal demand curve for the firm's product shifts upwards. Given the positive movement of the MC curve, each higher demand curve will intersect the given SMC curve at a point that lies to the right of the previous point of intersection such as e_1, e_2 and e_3 indicate in Figure 5-5 (at each of these points MR = MC). This means that the quantity that the firm produces increases as the price increases. We know that the firm will produce nothing if the price falls below e_1 in Figure 5-5 because variable cost is then not covered – thus a point such as e_1 will be the lowest starting point of the firm's supply curve. If the successive points such as e_1, e_2 and e_3, where the demand curve intersects the MC curve, are drawn in a separate graph (see Fig 5-6), the *short-run supply curve of the firm under perfect competition is represented by the section of the SMC curve above the variable cost curve (ie above the closing-down point)*. Below the closing-down point, the firm will offer nothing; as the price rises above the closing-down point, the quantity offered will increase.

Short-run supply curve

Figure 5-6

The short-run supply curve of the firm

The curve is represented by the rising section of the SMC curve above the AVC curve.

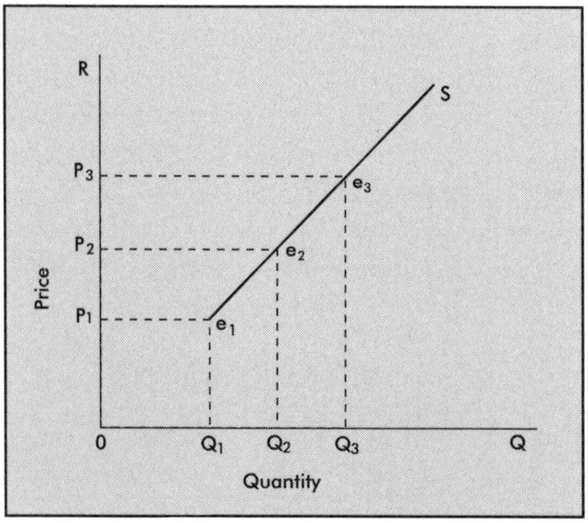

The industry's short-run supply curve

The industry's short-run supply curve (also referred to as the market supply curve) is obtained by horizontally adding together the supply curves of all the individual firms in the industry. (This technique was discussed in Chapter 2.) The underlying assumptions here are that the price of production factors and the technology remain unchanged and that the industry consists of a large number of firms. In these circumstances the total quantity offered at a particular price in the market is the sum of the quantities offered by the individual firms in the industry at that price.*

In Figure 5-7(a), the industry's supply curve is indicated as the straight line SS with a positive slope. The precise shape and position of this supply curve are determined by the technology and the price of production factors, as well as the size of the firms in the industry. Firms are not necessarily all the same size – the size of an individual firm under perfect competition is also determined by the ability of the particular entrepreneur and, of course, different people have different abilities.

Short-run equilibrium of the industry

Given the market demand and the market supply, the industry will be in equilibrium at the price that clears the market – that is, at the price where the quantity demanded is exactly equal to the quantity supplied. In Figure 5-7(a) the market is in equilibrium at the price P_e, in which case the quantity demanded and the quantity supplied are Q_e. However, if firms make an economic profit (Fig 5-7(b)) or loss (Fig 5-7(c)) at the prevailing price, this will only be a short-run equilibrium (which does not apply in the long run). In the long run firms that make a loss and are unable to adapt their plants will close down. Those firms that make an economic profit will expand their plants; what is more, the economic profit will also attract new firms to the industry. Entries, exits and readjustments by the remaining firms will lead to long-run equilibrium, where all the firms make normal profit – once this has happened there will be no further entries to or exits from the industry. This topic will be discussed in greater detail in the next section.

---

* The words 'market' and 'industry' are often used synonymously. This is understandable for the total supply of a product on the market is what the industry offers; the total market demand for a product is the demand an industry experiences for the product. Industrial equilibrium and market equilibrium will therefore also have the same meaning.

Figure 5-7(a)
Short-run equilibrium for the industry

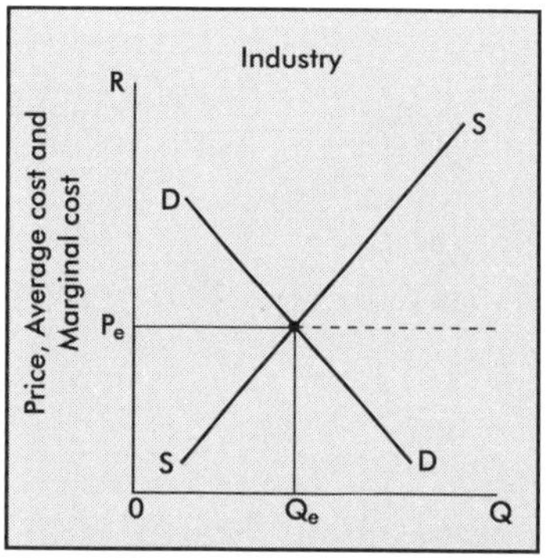

Figure 5-7(b)
Short-run equilibrium for a firm (economic profit)

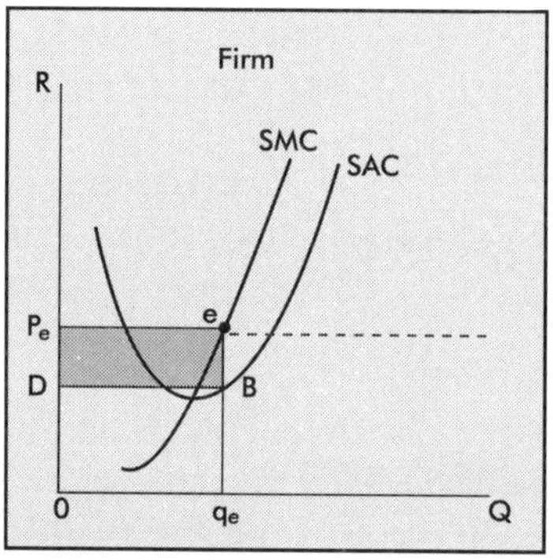

Figure 5-7(c)
Short-run equilibrium for a firm (loss)

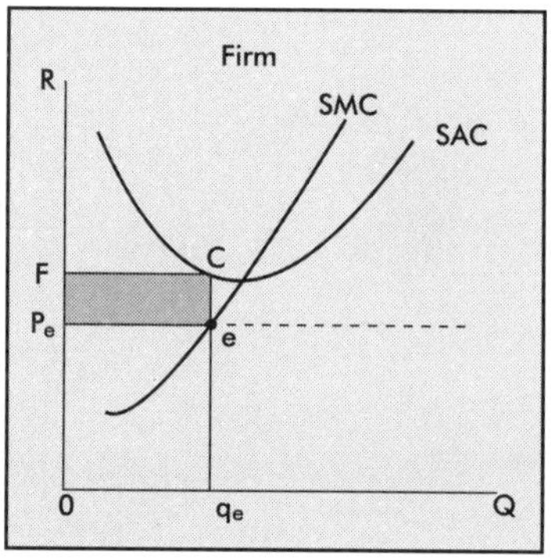

LONG-RUN EQUILIBRIUM

Long-run equilibrium of the firm

The principle that a firm can modify its plant size in the long run and that firms can enter or leave an industry plays a vital role in determining the long-run equilibrium of a firm. The way in which this long-run equilibrium is achieved will now be explained – first verbally, and then graphically.

It has already become clear that a firm makes economic profit if the market price, and therefore the demand curve, is higher than the minimum point of its average cost curve (Fig 5-7(b) indicates the short-run case). The previous section also mentioned that economic profit in an industry will attract new firms to that industry. The entry of new firms will increase the product supply and hence lead to a decrease in price, which will shift the horizontal demand curve of the individual firm downwards; but the entry of new firms will result in a greater demand for production factors. Production factors in turn will become more expensive, and this will lead to an upward shift of the cost curves. This dual process will continue until the LAC curve forms a tangent (at its minimum point) with the demand curve defined by the market price. Here the firm makes normal profit because it just covers its total cost (which includes normal profit). In contrast, if firms make losses in the long run (the market price and therefore the demand curve lie lower than the minimum point of the average cost curve), they will leave the industry in due course; this will cause prices to increase (because of the smaller supply) and costs will decrease as the industry becomes smaller and the demand for production factors declines. In this case the process will also continue until the LAC curve forms a tangent with the demand curve and the firms that remain in the industry just cover their total cost and make normal profit.

Long-run equilibrium

To sum up: in both cases (economic profit or loss), the firm achieves long-run equilibrium, when it has adapted the size of its plant in such a way that production occurs at the minimum point of the LAC curve and this point forms a tangent with the horizontal demand curve. At the point of equilibrium in the long run a firm makes only normal profit.

Figure 5-8

Long-run equilibrium of the firm

Under perfect competition, the price, in the long run, will converge on the minimum point of the LAC. At this price, all the firms in the industry make normal profit.

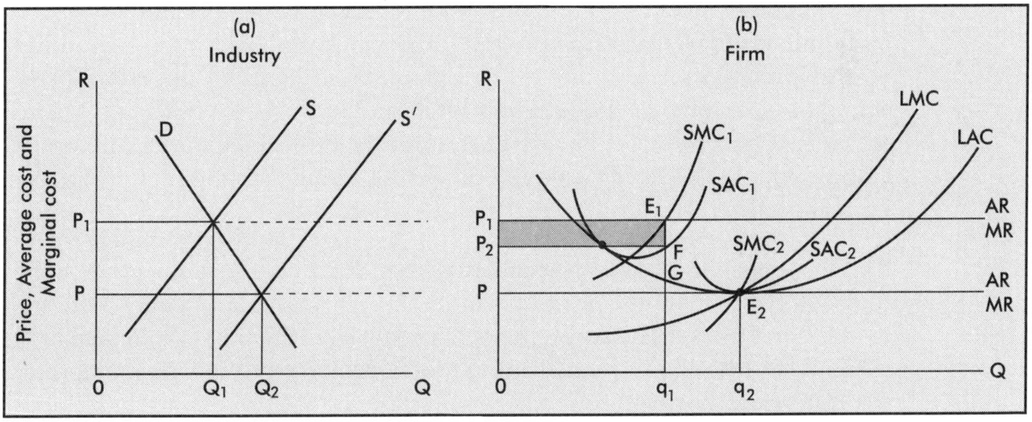

Graphic explanation of the firm's long-run equilibrium

Figure 5-8(b) illustrates graphically how under perfect competition firms that make economic profit adapt their equilibrium position in the long run. If the market price is P_1, the firm makes economic profit ($P_1E_1FP_2$) with the short-run plant represented by SAC_1. At a price of P_1 the firm will maximise profit in the short run at point E_1 where the principle for profit maximisation (MR = MC) applies; the quantity q_1 will be produced. At a production level of q_1 the total cost per unit amounts to q_1F in the short run (point F lies on SAC_1 and therefore represents average *total* cost); however, in the long run, the firm can produce at a lower total cost of q_1G per unit. Because of economies of scale, levels of output greater than q_1 can be produced at an even lower total cost in the long run, as indicated by the decreasing slope of the LAC between points G and E_2. Hence the firm will be spurred on by the possibility of greater profit to build a larger plant. The firm will not be interested in producing output levels greater than those represented by the minimum point of the LAC, since such levels of output are possible only at a higher cost – internal diseconomies of scale make the LAC rise to the right of point E_2. At the same time, the surplus profit will entice new firms to enter the industry. Because the quantity offered on the market increases as a result of expansion of existing firms and the entry of new ones, the market supply curve will shift to the right (from S to S′ in Fig 5-8(a)) and the price will decrease until it reaches P. At this price, which is at the same level as the minimum point of the LAC, total revenue ($0P \times 0q_2$) is equal to total cost ($0q_2 \times q_2E_2$), and the firm makes normal profit because it just covers its total cost (which includes normal profit). In time, all the firms in the industry will make normal profit and be in long-run equilibrium. (The LAC curve in Fig 5-8(b) includes any increases in cost as a result of the increase in the price of production factors if the industry expands.)

The above discussion explained the adjustment of firms that initially make economic profit. What is the process if firms initially make a loss – in other words, if the market price lies below the minimum point of the average cost curve? In such a case, the adjustment process simply works the other way round – hence it is unnecessary to discuss it here. Ultimately the LAC curve will form a tangent with the demand curve and the firms remaining in industry will make normal profit.

The above analysis leads to the conclusion that under perfect competition in the long run the price of the product will reach a level that corresponds with the lowest point of the LAC curve. A point such as E_2 in Figure 5-8(b) represents a point of rest (the point of equilibrium) for the firm. At the point of equilibrium the firm makes normal profit and there will be no incentive to either leave or enter the industry.

A long-run point of equilibrium such as E_2 in Figure 5-8(b) can also be defined in terms of symbols. An important fact about this point is that in the short run as well as the long run the firm reaches equilibrium because not only is marginal revenue (ie price) equal to short-run marginal cost (ie P = MR = SMC), but marginal revenue is also equal to long-run marginal cost (ie P = MR = LMC). Thus the following will apply:

$$P = MR = SMC = LMC$$

Furthermore, at a point of equilibrium such as E_2 in Figure 5-8(b), LAC = SAC because both these curves (LAC and SAC_2) will be at their minimum points. Because the point of equilibrium lies at the same level as the market price, LAC = SAC = P. The full condition that applies at the long-run point of equilibrium for the firm is therefore

$$P = MR = SMC = LMC = LAC = SAC$$

Long-run equilibrium of the industry

When a market price arises (in perfect competition) at such a level that each firm is in equilibrium at the minimum point of its LAC curve (which is the same for all firms) and only normal profit is made, the industry will also be in long-run equilibrium. If the long-run equilibrium situation is achieved, there will be no further entries or exits of firms provided that the technology and prices of production factors do not change.

The long-run equilibrium situation is indicated in Figure 5-9. At the market price P firms produce at the lowest possible cost at E and make only normal profit. Each firm is in equilibrium because it produces at a point where marginal cost is equal to marginal revenue (MR = MC), not only in the short run, but also in the long run.

At the price P each individual firm, and hence the industry too, is in long-run equilibrium: normal profit is made and all costs are covered, which means that there are no incentives for firms to leave or enter the industry. With all the firms in the industry in equilibrium, and with no entries or exits, the industry's supply will remain stable and, given the market demand (DD in Fig 5-9), the price P will be a long-run equilibrium price.

Figure 5-9

Long-run equilibrium of the industry

When each firm is in equilibrium at the minimum point of the LAC, the industry is also in equilibrium.

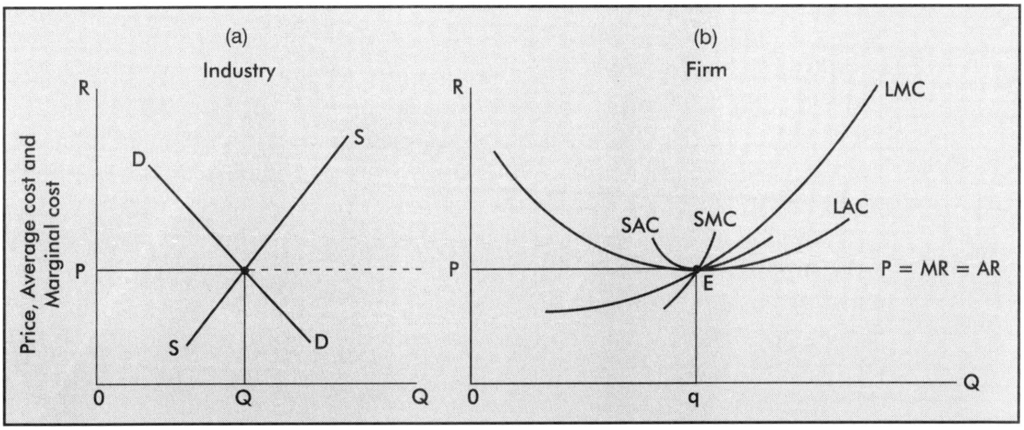

Optimal application of resources

On the basis of the above analyses, one can say that under perfect competition in the long run the market mechanism will lead to an optimal application of production factors. This is so because the following apply:

- The output is produced at the lowest possible cost (at the minimum point of the LAC).
- Consumers pay the lowest possible price for the product (the price is equal to the lowest cost at which the product can be produced).
- The price of the product equals the opportunity cost to produce the product.
- All firms make only normal profit.

DERIVATION OF LONG-RUN INDUSTRY SUPPLY CURVE UNDER CONDITIONS OF PERFECT COMPETITION

The previous section contained an analysis of the way a firm and an industry in a perfectly competitive environment achieve long-run equilibrium. With a situation of long-run equilibrium as the basic point of departure, it is now possible to examine how a perfectly competitive firmand industry react in the long run when the market demand for a particular product increases. This analysis also makes it possible to define a constant cost industry, an increasing cost industry, and a decreasing cost industry and explain their actions graphically.

Constant cost industry

When an industry (and consequently all the firms in the industry) is in long-run equilibrium and the market demand for the product increases, the market demand curve will shift to the right and the equilibrium price will increase. In the short run, a firm will expand production in its existing plant and in the process make economic profit. Other firms will become aware of the economic profit and, in the long run, enter the industry. This behaviour by firms (existing ones as well as new entrants) will increase the supply of the product in the market – the supply curve will shift to the right. If the price of production factors remains constant (although the growing industry requires more production factors), the market supply will increase until the original equilibrium price in the market is again reached. The supply curve of the industry in the long run therefore runs horizontally (at the same level as the minimum of the LAC curve). Such an industry is known as a constant cost industry.

Graphically, this analysis can be explained as follows:

Points E and e in Figures 5-10(a) and (b) show the long-run equilibrium position of the industry and the firm respectively before demand and supply change. The market demand now increases from D to D′ – in the short run this leads to an increase in the price from P to P_1. Each of the firms in the industry will apply the profit-maximisation principle (MR = MC) at the higher price P_1, and in the short run expand the production of its existing plant and produce at point e′, which means that its production increases from q_1 to q_2. The initial point of equilibrium of the industry as a whole moves in the short run from E to E′ and total output increases from Q_1 to Q_2.

At a price P_1, in the short run, each firm in the industry makes an economic profit of fe′ per unit, which in the long run will attract other firms (also requiring production factors) to the industry; this will cause the supply curve S to shift to the right. If the price of production factors remains constant, S shifts to S′ and the initial equilibrium price P comes into effect once again – the price is determined by the point of intersection of D′ and S′ at E″. At the price P, each firm produces at the minimum point of its LAC and makes only normal profit (see point e). By joining points E and E″ we obtain the supply curve (LS) of the industry in the long run. Since EE″ runs horizontally, it is a constant cost industry. The initial increase in demand has caused the number of firms in the industry to increase, which has caused the total production quantity to increase to Q_3. However, in the final instance, the equilibrium price is again at its original level.

Figure 5-10

Constant cost industry

If the industry expands, the price of production factors remains constant. The long-run supply curve of the industry runs horizontally.

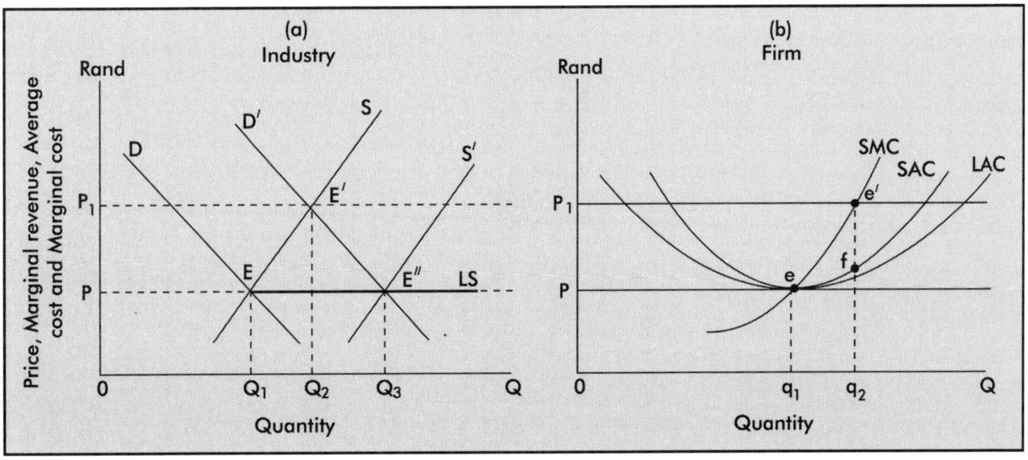

A constant cost industry will in all probability use production factors that are reasonably freely available; such an industry's demand for production factors will also constitute only a small portion of the total quantity applied in the economy. This will enable the industry to use more production factors without an increase in their price.

Increasing cost industry

If the price of production factors increases when firms enter a perfectly competitive industry in the long run and the total production of the industry increases, this is known as an increasing cost industry. The long-run supply curve of such an industry will run upwards from left to right – which means that in the long run greater quantities of the product will only be supplied at higher prices.

Graphically, the analysis initially proceeds exactly as the previous case. Points E and e in Figures 5-11(a) and (b) once again show the long-run equilibrium position of the industry and the firm respectively, before supply or demand change. Market demand now increases from D to D′ – in the short run, this leads to an increase in the price from P to P_2. Each of the firms in the industry will apply the profit-maximisation principle (MR = MC) at the higher price P_2, and in the short run increase its existing plant's production and produce at point e′, which means that its output will increase from q_1 to q_2. In the short run, the industry's initial point of equilibrium shifts from E to E′ and total output increases from Q_1 to Q_2.

At a price P_2, in the short run, each firm in the industry makes an economic profit of fe′ per unit, which in the long run attracts other firms (which also require production factors) to the industry; this will cause the supply curve S to shift to the right. (Up to this point, the analysis is the same as in Fig 5-10.) If the price of production factors were now to increase, costs would rise and the LAC and SAC curves of each firm would therefore shift upwards to LAC′ and SAC′ (see Fig 5-11). The supply curve shifts from S to S′ and a new equilibrium price P_1 comes into effect – the price is determined by the point of intersection of D′ and S′ at E″. At the price P_1 each firm again produces at the minimum point of its LAC (which now lies higher than before) and makes only normal profit (see point e″). (Economic profit disappears because of the increasing costs and decreasing prices.) By joining points E and E″, the supply curve of the industry in the long run (LS) is again obtained. Since EE″ runs upwards to the right, it is an increasing cost industry. The initial increase in demand has caused the number of firms in the industry to increase, which causes the total output to increase to Q_3; the equilibrium price in the final instance is at a higher level than it originally was.

An increasing cost industry will probably use specialised inputs, for instance labour with particular skills (such as highly trained laboratory technicians) or custom-made machinery that performs special tasks (an oil drill at sea). In such a case, the industry will probably have to pay higher prices if it requires larger quantities of inputs – this will result in an increasing cost industry.

Figure 5-11

Increasing cost industry

If the industry expands, the price of production factors increases. The long-run supply curve of the industry has a positive slope.

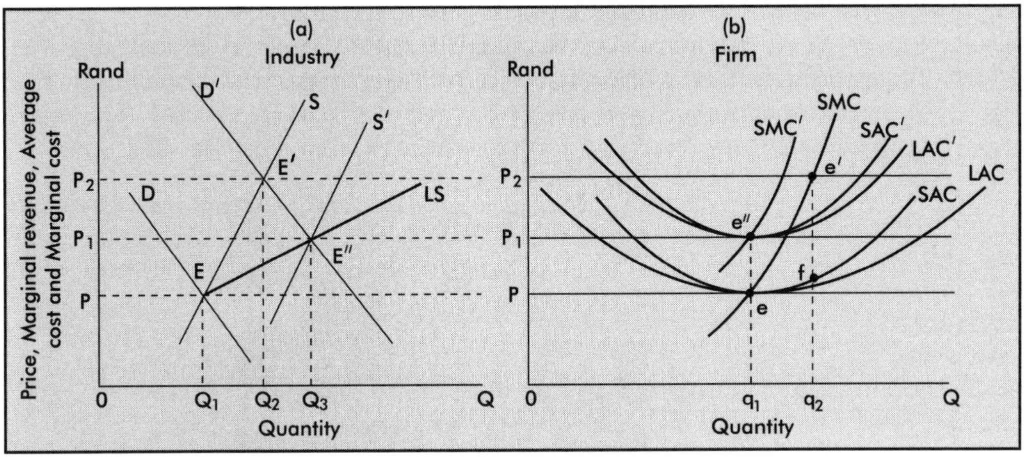

Decreasing cost industry

If the price of production factors decreases as more inputs are required by a growing industry, the long-run supply curve of the product will slope downwards from left to right. This is known as a decreasing cost industry, and means that larger quantities of the product will be provided in the long run at lower prices. (See Fig 5-12.)

The movement from E to E′ (as well as from e to e′) is the same as in the previous two examples. Since the typical firm will make economic profit at e′, in the long run more firms will enter the industry. The industry supply of the product will increase, and increased production will result in a greater demand for production factors. If the price of production factors decreases in the process, costs will decrease and firms' LAC and SAC curves will shift downwards (see LAC′ and SAC′). The industry supply will shift from S to S′ and cause a new equilibrium at price level P_2, which corresponds with the minimum of the lower LAC (see point e″). By joining points E and E″ the supply curve (LS) of the industry in the long run is again obtained. Since EE″ slopes downwards to the right, it is a decreasing cost industry. The initial increase in demand has caused the number of firms in the industry to increase, which causes the total output to increase to Q_3; in the final instance, the equilibrium price is at a lower level than it originally was.

Decreasing costs in a growing industry may be caused by factors such as the following: the creation of training institutions to provide the kind of labour the industry requires at a lower cost than before; the establishment of enterprises to supply equipment to the industry that was previously manufactured at a high cost by the firms themselves; and the exploitation of cheaper natural resources, which previously could not be economically utilised when the demand for them was smaller.

In practice, each growing industry should fall into one of the categories (constant, increasing or decreasing costs). Over time, a particular industry may even change from, say, a constant cost industry to an increasing cost industry. Increasing cost industries are probably the most common of the three.

Note that shifts in the firms' cost curves (LAC and SAC) in Figures 5-11 and 5-12 occur vertically upwards and downwards so that the lowest point of the LAC and LAC′ curves are at the same output q_1. This is so if the prices of all production factors change in the same ratio; if the prices do not change in the same ratio, the LAC and SAC curves will not move vertically upwards or downwards, but will simultaneously shift to the left or right in the movement.

Figure 5–12

Decreasing cost industry

If the industry expands, the price of production factors will decrease. The long-run supply curve of the industry has a negative slope.

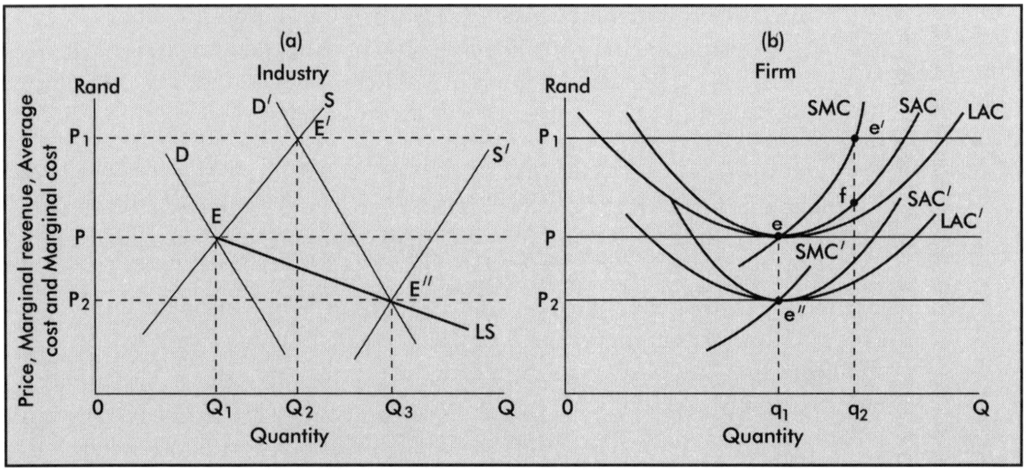

The downward shift of a firm's average cost curves (because of a decrease in input prices) when the industry becomes larger is known as external economies of scale; the upward shift of a firm's average cost curves (because of an increase in input prices) when the industry becomes larger is known as external diseconomies of scale. These should be clearly distinguished from internal economies or diseconomies of scale, which refer to a movement along a given LAC curve when a firm increases its production and builds a larger plant.

CONCLUDING REMARKS

This chapter provided an analysis of the theory of perfect competition. To sum up, the following may be said:

- The four primary conditions for perfect competition in a market are as follows: no participant in the market can influence the price; the product sold in the market is homogeneous; production factors can move around freely; and all buyers and sellers have full knowledge of all market conditions.
- A firm will maximise profit in the short run (or minimise losses) by producing that output where MR = MC. Under perfect competition MR = P - hence at the point of equilibrium, MR = MC = P. If the market price declines below the firm's average variable cost (AVC), the firm will minimise losses by stopping production. The firm's short-run supply curve is represented by the ascending part of the marginal cost curve (MC) above the AVC curve.
- The short-run price of a product is determined by the interaction between demand and supply in the market. The short-run supply curve of the industry is obtained by horizontally summing the supply curves of the firms in the industry. (The latter applies if the price of production factors and technology does not change.)
- In the short run, the equilibrium price is that price where the quantity supplied and the quantity demanded are the same in the short run. At the equilibrium price, MR = MC = P.
- In the long run, firms can change the size of their plants and enter or leave the industry. In the long run, the equilibrium price will be at the same level as the minimum point of the LAC.
- Industries can be divided into three groups: constant cost industries, increasing cost industries and decreasing cost industries. The long-run supply curves of the industries run horizontally, ascend from left to right, and slope downwards from left to right, respectively.

IMPORTANT CONCEPTS

- Homogeneous products
- Mobility of production factors
- Perfect knowledge
- Marginal revenue
- Market period
- Economic profit
- Short-run loss
- Market
- Industry
- Short-run equilibrium
- Long-run equilibrium
- Constant, increasing and decreasing cost industries

QUESTIONS

(1) Briefly discuss the conditions for perfect competition. (16)

(2) Compare perfect competition and monopolistic competition in table form in respect of the following:
 (a) number of firms
 (b) type of product
 (c) control over prices
 (d) path of the demand curve (8)

(3) Discuss the relationship between TR, AR and MR in perfectly competitive firms. (9)

(4) Why does the demand curve for the product of a perfectly competitive firm run horizontally? (4)

(5) Derive the short-run supply curve of the perfectly competitive firm. (Use only one figure.) (15)

(6) Explain why the perfectly competitive firm will maximise profits where SMC = MR. (10)

(7) Give the long-run equilibrium condition for the perfectly competitive firm and explain why each element is included therein. (12)

(8) Explain the difference between a constant cost industry and an increasing cost industry. (8)

(9) Derive the long-term industry supply curve for an increasing cost industry. (20)

6

MONOPOLY

Chapter 5 dealt with the market structure known as perfect competition. One of the main characteristics of perfect competition is that many buyers and sellers operate in the market and that the market mechanism determines both the price and the quantity traded. A monopoly is the opposite. A pure monopoly occurs when there is only one manufacturer of a product for which there are no close substitutes. Although the monopolist is also faced with a market demand curve for his product, because he is the only one offering the product, he himself can decide (within limits) at which point on the market demand curve he would like to be. The monopolist can therefore decide on both the price and the quantity of the product that he is prepared to offer – without expecting any repercussions from other market participants. A pure monopoly, like perfect competition, is seldom found in practice. The reasons for this will be explained later.

On completion of this chapter, you should know

- what a monopoly is
- the characteristics of a monopoly
- how a monopoly maximises profit
- the equilibrium condition for a monopolist
- how a monopolist can apply price discrimination
- how a monopoly and perfect competition compare
- why and how governments act against a monopolist

CHARACTERISTICS OF A MONOPOLY

The main characteristics of a monopoly are that there is only one manufacturer or seller of a product, there are no close substitutes for the product, and there are obstacles that impede other participants' entry to the market. Thus consumers cannot buy the product from anyone but the monopolist. Typical examples of monopolies in South Africa are diamond sales by De Beers's Central Selling Organisation (CSO) and SA Breweries' (SAB) production of beer. As far as SAB is concerned, there are a few small producers of beer, but their market share is so tiny that they are hardly worth mentioning. However, SA Breweries cannot be regarded as a pure monopoly but rather as a quasi-monopoly.

Natural monopoly

Other producers cannot provide the same product as a monopolist because obstacles make entry to the product market difficult. These obstacles may assume different forms – some are of an economic nature, and are referred to as *natural monopolies*. An example is exclusive ownership of raw materials such as an exclusive kind of mineral water which makes the manufacturer a monopolist. Another example of a natural monopolist could be an exceptionally high development cost, as with Iscor in the 1920s. Finally, if there is room for only one firm to produce a product efficiently in an industry (ie when one firm can serve the entire market at a lower price than two or more firms), economists also speak of a natural economy.

Artificial monopoly

If the obstacles to the entry of other firms are not economic in nature, one speaks of *artificial monopolies*. An example of such an obstacle is a *patent*, which is the legal right whereby the holder of the patent has the exclusive right to manufacture a product or use a specific technique or process. A case in point is the Polaroid camera – during the period for which the patent was valid other manufacturers were not allowed to copy this type of camera. *Licensing* is another way in which an artificial monopoly comes into being. A pertinent example here is the SABC, which was issued with a radio broadcasting licence in 1936 and a TV broadcasting licence in the 1970s. If there are no such obstacles to entry by other firms, one cannot really speak of a real monopoly, even if the firm is the only producer of a product – without obstacles to entry, monopoly profits would immediately attract competitors to the industry. In a town, for example, there may be only one producer of milk, but although such a supplier will have a certain degree of monopolistic power, this does not satisfy the definition of a monopolist. (This is why SA Breweries cannot be regarded as a pure monopolist – there are no obstacles that make it impossible for other producers to enter the market.)

Although a monopolist is the only supplier of a product, the product is still influenced by market forces in the economy. First, consumers have limited budgets and a monopolist cannot ask excessive prices for his product. As such, the product of a monopolist has to compete with all the other products available in the economy for the favour (and money) of consumers. Also few products have no close substitutes whatsoever. For many years in South Africa, for example, there was no competition in the provision of telephone services (ie before cell phones appeared on the scene), but even then consumers could consider alternative means of communication such as letters, messengers and amateur radio links. This applies to other products too.

Although one seldom finds a pure monopoly in practice, a study of this market form provides useful insight should market conditions move in the direction of a monopoly. These insights are essential to the formulation of public policy for industries with the characteristics of a monopoly. Knowledge of the theory of monopolies also provides a point of reference on the opposite end of the spectrum of market structures from perfect competition. Such knowledge is also important for any person planning an enterprise in which he or she may have the characteristics of a monopolist.

THE MARGINAL REVENUE CURVE AND AVERAGE REVENUE CURVE OF A MONOPOLIST

We have already mentioned that a monopolist is the sole provider of a product to the market. The demand for the product of a monopolist, however, is also determined by the market – hence the monopolist is confronted by a normal market demand curve that runs downwards from left to right. (This is in sharp contrast to the horizontal demand curve of the individual firm in perfect competition.)

D = AR

Any point on the demand curve of a monopolist is an indication of the quantity of the product that can be sold and also an indication of the price at which it will be traded. In Figure 6-1(a), for example, one can see that the monopolist can sell the quantity Q_1 at price P_1. Because *each* of the individual units (comprising Q_1) can be sold at P_1, this means that P_1 is also the average price or revenue that the monopolist will obtain per unit at the particular point on the demand curve. This applies to any price-quantity combination on the demand curve, which means that the *demand curve* of the monopolist is also its *average revenue curve*.

The fact that the monopolist's average revenue curve (or demand curve) slopes downward from left to right has an important effect on the path of the marginal revenue curve. In contrast to perfect competition, where the marginal revenue curve and the average revenue curve coincide at the market price, the monopolist's marginal curve runs downwards from left to right but it is steeper than (and therefore runs below) the average revenue curve. Because of the downward sloping demand curve, the monopolist can only increase his sales (by, say, one unit), by asking a lower unit price for his product. Because this reduction in price relates not only to the marginal unit, but also to all previous units, the increase in total revenue (ie marginal revenue) that follows the sale of the additional unit is less than the asking price (ie average revenue). The marginal revenue curve therefore runs below the average revenue curve. (For a numerical explanation of this, read Box 6-1.)

Figure 6-1

Average, marginal and total revenue

The AR curve is also the monopolist's demand curve. The MR curve can be derived by calculating the slope of the TR curve. The intercept of the MR curve on the horizontal axis is precisely half of that of the AR curve. Thus $0Q_1 = Q_1Q_2$.

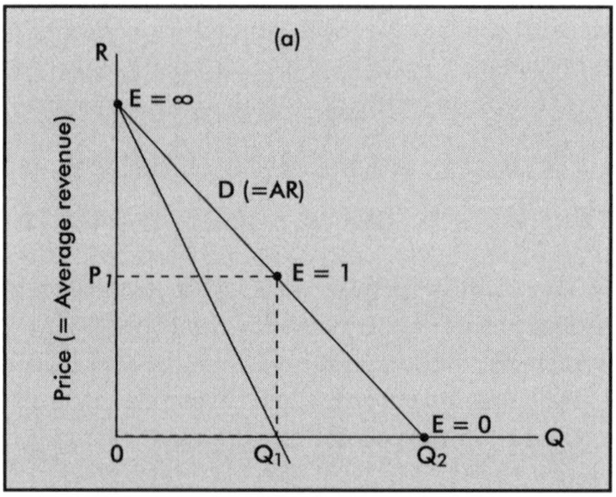

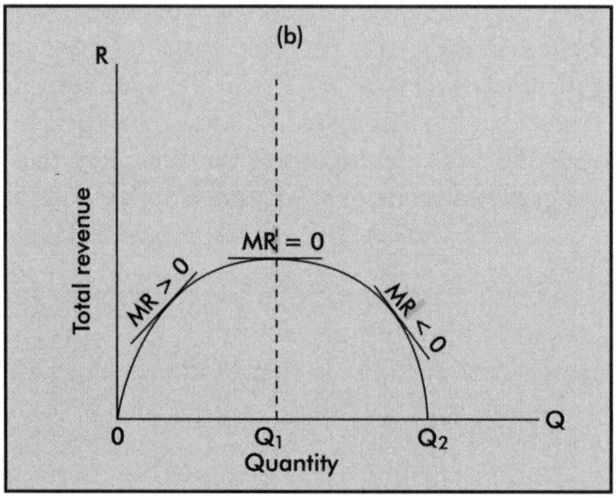

Box 6–1

AVERAGE REVENUE (PRICE) AND MARGINAL REVENUE IN A PURE MONOPOLY

The figure below shows an imaginary demand curve for a monopolist. At the price of R142, a monopolist can sell three units and at the price of R132, four. This means that if he reduces his price from R142 to R132, he can sell one additional unit and therefore increase his total revenue by the price of the additional unit, that is by R132. It is now assumed that if the monopolist reduces his price to sell the fourth unit for R132, he will also have to sell the first three units for the same price. However, the price reduction of R10 on the first three units means of a 'loss' of R30 on those units. The net change in total revenue (ie marginal revenue) resulting from the sale of the fourth unit is therefore R102 (ie R132 minus the loss of R30). Hence marginal revenue is considerably less than average revenue (marginal revenue = R102 and average revenue = price = R132).

Price and marginal revenue in a pure monopoly

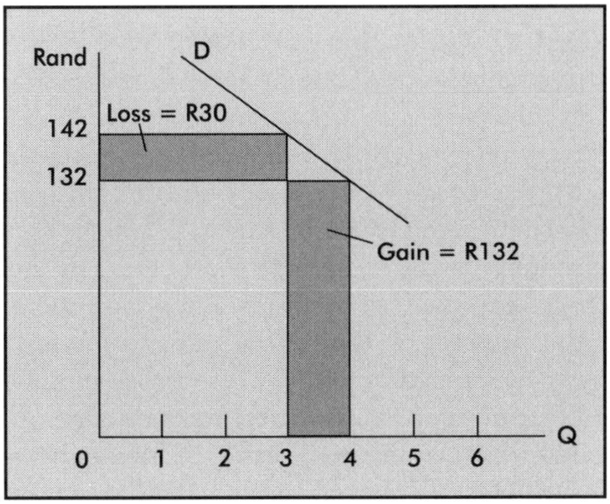

Location of the marginal revenue curve graphically

The marginal revenue curve has a very specific location in relation to the average revenue curve, namely it cuts the horizontal axis (quantity axis) precisely halfway between the origin and the intercept of the average revenue curve. Thus if the average revenue curve is known, it is very easy to determine the marginal revenue curve. The following explanation should simplify this.

Figure 6-1(a) shows a demand curve with the usual slope, namely sloping downwards from left to right. In the previous section it was apparent that this demand curve is also the average revenue curve of the monopolist. Figure 6-1(b) depicts a total revenue curve, which is obtained each time by multiplying the price by the corresponding quantity in Figure 6-1(a) (see the discussion of Fig 2-4 in Chapter 2).

By definition, marginal revenue reflects the change in total revenue stemming from the sale of one additional unit of a product. A change in total revenue (ie marginal revenue) is also indicated by the slopes of the tangents of the total revenue curve. See the total revenue curve in Figure 6-1(b). For a production level between 0 and Q_1, the slope of the total revenue curve is positive – hence the marginal revenue in this area is also positive. When output is exactly equal to Q_1 the slope of the total revenue curve is 0 – hence marginal revenue is also 0 at output Q_1. For production levels between Q_1 and Q_2 the total revenue curve has a negative slope, which means that marginal revenue in this area is also negative.

With the above information, it is easy to draw a monopolist's marginal revenue curve (see Fig 6-1). The marginal revenue curve that can be derived from a linear demand curve will also be a straight line – thus if two points are known on the marginal revenue curve, the curve can be drawn. The marginal revenue curve and the average revenue curve will have the same starting point on the vertical axis because if the monopolist sells only one unit, marginal revenue and average revenue will be the same. We indicated in the previous paragraph that marginal revenue at output Q_1 will be nil, which provides a further point on the marginal revenue curve. Because two points are known on the marginal revenue curve, namely at the intercept on the vertical axis and at output Q_1 on the horizontal axis, the curve is obtained by joining these two points. This is an important characteristic of the monopolist's marginal revenue curve, namely that it intercepts the horizontal axis (quantity axis) exactly halfway between the origin and the intercept of the average revenue curve – the distance $0Q_1$ is just as long as the distance Q_1Q_2. The slope of the marginal revenue curve is therefore twice that of the average revenue curve.

Total revenue, average revenue and marginal revenue: a numerical example

Average revenue and marginal revenue can also be deduced with the aid of a numerical example. Table 6-1 contains such an example.

Table 6-1
Average and marginal revenue

P	Q	TR	AR	MR
6	0	0	–	–
5	1	5	5	5
4	2	8	4	3 (8 – 5 = 3)
3	3	9	3	1 (9 – 8 = 1)
2	4	8	2	–1 (8 – 9 = –1)
1	5	5	1	–3 (5 – 8 = –3)
0	6	0	0	–5 (0 – 5 = –5)

In Table 6-1 the first two columns represent a demand schedule for a monopolist's product – in other words, P shows the different prices and Q the quantities asked at each of the prices. Total revenue (TR) is calculated each time by multiplying price (P) by quantity (Q). Average revenue (AR) is calculated by dividing total revenue (TR) by quantity (Q). Marginal revenue is obtained by calculating the change in total revenue for each unit change in quantity (calculations appear in the table).

It is clear from the table that except for the first unit, marginal revenue is lower than average revenue throughout – this tallies with the graphic analysis in the previous section. The figures show that marginal revenue remains positive until a price of R3 is reached, after which marginal revenue becomes negative, which means that a further increase in the quantity results in a decline in total revenue. Of course the monopolist is not interested in producing an output in the area in which marginal revenue is negative because his total revenue will decline there.

MARKET EQUILIBRIUM

At this point it should be clear that as far as competition is concerned, a monopolist is subject to different conditions from the perfectly competitive firm. When it comes to production, however, it is reasonable to assume that the monopolist has the same costs as the perfectly competitive firm. Hence the general shape of the monopolist's cost curves will be the same as that of the perfectly competitive firm.

Short-run equilibrium

As in perfect competition, it is assumed that a monopolist will try to maximise profit in both the short and long run. Figure 6-2 shows the total revenue curve

(TR) and short-run total cost curve (STC) of a typical monopolist. The STC curve cuts the vertical axis at a positive value which indicates the existence of fixed cost – hence the diagram illustrates a short-run cost function.

Figure 6-2

Total revenue and short-run total cost curve of a monopolist

Profit is maximised at output Q_1 where the positive difference between TR and STC is a maximum.

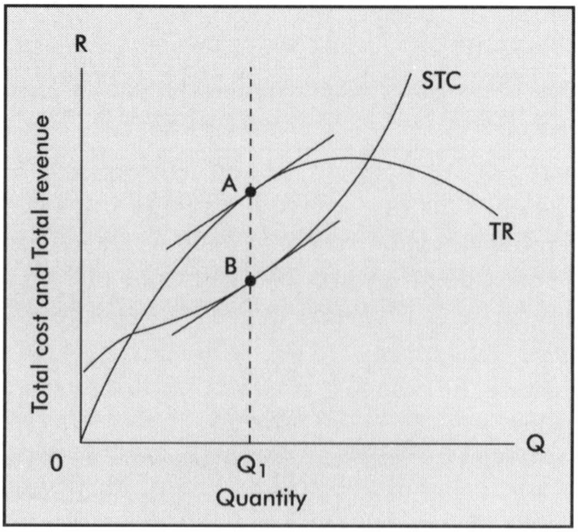

Total profit can be defined as the difference between total revenue and total cost. In Figure 6-2 profit is maximised at an output of Q_1 where the positive difference between TR and STC is a maximum. According to the principles explained in Chapter 4, the slope of the total revenue curve indicates the marginal revenue, while the slope of the short-run total cost curve indicates the marginal cost. At points A and B the slope of these two curves is the same – hence one can say that when the monopolist's total profit is maximised in the short run (and the short-run equilibrium is therefore reached),

Maximising profit

MR = SMC

applies.

The same condition for profit maximisation is encountered in perfect competition, with one difference. In perfect competition, MR = P and the condition for profit maximisation can therefore be written as SMC = MR = P. In the monopolist's case, MR is smaller that P (the MR curve runs below the AR), and if profit maximisation occurs, MR = SMC but MR is smaller than P. This will become clear in the discussion of Figure 6-3.

The short-run equilibrium situation of the monopolist can also be illustrated in another way, as depicted in Figure 6-3. The demand curve of the monopolist is a straight line and the MR curve is constructed as explained in a previous section. The cost curves are the typical SMC and SAC curves derived in Chapter 4. The way in which this information is used to determine the price-quantity combination when the monopolist is in short-run equilibrium is important: At point A, SMC = MR, which determines the profit-maximising output Q_1 on the horizontal axis. The price at which Q_1 can be sold is obtained by moving upwards from point A as far as C on the demand curve. The price that corresponds to C is indicated by P_1 on the vertical axis.

The short-run average cost curve (SAC) indicated in Figure 6-3 enables us to calculate the monopolist's short-run profit. The monopolist's total revenue is $P_1 \times Q_1$, which is equal to $0P_1CQ_1$. Total cost equals average cost multiplied by the quantity produced, or the area $0DBQ_1$. The difference between the two areas is the monopolist's total profit, which is indicated by the area DP_1CB in Figure 6-3. Because total revenue is greater than short-run total cost, the monopolist in this example makes an economic profit.

Figure 6-3
Monopolist in short-run equilibrium

Profit is maximised if MR = SMC, which determines output Q_1 and price P_1. Economic profit is P_1CBD.

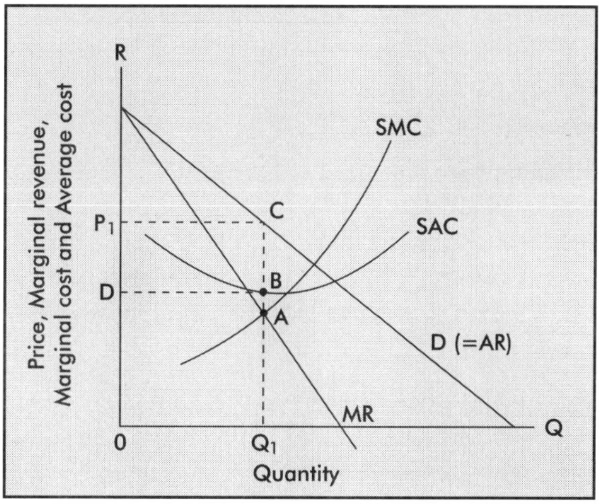

Not always economic profit for monopolist

Some people believe that because a monopolist is the only supplier of a product he or she will, without exception, make a profit. However, this is not always so – having a monopoly does not guarantee profit. The profitability of a monopoly depends on the demand for the product as well as the cost of production. Figure 6–4 represents the demand and cost curves of a monopolist who makes short-term losses. Equilibrium is again obtained where MR = SMC, but here it is a loss-minimising situation (as opposed to a profit-maximising situation). In equilibrium, the monopolist will produce quantity Q_1 and sell it at price P_1. Price P_1 is lower than the short-run average cost, as indicated by BD. The monopolist therefore makes a loss represented by the rectangle $ABDP_1$.

Loss

Figure 6–4

Short-run loss for the monopolist

The SAC curve lies above the demand curve, hence price P_1 is lower than the SAC. The loss is $ABDP_1$.

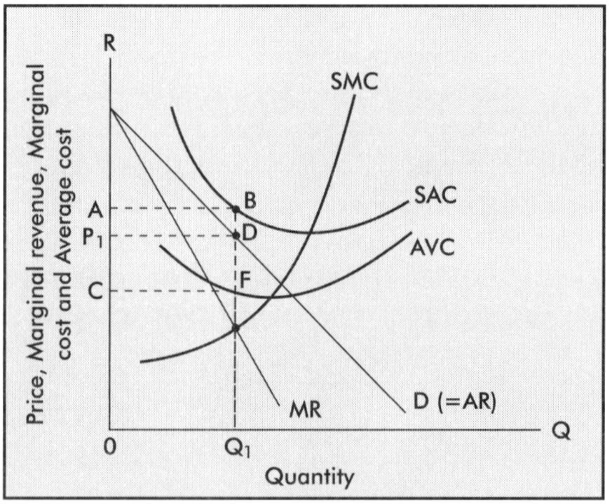

We saw in Chapter 4 that total cost is equal to constant cost plus variable cost. At output Q_1 in Figure 6–4, the monopolist's total cost ($0Q_1 \times Q_1B$) is equal to $0Q_1BA$, while his variable cost ($0Q_1 \times Q_1F$) is equal to $0Q_1FC$ – hence constant cost is CFBA. At the same time, the monopolist's total revenue ($0Q_1 \times Q_1D$) at output Q_1 is equal to $0Q_1DP_1$. The monopolist can therefore pay all his variable costs plus a portion ($CFDP_1$) of the constant (ie fixed) cost. (The portion that is not paid, is the loss $ABDP_1$.) In the short term, constant costs must be paid and, by staying in production, a portion of these costs can be paid out of the firm's revenue. Obviously, a situation in which a monopolist makes a loss cannot continue indefinitely.

Not always the highest price for the monopolist

Another misconception is that a monopolist can increase his price arbitrarily and will always ask for the highest price he can obtain. However, this is not true, for a price increase can also mean a loss in total revenue (and total profit) for a monopolist.

If a monopolist with his price-quantity combination finds himself on the inelastic part of the demand curve, then a price increase will always mean a rise in total revenue (see Fig 6-1 and Fig 2-4 in Chapter 2). However, a monopolist will not want to be on the inelastic part of the demand curve because he cannot maximise total profit there. To maximise total profit, he will produce where marginal revenue is equal to marginal cost (MR = SMC) and use this point of intersection (see point A in Fig 6-3) to determine his price on the demand curve – this price will always fall on the elastic part of the demand curve (see point C in Fig 6-3), where a price increase will reduce total revenue.

How do we know with certainty that the equilibrium price at which the monopolist maximises total profit will fall on the elastic part of the demand curve? Cost is always positive (no cost curve lies below the horizontal axis) and SMC is therefore also positive, which means that if SMC = MR, the point of intersection will also be at a positive value of MR – that is, above the horizontal axis. If this is so, the price that is determined by means of this point of intersection will always fall on the top half of the demand curve (see point C in Fig 6-3). In this half of the demand curve, demand elasticity is greater than 1 and we know that a price increase will lead to a decline in revenue.

If the monopolist was in the equilibrium position (or to the left of it), and total revenue declines, total profit will also decline. Hence it is a misconception that a monopolist will randomly increase his price and always ask for the highest possible price. A monopolist will be satisfied with selling his product at the equilibrium price and making maximum total profit.

The monopolist's supply

We saw in Chapter 5 that for each price there is a unique quantity that will be offered by a perfectly competitive firm which is determined by the short-run marginal cost curve. Thus a unique price-quantity relationship exists. The supply curve of the perfectly competitive firm is therefore that portion of the SMC curve above the minimum point of the average variable cost curve. However, this is not so for a monopolist. This is illustrated with the aid of Figures 6-5(a) and 6-5(b).

Figure 6-5(a) shows the SMC curve of a monopolist. Two possible demand curves, D_1 and D_2, are indicated. The marginal revenue curves, MR_1 and MR_2, that correspond to the demand curves intersect the SMC curve at the same output level Q_1 (the equilibrium condition SMC = MR therefore applies to both demand curves). In the diagram we can see that if demand is D_1, the monopolist determines the price for his product at P_1; if demand is D_2, the price will be

P_2. For a given output level Q_1, determined according to the equilibrium condition SMC = MR, there are two prices for this monopolist. In Figure 6-5(b) the other possibility is indicated in the same way, namely that at a given price two quantities, Q_1 and Q_2 are offered. Once again, two demand curves, D_1 and D_2, with their matching marginal revenue curves, MR_1 and MR_2, are indicated. According to the points of intersection, e_1 and e_2, of the SMC curve with the MR curves, a price P is determined, but two quantities, Q_1 and Q_2, are offered at this price.

Figures 6-5(a) and (b)

No supply curve for the monopolist

There is no unique price–quantity relationship. In 6-5(a) there are two prices for a given output level; in 6-5(b) there are two output levels for a given price. Supply curves cannot therefore be derived.

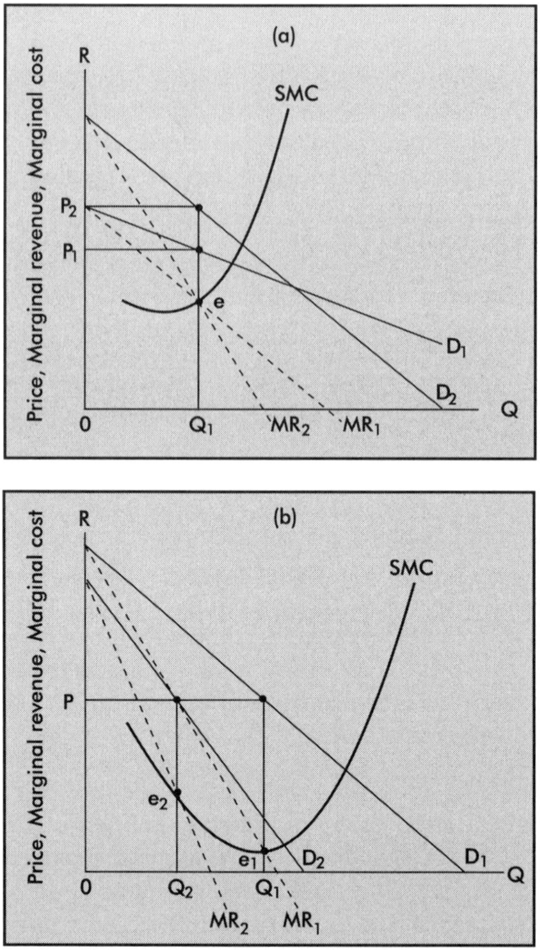

No supply curve These two examples illustrate that one cannot determine a unique price-quantity relationship for the monopolist and therefore one cannot derive a supply curve as one can for the perfectly competitive firm. This is not to say that the monopolist is not in a position to determine a price for his product, but that we cannot say with certainty what his supply curve will look like – the monopolist will allow himself to be led by the elasticity of the demand curve, and then, with due consideration of his marginal cost, determine the price.

Long-run equilibrium

As with the perfectly competitive firm, there is no fixed cost for a monopolist in the long run. A monopolist can therefore extend his plant in the long run and construct the particular plant size that maximises long-run profit. If the monopolist makes losses in the short run, he will endeavour to build a plant of such a size that it will make a profit. If no plant size can make a normal or economic profit, the monopolist will close his enterprise. If the monopolist makes an economic profit in the short run, it will change the plant size in the long run, in order to make more economic profit (if it is not already a maximum).

Figure 6–6
The monopolist in long-run equilibrium

Profit is maximised if MR = LMC, which determines Q_1 and price P_1. Economic profit is P_1CBE, and the monopolist can also make it in the long run.

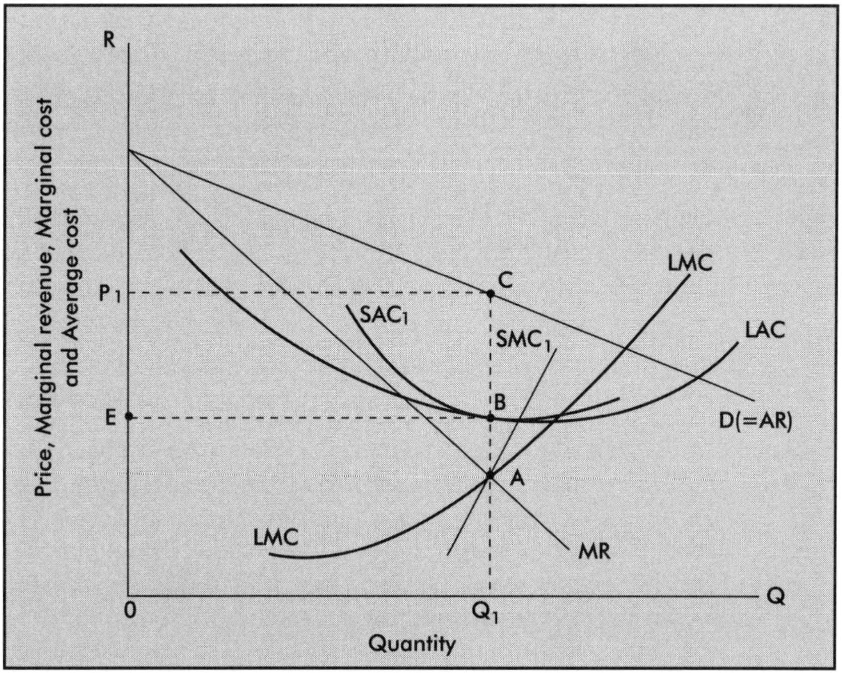

Long-run profit is maximised by making marginal revenue equal to long-run marginal costs, that is, MR = LMC. This is illustrated in Figure 6-6, where the MR curve and the LMC curve intersect at A, which determines the long-run profit-maximising quantity Q_1 at a price P_1. The plant size that maximises profit in the long run is represented by the short-run average cost curve SAC_1, which has a point of tangency at B with the long-run average cost curve LAC and can therefore produce the output level Q_1 at a lower average cost than any other plant size. Also, if the plant size SAC_1 which maximises profit in the long run is operated at the profit-maximising output level Q_1, profit is simultaneously maximised in the short run. This is indicated by the fact that in Figure 6-6 both the LMC curve and the SMC_1 curve intersect the MR curve at point A.

The demand curve and the cost curves that appear in Figure 6-6 show that this particular monopolist's selling price P_1 is higher than the LAC at output level Q_1 (compare C with B). The monopolist therefore makes economic profit equal to the area P_1EBC. Unless the demand curve shifts as the result of changes in taste, rising incomes, or the development of close substitutes for the monopolist's product, he will be able to make economic profit for an unlimited period in the long run. This favourable position is possible only because constraints prevent other firms from entering the market.

THE MULTIPLANT MONOPOLIST

Although a monopolist is the only supplier of a product this does not mean that he will necessarily produce his total output in one plant. With a monopolist who is the sole owner of a scarce resource such as a unique kind of mineral water, it may happen that, because of the physical location of the resource, production is confined to the immediate environment. Usually, however, it is possible for a monopolist to have different plants in different parts of the country. For such a monopolist it is important to look at his position as a whole and not to view each plant individually in a fragmented way. The question now is how such a monopolist will set about maximising profit. To answer this question, we shall examine the case of a monopolist with two plants – although the analysis can easily be extended to any number of plants.

Two plants Assume that a monopolist operates two plants, A and B, and that the cost structures differ – this is reflected in Figure 6-7 by the fact that the SAC curve in plant B is higher than in plant A. Costs at plant B for example, can be higher because labour is more expensive in the vicinity of plant B than at plant A. The monopolist must now make two decisions: first, how much output should be produced in total and at what price it should be sold to maximise profit, and second, how should the profit-maximising output be divided between the two plants.

Figure 6–7

Multiplant monopolist. Total output and price are determined by equating SMC with MR

To maximise profit, total output is divided between the two plants in such a way that $SMC_1 = SMC_2 = MR$. The plant with the lower costs produces more than the plant with the higher costs.

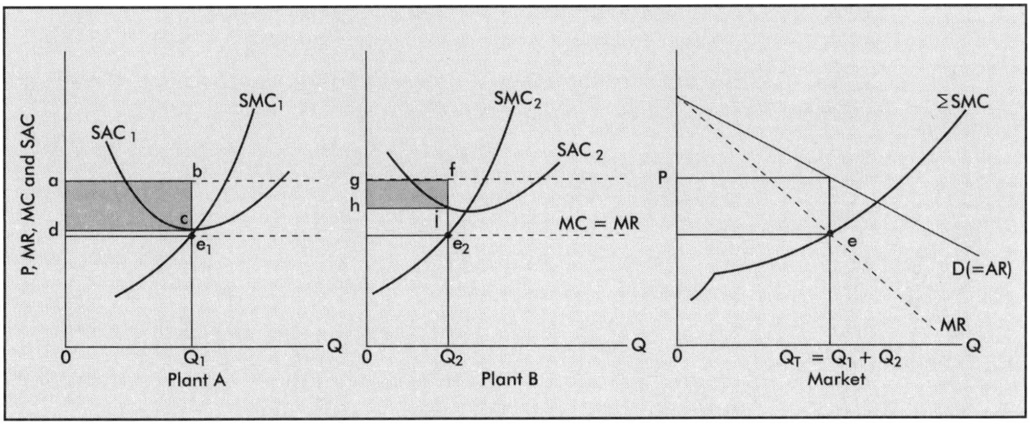

We assume that the monopolist does not face separate demand curves for each plant – that is, the monopolist has only one demand curve (the market demand curve) for the economy as a whole. We also accept that the monopolist knows what his market demand curve looks like (and the matching MR curve) as well as the cost structures of the various plants. To determine his equilibrium position, the monopolist must make his *marginal revenue* equal to the *total marginal cost* of the two plants. The total SMC curve of the monopolist in Figure 6-7(c) can be determined by horizontally adding together the SMC curves of the individual plants, that is:

$$\Sigma SMC = SMC_1 + SMC_2$$

Once the MR and ΣSMC curves are known, the monopolist can determine *total output and price* (Fig 6-7(c)) that will maximise his profit (ie the equilibrium position) – he simply looks to see where ΣSMC = MR, in other words, where the two curves intersect in Figure 6-7(c) (point e).

Dividing output

To divide total output between the two plants, the monopolist must work in such a way that $SMC_1 = SMC_2 = MR$. This means that the monopolist maximises profit if he produces so much in each plant that the marginal cost in both is the same, and at the same time it is equal to the common marginal revenue. If the marginal cost in one plant, say A, is lower than the marginal cost in B, the monopolist can increase his profit by producing more in plant A and less in plant

B – until the stage is reached that $SMC_1 = SMC_2 = MR$, then profit cannot be further increased.

Graphically, the equilibrium position of the monopolist with two plants can be explained as follows. As mentioned previously, the total profit-maximising output and price are determined by the point of intersection of the ΣSMC and MR curves, that is at point e in Figure 6-7(c). This point of intersection is carried over to Figures 6-7(b) and 6-7(a) by means of a horizontal line to intersect the individual curves SMC_2 and SMC_1 of the two plants at e_2 and e_1 respectively. At these points the equilibrium condition, namely $\Sigma SMC = MR = SMC_1 = SMC_2$, is satisfied. From these two points (e_1 and e_2), lines are drawn vertically downwards to the Q-axes of Figures 6-7(a) and 6-7(b), which indicate the quantity that will be produced in each plant. It is clear that $Q_1 + Q_2$ must be equal to the profit-maximising quantity Q_T. The total profit is the sum total of the profit earned in the two plants. The price at which the product is sold is also determined in Figure 6-7(c) and transferred from there to Figures 6-7(b) and 6-7(a). The profit in plant A is the rectangle abcd and the profit in plant B the rectangle gfjh. It is clear that more profit is made in the plant with the lower cost structure (A) than in the plant with the higher cost structure (B). It is also clear from Figure 6-7 that more is produced in the plant with the lower cost structure (A) than in the plant with the higher cost structure (B) – which is why Q_1 is greater than Q_2.

Box 6-2

CONSUMER SURPLUS

When a consumer, Sarah Smith, goes into a shop to buy bread, the price that she pays is per definition the market price. However, the market price is not necessarily a precise indication of the value that Sarah attaches to the bread. What can be said with certainty is that if Sarah buys the bread, the value that she attaches to it cannot be less than the price of the bread – because if that had been so she would not have bought it. What can also happen (and this is often so) is that the value that Sarah attaches to the bread is a great deal higher than the price of the bread.

An experiment would show by how much the value that Sarah attaches to the bread could exceed the price. Suppose that Sarah normally buys ten loaves of bread a month and the bread is obtainable at only one shop in the town (thus she cannot buy it anywhere else). If the price of the bread is not regulated by the government, the owner and Sarah would be able to negotiate the price she would be prepared to pay for the ten loaves of bread rather than do without them. The maximum that she would be prepared to pay will be the rand value of the utility (or satisfaction) that Sarah gets out of having ten loaves of bread rather than doing without them. The difference between what Sarah would be prepared to pay for the ten loaves of bread and the price that she does pay for them is known as the *consumer surplus*.

Graphically, the consumer surplus is represented by the area between the demand curve and the price line (ie the horizontal line drawn on the level of the market price). This is indicated by the shaded area in the figure below. It is clear in the figure that the consumer surplus is the difference between the total value consumers are prepared to attach to a specific quantity (C) of the product (ie the surface 0ABC) and the total amount they must pay to buy that particular quantity of the product (0PBC). Put differently, the consumer surplus is the difference between the total value attached to a certain quantity of the product and the market value (P x Q) of that quantity.

The consumer surplus is a reality that occurs in practice. Because consumers are prepared to pay more than the market price for a product, rather than do without it, this creates the opportunity for an entrepreneur such as a monopolist to apply price discrimination and in so doing increase his profit. What this amounts to is that a monopolist can sell his goods at a higher price to those consumers who have greater desire for his product and who therefore attach greater value to it.

Consumer surplus

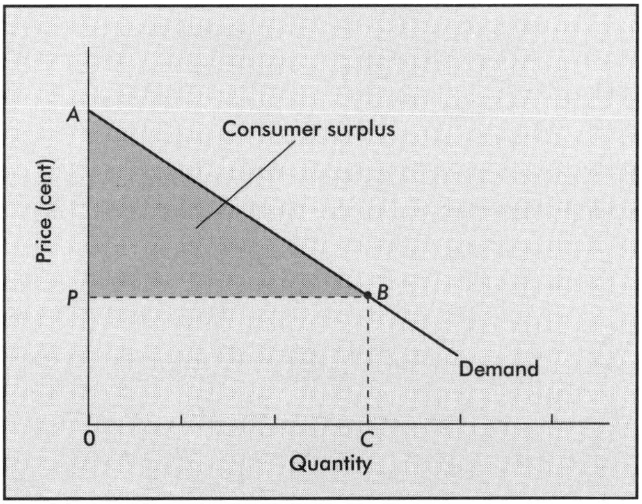

PRICE DISCRIMINATION

Background to price discrimination

A monopolist is in a unique position in that he or she is the only supplier of a product. Frame 6-2 showed that the existence of the consumer surplus makes it possible for the monopolist to apply price discrimination. Price discrimination occurs when a firm asks a higher price from some consumers than others for the same product and the price difference cannot be attributed to cost differences in supplying the product. By applying price discrimination, an entrepreneur can increase his total revenue and thus also increase his profit.

Price discrimination is applied most easily by the monopolist, because he can control the supply of his product, although non-monopolists also often use this price policy. Different clients are asked for different prices on the basis of factors such as the quantity that is purchased, or how well the seller knows the buyer. In this section the focus will be on the monopolist who sells an identical product (all units produced at the same cost) at different prices, depending on the consumers' preferences, their income, location and possible substitutes that are available. These factors give rise to demand curves with different elasticities.

Conditions

Two conditions have to be met before a monopolist can apply price discrimination. First, it must be possible to divide the market into submarkets, with different price elasticities. Second, it should not be possible to resell from a low-price market to a high-price market. The question of resale gives rise to another point, namely that price discrimination can be applied more easily to a product such as electricity or services as rendered by a doctor, hairdresser, bus company or cinema – such products or services are usually 'consumed' by the buyer and cannot be resold. Physical products such as furniture, motor vehicles and clothes, however, can be stored and resold later.

In practice, there are numerous examples of price discrimination. Electricity, for example, is provided at a higher tariff to households than to large industrial plants. Airline tickets differ in price, depending on whether the reservation is made a long or a short time prior to the date of departure. Telephone tariffs are cheaper at night and over weekends than during the day. Students and pensioners often receive special discounts which other people do not receive. What is the theoretical explanation for this? This will be discussed in the next section.

Segmented-market price discrimination

We mentioned earlier that a monopolist (or any other firm) applies price discrimination to increase his total revenue, and hence also his profit. By selling the quantity which is determined by the equilibrium condition MC = MR at different prices in different markets, the monopolist can obtain a higher total revenue and therefore also higher profit than if he were to ask a uniform price.

Two markets

The case that we are studying is that of a monopolist who sells his product at two different prices in two markets.

We accept that the monopolist has two markets that are totally separate from each other and that the elasticity of the demand curves also differs. In Figure 6-8 the demand curve D_2 is more elastic than D_1 at any given price. The total demand curve ΣD is obtained by the horizontal summation of D_1 and D_2. The total marginal revenue curve ΣMR is likewise the horizontal summation of the marginal revenue curves MR_1 and MR_2. We also accept that the monopolist has only one plant and the marginal revenue curve is therefore represented by MC.

A monopolist who wishes to apply price discrimination and to maximise his profit must first decide the total output that he must produce and, second, how much needs to be sold in each market and at what price.

The profit-maximising total output is determined by the point of intersection of the MC curve and the monopolist's total marginal revenue curve ΣMR. In Figure 6-8 the two curves intersect at A and the total output determined by this point of intersection is Q_T. If the monopolist wishes to ask a uniform price, it will be P_T (also determined by the point of intersection A and read off by means of point F on the vertical axis) and his total revenue will be $0Q_TFP_T$.

Maximising profit

The monopolist's profit will be the difference between his revenue and the production cost of the quantity Q_T. However, the monopolist can make a higher profit by asking different prices in the two markets. To maximise total profit, it is important for the monopolist to determine the price and quantity in such a way that the maximum profit is made in each market – hence *in each market the marginal revenue is made equal to the marginal cost*. Marginal cost to produce the total quantity Q_T is determined at point A and remains the same regardless of the market in which the products are sold. By contrast, the marginal revenue differs between the two markets because of the difference in elasticity of the two demand curves. The profit in each market is maximised by equating MC (as determined at A) to MR in each market. In the first market, profit is therefore maximised if

$MR_1 = MC$ (at point C in Fig 6-8)

and profit is maximised in the second market if

$MR_2 = MC$ (at point B in Fig 6-8)

It is therefore clear that total profit is maximised if the marginal revenues are set equal to the common MC, that is

$MR_1 = MR_2 = MC$

Figure 6-8
Price discrimination: segmented markets

Profit is maximised by making maximum profit in each market. The profit-maximising total output is determined by $MC = \Sigma MR$. P and Q in each market are determined by making $MR = MC$, that is, $MR_1 = MC$ and $MR_2 = MC$. Higher profit is earned with price discrimination than with a uniform price.

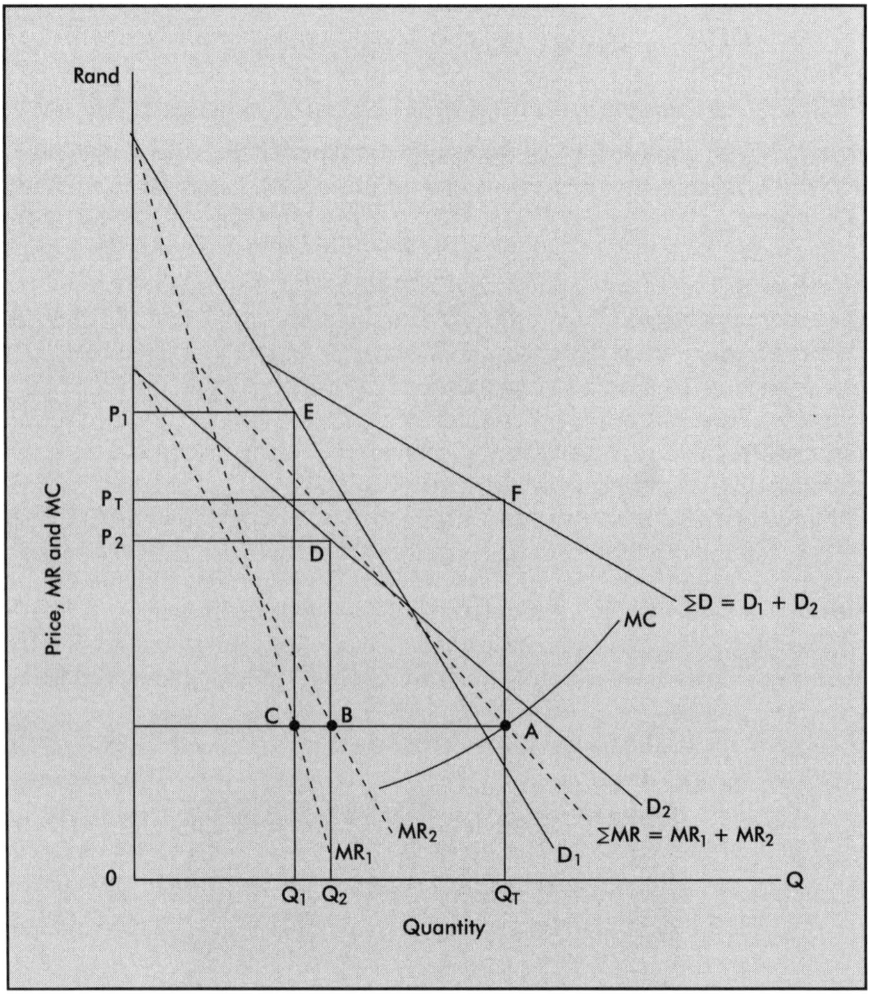

If marginal revenue MR is higher in the first market than in the second, the monopolist will sell more in the first market and less in the second until the above precondition is met. Determination of the various prices and quantities can be explained graphically as follows: from the equilibrium point A, a line is drawn *parallel* to the horizontal axis to cut the marginal revenue curve MR_1 at C and the marginal revenue curve MR_2 at B. This line runs at the same level as the

MC at A – hence $MC = MR_1 = MR_2$ applies. From points C and B lines are drawn downwards as far as the quantity axis, and upwards until they reach the respective demand curves D_1 and D_2. These vertical lines determine the output and price in each market. In the first market the monopolist will therefore sell quantity Q_1 at price P_1 and in the second market, quantity Q_2 at price P_2. In the market with the higher price elasticity (D_2) the price is therefore lower than in the market with the lower price elasticity (D_1). It stands to reason that the sum of the quantities sold in the respective markets is equal to the total sales, therefore $0Q_1 + 0Q_2 = 0Q_T$.

One can deduce from Figure 6-8 that the total revenue earned from price discrimination is greater than the revenue that would be earned with a uniform price. With price discrimination the monopolist's total revenue is

$$(P_1 \times Q_1) + (P_2 \times Q_2) = 0P_1EQ_1 + 0P_2DQ_2$$

This total revenue should be compared with the amount the monopolist would earn without price discrimination with a uniform price P_T, namely $P_T \times Q_T = 0P_TFQ_T$. By comparing the areas one can determine that the total revenue obtained with price discrimination is larger than the total revenue obtained with a uniform price. Since the cost to produce Q_T is the same, regardless of the price at which it is sold, the profit that is earned with price discrimination is larger than that earned with a uniform price.

Segmented-market price discrimination in practice

We mentioned earlier that examples of segmented-market price discrimination are frequently found in practice. In the light of the theoretical discussion above, we can briefly look at these examples again. Electricity is one such example. If electricity becomes very expensive, if need be, an industrial enterprise may generate its own power – such an enterprise's price elasticity (or sensitivity to price changes) for electricity is therefore fairly high. It is more difficult for households to generate their own electricity than it is for an industrial enterprise – hence households' price elasticity is less than that of industrial enterprises. In practice it is common for industrial enterprises' electricity tariffs to be lower than those of households. Similarly, a traveller who has an urgent reason to fly from Johannesburg to Cape Town will be prepared to pay more for the airline ticket than someone who has months to plan the trip and can consider other alternatives – the price elasticity of the traveller who is in a hurry is therefore relatively low. Airlines use this phenomenon to their advantage and travellers who are in a hurry have to pay higher prices.

Examples

Another example is telephone tariffs. Business calls usually have to be made during the day, which makes the price elasticity of telephone calls during working time fairly low – this allows Telkom to ask higher tariffs for such calls.

Similarly, students and pensioners, who are usually regarded as groups with a greater sensitivity to price changes (thus greater price elasticity), often obtain discounts which other groups are denied.

In each of these examples, the group with the higher price elasticity will be represented by a demand curve such as D_2 in Figure 6-8, while the group with lower price elasticity will be represented by D_1. Again it can be seen that in the market with the higher price elasticity (D_2), the price is lower than in the market with the lower price elasticity (D_1).

Multipart price discrimination

The preceding section showed that a monopolist can increase his profit if his customers can be divided into different submarkets with different price elasticities. If segmented-market price discrimination is applied, the price differs from one market to the next, but all the customers in a given submarket pay the same price. Another form of price discrimination is known as multipart price discrimination. In practice it means that a customer pays a high price for the first unit, a lower price for the next unit, and so forth. An example of multipart price discrimination is often found in supermarkets – for example, a container with fruit juice will sell for R1,89, but a package with two containers is sold for only R3,40. In such a case, the first container in the package cost R1,89 while the second cost only R1,51.

Figure 6-9

Price discrimination: multipart

By selling different quantities at different prices, total revenue increases and therefore so does profit.

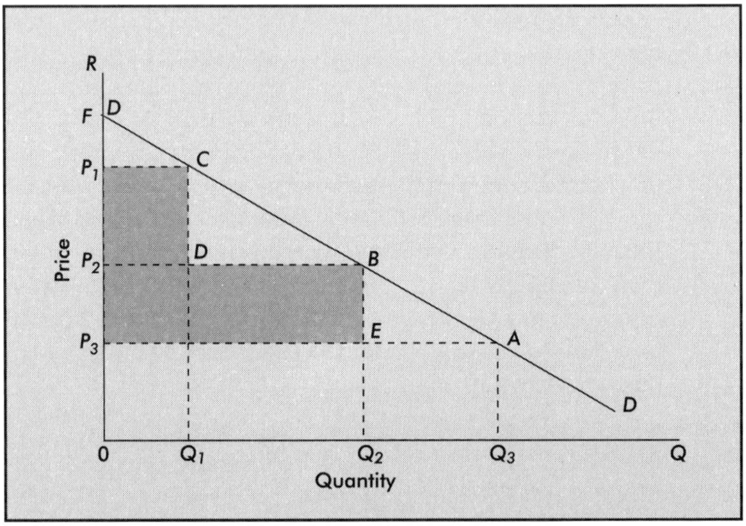

Multipart price discrimination is illustrated in Figure 6-9. A consumer's demand curve is represented by DD. The monopolist offers the initial quantity from 0 to Q_1 at a price of P_1 to the consumer. Between Q_1 and Q_2 the consumer can purchase the product at a price of P_2. Finally, the consumer can buy the quantity between Q_2 and Q_3 at a price of P_3.

What is the motivation behind the monopolist applying multipart price discrimination? Suppose that the monopolist does not apply price discrimination and asks only the single price P_3 and that this price is determined by the point of intersection of the MR and MC curves. The total revenue ($P \times Q$) of the monopolist will therefore be $0P_3AQ_3$. These total takings should be compared with what the monopolist receives if he does apply price discrimination, namely $0P_1CQ_1 + Q_1DBQ_2 + Q_2EAQ_3$. It is clear that by applying multipart price discrimination the monopolist can increase his total revenue by an amount equal to the shaded area in Figure 6-9 – what is more, without production costs rising in the process. Because the monopolist's total revenue has increased as a result of price discrimination, his profit will also increase.

The monopolist who applies price discrimination succeeds in increasing his total revenue by receiving part of the consumer surplus in addition. In the most extreme case, where the monopolist can negotiate with each consumer and can sell each unit of his product at the corresponding price (as indicated by DD in Figure 6-9), he will receive the entire consumer surplus P_3AF.

Box 6-3

PREDATORY PRICING

The use of predatory prices by a firm to obtain or maintain a monopoly is a common practice.

Definitions of predatory prices sometimes differ, but in general one can say that a firm uses predatory pricing when it keeps the price of its product very low in an effort to force a competitor out of the business, or to make it extremely difficult for a potential opponent to enter it. For example, suppose that a monopolist is being threatened by a competitor. The monopolist's average and marginal cost curves appear below. (To avoid long-windedness, we shall continue to refer to the firm as a monopolist, although it will no longer be one once the opponent enters the industry.)

The monopolist can set a price such as P_0, which lies below the AC curve. If this curve is also below the opposition's average cost, the opposition will make losses. The question arises whether the monopolist acts rationally, since in the process he also makes losses. This will depend on whether (and how quickly) the competitor can be forced out of the business. Since the monopolist is supposed to have a greater output, he will lose more money than the competitor. However, the monopolist will probably have greater financial reserves and be in a position to temporarily bear such losses.

Of course, other competitors may appear on the scene later. However, if the monopolist ruthlessly disposes of the first competitor, the idea will probably take root that it is not worth trying to compete with the monopolist. This will frighten off potential competitors.

Predatory pricing

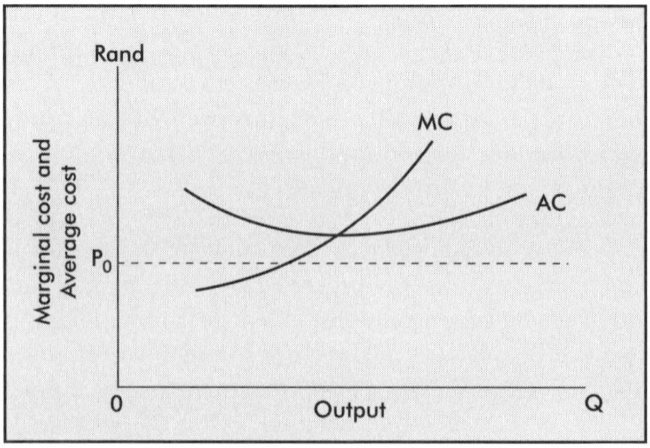

LONG-RUN EQUILIBRIUM: COMPARISON OF A MONOPOLY AND PERFECT COMPETITION

A comparison of the long-run equilibrium situation of a pure monopolist with a firm under perfect competition reveals interesting differences between the two market forms.

Figure 6-10(a) shows the long-run equilibrium situation of the firm under perfect competition and Figure 6-10(b) that of a monopolist. We know that a firm under perfect competition is one of a large number of firms and that it is insignificantly small compared with the industry as a whole. A monopolist, by contrast, is the only producer in the market and can therefore be regarded as the whole industry. To compare the two market forms, we have to make three assumptions. First, we assume that we can add together all the data of all the firms in a perfectly competitive market, that is, to allow them to 'merge' for the sake of the analysis, but we assume that their cost curves do not change and the joint cost curves are represented by Figure 6-10(a). Second, after this merging, the cost structure of the new 'enterprise' is the same as that of the monopoly illustrated in Figure 6-10(b). Third, the firms retain all the characteristics of perfect competition and do not act like a monopoly. With these assumptions, we can compare the long-run equilibrium situation of the two market forms.

Figure 6-10
Long-run equilibrium: comparison of monopolist and perfectly competitive firm

Monopolist: produces less, asks higher price, earns economic profit, does not build optimum plant size, does not utilise plant optimally, P higher than MC.

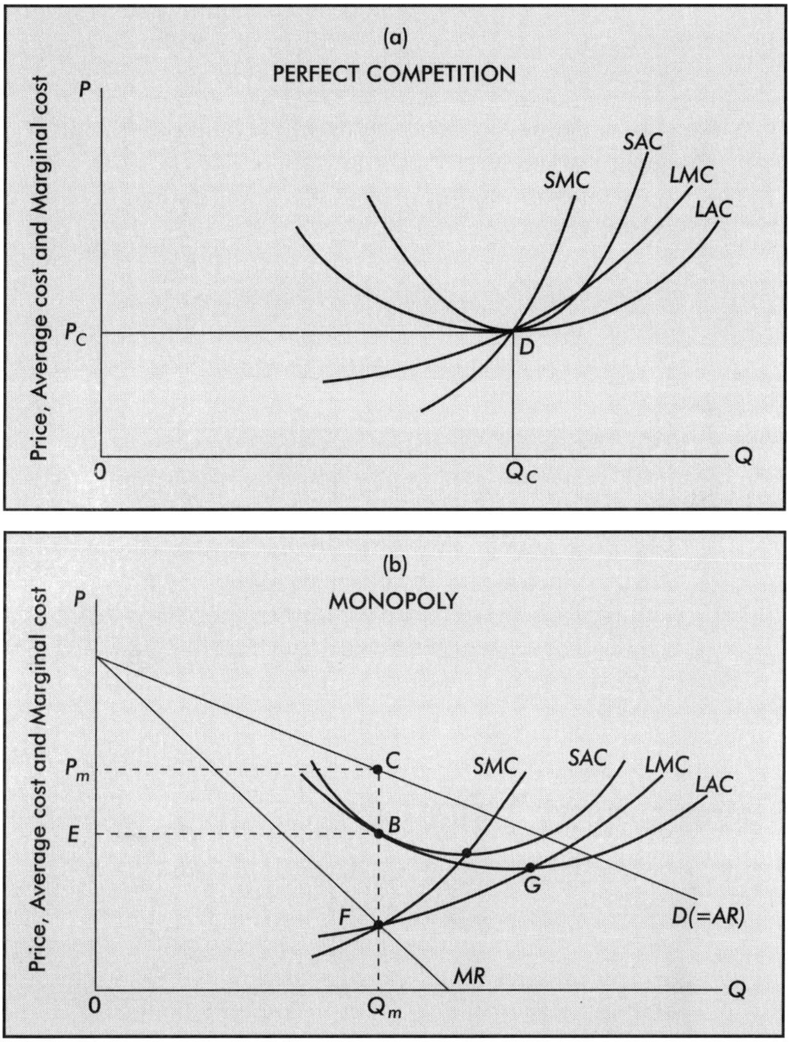

Figures 6-10(a) and 6-10(b) are drawn according to the same scale and can therefore be compared directly. When the 'firm' (the newly formed one) under perfect competition is in long-run equilibrium, it will produce quantity Q_c and sell it at the price P_c. The monopolist will produce quantity Q_m and sell it at P_m. A comparison of the two situations shows that the monopolist will produce less ($Q_m < Q_c$) and ask a higher price ($P_m > P_c$) than the perfect competitor. This is because under perfect competition in the long-run equilibrium situation production occurs at the minimum point on the LAC curve, while this is not so with the monopolist.

Under perfect competition, only normal profit will be made in the long run – the monopolist, by contrast, can earn economic profit both in the short run and the long run. In Figure 6-10(a) the firm under perfect competition only makes normal profit at D. Figure 6-10(b), however, shows that the monopolist makes an economic profit of P_mCBE in the long run.

Also, under perfect competition in the long run, the product is produced and supplied to consumers at the lowest possible cost. This means that under perfect competition the optimum plant size (at the minimum of the LAC) is used in the production process; this plant size is also utilised to its full capacity – that is, production occurs at the minimum of the SAC. For the monopolist there is no guarantee that this will happen – as can be seen in Figure 6-10(b) the monopolist does not utilise the plant optimally at point B (it is not at the minimum of the SAC) and the optimum plant size (at the minimum of the LAC) is also not used.

Under conditions of perfect competition, the price is equal to marginal cost (P = MC). For the monopolist, the price will exceed the cost of the last unit produced (P is higher than MC). If price (P) is higher than marginal cost (MC), this means that the community attaches a greater value to an additional unit of the product than to the sources required to produce it. In such an instance the community's welfare is increased by producing more of the product. Efficient allocation of resources is achieved when the price of each product is made equal to the marginal cost thereof (P = MC). Therefore the community's welfare is increased by moving from a condition of pure monopoly to one of perfect competition.

GOVERNMENT REGULATION OF A MONOPOLIST

There is always a chance that a monopolist will exploit consumers (although this does not necessarily always happen). Authorities worldwide monitor the situation well and if a monopolist abuses his economic power (market power), the government may decide to intervene and take action against him. Government intervention, in whatever form, to control a monopolist usually has one or more

Objectives of the following objectives: a *decrease in the price* of the product for the consumer;

an *increase in the quantity* the monopolist produces, so that more people can enjoy the particular product; and a *decrease* in the monopolist's *economic profit*.

Governments can adopt various methods of intervention. In the following section we look at *price control* where the maximum price that a monopolist may ask for his product is prescribed by the government.

Price control

Figure 6-11 illustrates the long-run cost structure and market conditions relating to a specific monopolist. The diagram therefore shows the demand curve (ie the AR curve) and the accompanying MR curve as well as the marginal cost and average cost curves of the monopolist.

If the monopolist himself, without government intervention, can set the price, the principle of equating marginal revenue to marginal cost (MR = MC) to determine the price-quantity combination is again applied. This happens at point e, which means that the monopolist will set the price at P_m and produce the quantity Q_m. As we have seen previously, the monopolist will make an economic profit at this price, which indicates a certain degree of consumer exploitation. If the government wishes to set a lower (maximum) price, the question arises at what level this should be – two possible price levels received close attention in both the theory and the practice.

Which price?

First, the government can fix the price at such a level that P = MC; in Figure 6-11 this occurs at the price P_1. If the government sets the price at P_1 the monopolist must accept this price as given; his demand curve will then change and run horizontally (like that of a perfectly competitive firm) for the section P_1A; from A it follows the normal course downwards to the right as far as F. Because the demand curve runs horizontally for the section P_1A, the MR curve runs concurrently with the demand curve for this part (once again, like that of the perfectly competitive firm). The monopolist will still try to maximise his profit at price P_1 – in other words, to produce at the point where MR = MC; this will happen at point A (where the horizontal MR curve intersects the MC curve) and results in output Q_1. By setting the price at P_1, the government has therefore brought about the following: the price is lower than it was (P_1 instead of P_m), output is higher (Q_1 instead of Q_m), the quantity demanded is equal to the quantity supplied (at point A), price is equal to marginal cost and, finally, the monopolist's economic profit is less than it was. However, note that economic profit is not totally eliminated, because at A average revenue (ie the price P_1) is still higher than average cost.

Second, the government can set the price at such a level that P = AC; in Figure 6-11 at first glance it would appear that this is at price P_2. However, the situation is not as simple as it seems. At a fixed price P_2, the monopolist's demand curve changes to P_2B (thereafter it runs downwards to the right) and the MR curve again runs concurrently along the section P_2B. Therefore, at price P_2 the monopolist would prefer to produce at point C (where MR = MC), which will result in a smaller output than Q_1. Thus the situation is that the monopolist maximises profit by offering P_2C (ie Q_3), while the quantity demanded at P_2 is actually P_2B. Hence there is a surplus demand equal to CB and the market is therefore not in equilibrium.

Figure 6–11

Price control of the monopolist

With price P_1, the government's goals (lower P, greater Q, less profit) can be realised. At P_2 there is excess demand and additional measures are necessary.

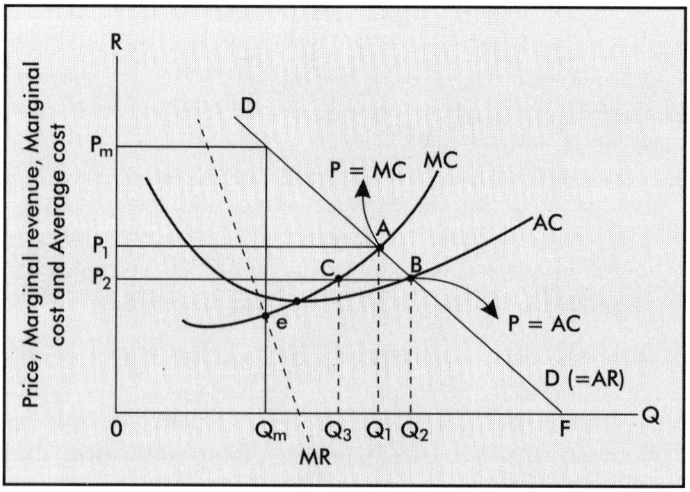

If the government does nothing, this surplus demand will give rise to black market prices. Some consumers are prepared to pay higher prices. (Think, for example, what happens when all the tickets for a rugby or soccer test are sold out – black market prices arise.) The primary goal of the government in reducing prices is therefore being thwarted.

In a situation such as this, the government could introduce additional measures. First, it could *ration* production to consumers. However, this is a clumsy system with high administrative costs. Alternatively, the government could *force* the monopolist to produce the output P_2B (ie Q_2). If they succeed in doing this, they will also succeed in making price equal to average cost. The monopolist will then make only normal profit.

Of course there is always the possibility that the government can set a price even lower than P_2. However, there is a danger here, namely that the price may be lower than the average cost (AC). As indicated earlier in the chapter, such a situation cannot continue in the long run, because the monopolist will suffer losses and cease production – as the only producer of his product, this could create serious problems in the economy if the product is no longer available. In such an event, the government would have to *subsidise* the monopolist to remain in production.

It is important to note that the application of these theoretical principles is no easy task in practice. The government is faced with the difficult task of collecting information on the monopolist's cost structure and market demand. The implementation of theoretical guidelines therefore cannot guarantee the optimal allocation of economic resources.

Taxation as control measure

A government can also use tax methods to reduce a monopolist's profit. However, this method is also not without problems because the monopolist can shift a portion of the tax on to consumers. It may easily happen that the economic profit of the monopolist declines, but the price of the product rises and the quantity offered diminishes – this is in contrast to the goals of government intervention mentioned earlier. The discussion below illustrates the government's dilemma in such a situation.

Figure 6–12

The effect of per-unit tax on the monopolist

Economic profit declines, but Q decreases and P rises. Welfare diminishes.

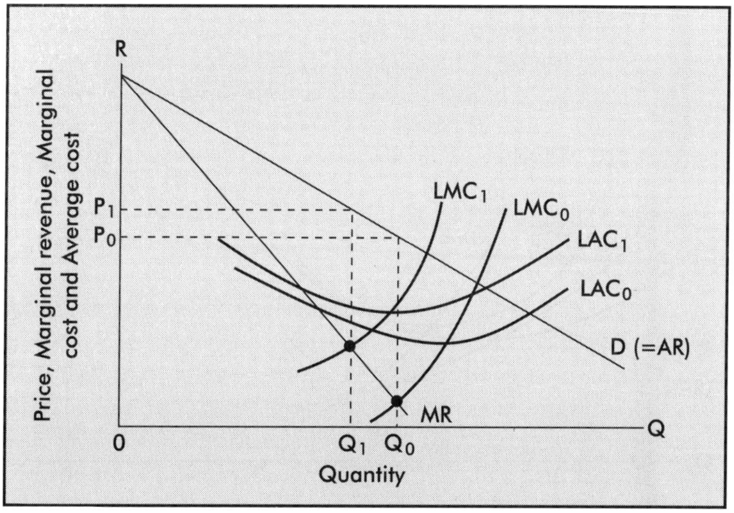

Per-unit tax

The effect of *per-unit taxation,* whereby the monopolist must pay a tax for each unit he sells, is indicated in Figure 6-12. LAC_0 and LMC_0 represent the monopolist's long-term average cost and long-term marginal cost curve respectively before the introduction of the tax. The equilibrium situation, in which the monopolist maximises profit, will be determined according to the customary rule (MR = MC) and the monopolist will therefore produce quantity Q_0 and sell it at price P_0. Because the per-unit taxation causes an increase in the monopolist's total taxation as production (and sales) increase, the firm will regard it as a variable cost item. The implication here is that the LMC and LAC curves both move upwards as the per-unit taxation is introduced; this is shown in Figure 6-12 by the shift of LAC_0 and LMC_0 to LAC_1 and LMC_1. Because of the shift of LMC_0 to LMC_1, the monopolist produces quantity Q_1 and sells it at price P_1. In Figure 6-12 we can see that the economic profit of the monopolist has decreased, but it is accompanied by a *decrease in output* and an *increase in price*. Since the per-unit taxation method reduces the welfare of consumers instead of increasing it, it is not very popular among economists.

Figure 6-13

The effect of lump-sum taxation on the monopolist

Economic profit decreases, P and Q remain the same.

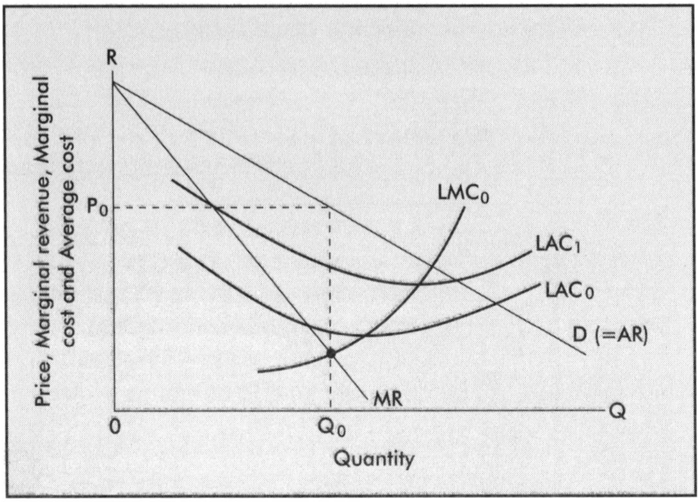

Lump-sum tax

The effect of *lump-sum taxation* is shown in Figure 6-13. As in the previous case, the monopolist's initial situation is represented by curves LAC_0 and LMC_0. Since the firm has to pay the lump-sum tax regardless of its revenue or size, the monopolist will regard it as a fixed cost. The introduction of a lump-sum tax will consequently shift the monopolist's long-run average cost curve upwards from LAC_0 to LAC_1, as shown in Figure 6-13. On the other hand, because the introduction of the lump-sum tax does not change the *slope* of the long-run total cost curve, the long-run marginal cost curve will remain unchanged at LMC_0. Since LMC_0 does not shift, the point of equilibrium remains where it was and the lump-sum tax therefore does not result in a reduction in the monopolist's output (Q_0) or increase in his price (P_0). The upward shift of the long-run average cost curve to LAC_1 will reduce the monopolist's economic profit, but will not influence his price or output.

Profit tax A third taxation method, namely a *profit tax*, gives the same results as the lump-sum tax.

It is understandable that the lump-sum and profit tax methods are preferred to the per-unit tax method because the first two reduce the monopolist's economic profit, but the price and quantity produced remain the same, while the per-unit tax reduces the monopolist's economic profit but leads to a reduction in the quantity produced and an increase in price. Nonetheless neither of these tax methods favours the consumer directly with price reductions and/or increased output. If the government is in a position to obtain sufficient information on the monopolist's cost and demand conditions, price control would be a preferable method to recover some of the welfare losses imputable to monopolies. However, as mentioned earlier, this is no easy task.

Other methods of control over a monopoly

Besides the fixing of maximum prices or the imposition of taxes, governments can apply other methods to control monopolies.

- *Government ownership* is one such option. Certain products (eg water and electricity) are produced effectively by a monopolist. The government often owns such natural monopolies. Governments may also buy or take over private monopolies, which is known as nationalisation. These days, however, it is generally accepted that production should be left to private firms, and that government should regulate these firms rather than nationalise them.

- A fourth alternative is *regulation*. Most countries have a policy on monopolies, economic concentration and the possible misuse of economic power. In the USA, this is referred to as anti-trust policy, while in South Africa it is known as competition policy. The aim is to promote effective competition instead of trying to summarily eliminate large enterprises (or monopolies). As far as monopolies and large enterprises in particular are concerned, the aim is to curb the potential misuse of monopolistic power and allow the benefits of large-scale production to filter through to society as a whole.

- Creating opportunities for increased competition is a fifth possibility. The exposure of firms to *import competition* in particular is an effective way of preventing monopolies and the misuse of economic power.

Box 6–4

The following extract from a report in *Business Day* in October 1997 shows that governments keep a watchful eye over the possible misuse of monopolistic powers.

MICROSOFT IN $1M-A-DAY ANTI-MONOPOLY SUIT

WASHINGTON – The US Justice Department asked the Federal Court yesterday to fine the world's leading software company, Microsoft, $1m for each day that it violated anti-monopoly laws in marketing its Internet browser.

The petition, filed by the department's anti-trust division, said Microsoft violated a 1995 court order by requiring personal computer manufacturers to distribute its Internet Explorer browser if they wanted to include its Window 95 software.

The 1995 order prohibited Microsoft from forcing manufacturers to license any other Microsoft product as a condition for licensing Windows 95.

'Microsoft is unlawfully taking advantage of its Windows monopoly to protect and extend that monopoly and undermine consumer choice', attorney-general Janet Reno said. More than 85% of personal computers manufactured today contain Windows 95.

Assistant attorney-general Joel Klein said: 'Our main concern is that . . . Microsoft is using an unlawful advantage to beat back an important competitive challenge to its Windows monopoly.' The government also asked the court to require Microsoft to notify Windows 95 users that they were not required to use Internet Explorer and to give them instructions on how to remove the browser's visual icon. Sapa-AFP-AP.

MONOPOLY IN PRACTICE

At the beginning of this chapter we stated that pure monopolies are seldom encountered in practice. Yet they do occur. The Central Selling Organisation (CSO) of De Beers Consolidated Mines Ltd, with its head office in South Africa, has been described as one of the most successful monopolies in the world. De Beers, which was founded by Cecil John Rhodes in 1880, controlled more than 99 per cent of the world's diamond production until approximately 1900. At present the company produces only about 15 per cent of the world's diamonds, but through its Central Selling Organisation it still controls more than 80 per cent of the world's sales of brilliant diamonds. This organisation markets De Beers's own diamonds as well as those of other important diamond producers such as the Democratic Republic of Congo, the Soviet Union, Botswana, Namibia and Australia.

There is no doubt that De Beers control the price of diamonds. Buyers are offered small holders with assorted diamonds on a 'take it or leave it' basis at a price fixed by De Beers. Those who decide not to buy have to wait for the next opportunity. If the demand for diamonds declines, which is what happened in the early eighties, De Beers buy in diamonds to support the price.

Besides limiting supply, De Beers also go to great pains to shift the demand curve for diamonds to the right. An important part of the marketing campaign involves linking diamonds to romance. (The company motto, 'A diamond is forever', has been going strong for more than fifty years.) This approach also helps to keep diamonds, once they are sold, out of the market. A product to which people attach so much sentimental value will not easily be sold during difficult economic times. De Beers' policy has made considerable profits for the company, but consumers have had to pay higher prices than they would have if the market had been competitive.

IMPORTANT CONCEPTS

- Monopoly
- Natural monopoly
- Artificial monopoly
- Marginal revenue (MR)
- Average revenue (AR)
- Short-run equilibrium (profit maximisation)
- Monopolists' 'supply'
- Long-run equilibrium (profit maximisation)
- Multiplant monopolist
- Consumer surplus
- Price discrimination
- Segmented-market price discrimination
- Multi-unit price discrimination
- Government regulation (goals)
- Price control
- Taxation as a control measure
- Per-unit taxation
- Lump-sum taxation
- Profit taxation

QUESTIONS

(1) Explain the concept 'monopolist' as well as the meaning of the terms 'natural monopoly' and 'artificial monopoly'. (5)

(2) (a) Explain why a monopolist's marginal revenue is always less than the price. (10)
(b) Explain why average revenue is always equal to price for a nonprice-discriminating monopolist. (4)

(3) Illustrate a situation of short-run (or long-run) equilibrium, in which the monopolist makes only normal profit. Explain the derivation of the equilibrium situation in detail. (12)

(4) Explain why a monopolist does not have a fixed supply curve. Use a diagram to illustrate your explanation. (8)

(5) You are the financial manager of a firm that has a monopoly on a particular product. The firm has two production plants. Explain in writing to your directors the theoretical principles one would use to maximise profit and to determine the output to be produced in each plant. Use a diagram to illustrate your explanation. (12)

(6) Compare the long-run equilibrium position of a monopolist with that of a perfectly competitive firm. Use diagrams to illustrate your discussion. (12)

(7) Explain the problems experienced when price regulation is used to ensure that a monopolist makes only normal profit in the long run. Use a diagram to illustrate your discussion. (Assume that the monopolist will in fact make economic profit without price regulation.) (15)

(8) Explain why a monopolist who applies price discrimination will sell his product at a higher price to those consumers who have a greater desire for the product. Use a diagram to illustrate your explanation. (15)

(9) Explain how a monopolist will apply multi-unit price discrimination. Use a diagram to illustrate your explanation. (15)

(10) (a) Explain in your own words with the aid of a diagram why governments seldom make use of a per-unit tax to curb monopolists. (10)
(b) Explain in your own words with the aid of a diagram how the government can use the lump-sum taxation method to reduce a monopolist's profit. (10)

7

IMPERFECT COMPETITION: MONOPOLISTIC COMPETITION AND OLIGOPOLY

The models of perfect competition and monopoly discussed in the previous two chapters represent two extreme market structures. Although these models are useful in explaining how markets operate, in practice most markets fall somewhere between the two extremes. In this chapter we discuss two such market forms, namely monopolistic competition and oligopoly. The theoretical analysis in this chapter can be far more easily reconciled with reality than the preceding market structures could.

As the name indicates, monopolistic competition is a hybrid: it constitutes a fair amount of competition but it also contains elements of a monopoly. The theory of monopolistic competition was developed in the early thirties by a British economist, Joan Robinson, and an American economist, Edward Chamberlin, working independently of one another. Neither of these economists had been satisfied with the two models (perfect competition and monopoly) which had been used up to that stage to analyse markets. They pointed out that most goods and services are heterogeneous rather than homogeneous, and that many sellers are really monopolists in respect of their own goods and services. These monopolists compete with one another in markets for goods which are much the same but nevertheless show slight differences. Many firms can therefore be regarded as 'competing monopolists', hence the term monopolistic competition. The theory of monopolistic competition is applied mainly to the retail trade and is therefore important not only to economists but also to marketers, managers, manufacturers and other businessmen.

In the second half of the chapter we discuss oligopoly as a market form. A characteristic of oligopoly is that the market is dominated by a few big firms and that there is usually a great deal of interdependence between the firms. Interdependence refers to the extent to which the actions of one firm are influenced by the actions of other firms. Because there are so few firms in an oligopoly, any change in a firm's policy on factors such as price or output could affect its competitors' sales and profits. Any firm which forms part of an oligopoly would therefore be likely to bear in mind the possible reaction from other firms when formulating its policy. Another important characteristic of the oligopoly is market uncertainty. Because firms are interdependent, and no firm can ever be sure of the policy of its competitors, companies function in a very uncertain environment. As a result there is often collusion between oligopolistic firms, that is to say, they agree on the prices they will charge and the quantities they will manufacture. Oligopoly is the market structure most frequently found in modern economies, for example in the motor industry and in general manufacturing. The study of this market form is therefore extremely important for people in a wide variety of occupations.

After having studied this chapter you should be able to

- define the monopolistic competitor
- explain how the monopolistic competitor achieves equilibrium in both the long run and the short run
- compare the monopolistic competitor with the perfect competitor
- explain non-price competition by monopolistic competitors
- describe the characteristics of an oligopoly and explain how this market form arises
- describe cartels and explain how they work
- explain why cartels frequently fail
- describe price leadership (and in particular the dominant price leader)
- analyse the model of the kinked demand curve

MONOPOLISTIC COMPETITION

Characteristics

The two most important characteristics of a market in which there is monopolistic competition are that a large number of firms manufacture differentiated products, and entry to the market is unrestricted.

Product differentiation

Differentiated products are products which are much the same but are not identical. Similarities between products arise because they satisfy the same consumer need. A few examples of differentiated products which are sold by monopolistic competitors in South Africa are the large varieties of men's clothing, women's clothing, shoes, beauty preparations, stationery, wine and furniture which are available in the trade. Product differentiation may involve real differences, as in wines, which may differ in origin, vintage and variety, or men's clothing, where there are differences in cut and quality. The differences may be imaginary, as in medicines which bear different trade names but contain the same basic ingredient. Sometimes merely the service offered by the seller sets his product apart. Even the packaging of a product can make it different from other similar products. Because the products of monopolistic competitors are differentiated this creates opportunities for non-price competition, that is competition which is not based on prices but on factors related to the uniqueness of the product. As will become apparent later, advertising is of major importance here.

Some monopolistic power

As we have already said, monopolistic competition is a combination of competition and monopoly. The competitive element arises because there are many sellers of the differentiated product, and each is relatively small in comparison with the market as a whole. Firms are able to enter or leave a monopolistically competitive market quite freely in the long run and this also contributes to the element of competition. On the other hand, the element of monopoly is the result of product differentiation. Each monopolistically competitive firm possesses a certain amount of monopolistic power and is a mini-monopolist, since it is the only producer of that specific trademark or variant of the product.

Monopolistic competition is common in the retail and services sector of the economy. We have already mentioned products such as clothing, wine and furniture which are examples of monopolistic competition at the national level. At the local level the best examples of monopolistic competition are the large numbers of filling stations, pharmacies, grocers, hairdressers, restaurants, take-aways and bottle stores, particularly in urban areas. Each of these enterprises enjoys a certain degree of monopolistic power over its competitors as a result of the uniqueness of its product, or possibly because of a better location, or slightly lower prices, better service, a greater variety of products, etc. This monopolistic power is not very strong, however, because good substitutes are always available.

Under a system of monopolistic competition each firm has its own identity and produces its own variant of a differentiated product. It is therefore impossible to define an industry for monopolistic competition (an industry refers to producers of an identical product). A further consequence is that a general theory or model of a monopolistically competitive industry cannot be formulated either. Although there is a market for, say, men's clothing, there is not just one product or one market price in that market, but a whole range of similar products and a range of prices. Chamberlin overcame this problem by grouping the sellers of products that are virtually the same into *product groups*. For convenience the term 'industry' is used in this discussion, but it actually refers to all the sellers of a differentiated product in a particular product group (eg men's trousers). Because of product differentiation we cannot derive demand and supply curves for an industry, as we did under conditions of perfect competition; a single equilibrium price is not determined for the differentiated product either, because there would have to be a range of prices. Our graphic analysis therefore has as its subject not the industry but a typical or *representative firm*.

Represen-tative firm

The characteristics of monopolistic competition may be summed up as follows:

- Each firm produces a particular differentiated product.
- Each firm therefore encounters a demand curve for its specific product, and these curves have a downward slope.
- There are a large number of firms in the industry.
- There are no restrictions on entry (or exit).

The equilibrium of the firm under monopolistic competition

Because the product of any firm operating under conditions of monopolistic competitive differs slightly from those of its competitors, giving that firm a certain amount of competitive power, the demand curve for its product also slopes downwards like that of a monopolist. This similarity with a monopolist does not mean that a monopolistic competitor will necessarily make big profits. Because entry to the industry is unrestricted, in the long run economic profit will attract new firms with competitive products to the industry and this will eventually put paid to the economic profit.

Short-run equi-librium

The short- and long-run equilibrium of a firm operating under conditions of monopolistic competition will now be analysed. The *short-run equilibrium* of a monopolistic competitor corresponds with that of a monopolist, except that the demand curve of a product of a monopolistic competitor will be more price-elastic than that of a monopolist. There would be a number of good substitutes for the product of the monopolistic competitor, which is not true of the product of a monopolist. Figure 7-1(a) illustrates the short-run situation of the representative firm. The figure shows the downward sloping demand curve of the monopolistic competitor, which is also his average revenue curve (AR), and the corresponding marginal revenue curve (MR). The SAC and SMC curves are also shown. The profit maximising price P_1 and output Q_1 are again determined by the point where marginal revenue is equivalent to marginal costs (MR = MC), that is point E in Figure 7-1(a). Since the price P_1 exceeds the average costs (see points F and G), the monopolistically competitive firm would make an economic profit, as indicated by the shaded area. (The firm could naturally also make a loss, but that is not discussed here.)

Figure 7-1

Equilibrium of the monopolistic competitor in the short and long run

Because the monopolistic competitor is the only producer of his particular product, his demand curve slopes downwards. In the short run the firm will earn an economic profit (Fig 7-1(a)), but in the long run it will attract other firms to the industry. The firm's demand curve shifts to the left (Fig 7-1(b)) and the firm makes only normal profit.

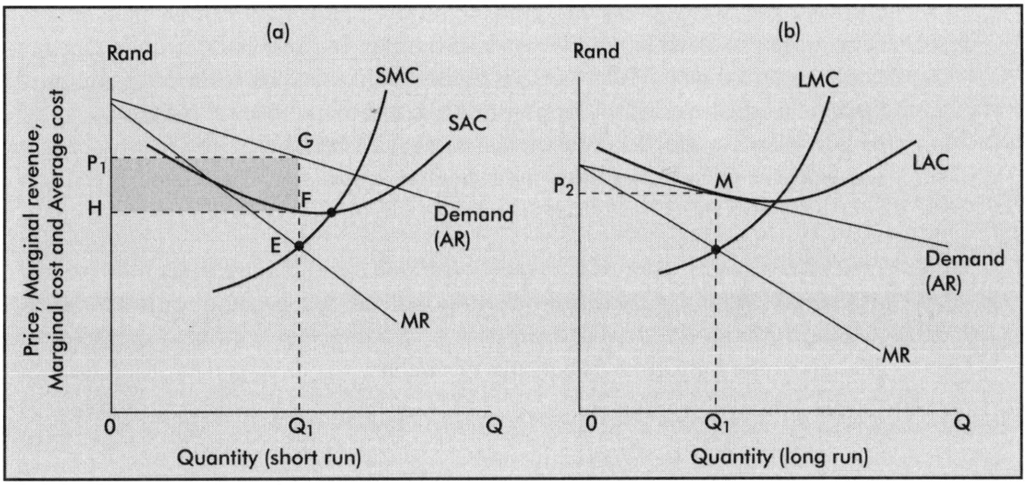

In the *long run* there are major differences between the situation of the monopolistic competitor and the monopolist. The monopolist is protected by restrictions on entry into the industry and is therefore able to make an economic profit in the long run. In contrast, monopolistic competition is characterised by free entry. The economic profit which the firm makes in the short run (Fig 7-1(a)) attracts new entrants to the industry in the long run. This increase in the number of firms in the industry will cause the demand curve for the product of the representative firm to shift to the left, because the market demand has now to be divided among more firms so that each firm's share is correspondingly smaller. The demand curve will also become more elastic, because there are now more substitutes for the firm's product than before. The demand curve shifts to the left, which may mean that some firms in the industry are unable to survive because the demand for their products is too small. Such firms are likely to leave the industry, which would cause the demand curve to shift to the right again. This process will continue until a condition is reached where no firms are entering or leaving the market and all economic profit has been eliminated. Long-run equilibrium has then been achieved, where all the representative firms are making a normal profit; in this situation the firm's demand curve would form a tangent to the long-run average cost curve. (Understandably this is also known as the tangential situation of the monopolistic competitor.)

Tangential situation

Figure 7-1(b) contains a graphic illustration of the long-run equilibrium of the monopolistically competitive firm. The economic profit which the firm made in the short run (Fig 7-1(a)) attracted new firms to the market, with the result that the demand curve shifted to the left. The competition caused all economic profit to disappear, which meant that the average costs were equal to the price. Given the slopes of the cost curve and the demand curve (AR) of the monopolistic competitor, the implication is that the AR curve must form a tangent to the LAC curve (see point M). Although only a normal profit is made, it is the maximum profit which can be made given the circumstances, because the equilibrium condition (LMC = MR) is observed. In this respect the long-run profit position of the firm in a monopolistically competitive market is the same as that of a firm in a perfectly competitive market. Nevertheless the firm does have some degree of monopolistic power because its product is unique – as is shown because its demand curve slopes downwards from left to right.

For the reasons mentioned previously it is not possible to represent the position of the *industry* under conditions of monopolistic competition with the aid of a diagram, as it is with perfect competition. We therefore confine ourselves to the analysis of the long-run equilibrium of the *firm*.

Monopolistic competition versus perfect competition: price, excess capacity and product variety

Perfectly competitive markets lead to economic efficiency and are therefore a model to strive for. As long as nothing hampers the operation of the market mechanism, producers will make normal profit in the long run and consumers will be able to buy the product at the lowest possible cost. Production therefore takes place at the minimum point of the long-run average cost curve (LAC). Monopolistic competition shows certain similarities with perfect competition, but the question is whether it is an equally effective market structure. To answer this question, we shall compare the long-run equilibrium position of a monopolistic competitor with that of a perfect competitor.

In Figures 7-2(a) and 7-2(b), the long-run equilibrium position of a firm is represented under conditions of perfect competition and monopolistic competition respectively. For comparison it is assumed that the two firms are the same size and have the same cost structures. In both cases the price of the product is equal to the average cost (see points H and I) and therefore only a normal profit is made. From the point of view of profit, therefore, there is no difference between the perfect competitor and the monopolistic competitor.

Figure 7-2

Monopolistic competition versus perfect competition

In both cases only a normal profit is made. Consumers pay a higher price for the product of the monopolistic competitor, as indicated in (b). The monopolistic competitor does not produce at the minimum point of the LAC curve and the output is therefore less than that of the perfect competitor in (a). There is also excess capacity.

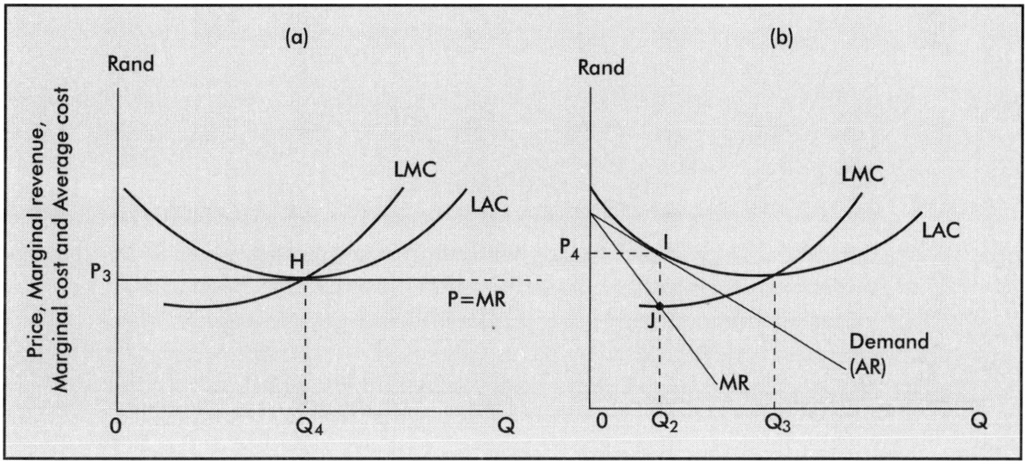

The two market forms do differ in the area of pricing. In the long run the perfect competitor produces at point H, where the price is equivalent to the marginal cost and the average cost is a minimum. In contrast, the monopolistic competitor produces at point I in the long run, which means that the price of his product is higher than the marginal cost and the average cost is not a minimum. Consumers therefore pay a higher price under conditions of monopolistic competition than under conditions of perfect competition (compare P_3 with P_4 in Fig 7-2). Because the price is higher than the marginal cost this also means that society attaches greater value to an additional unit of the product than to the resources required to produce it. This points to an inefficient utilisation of resources because social welfare could be increased by producing more of the product.

Another comparison which could be made between the two market forms relates to quantities produced. As we all know, the perfect competitor has a horizontal demand curve and production takes place in the long run at the minimum point of the long-run average cost curve (LAC). The output is indicated as Q_4 in Figure 7-2(a). For the monopolistic competitor the demand curve slopes downwards from left to right and the tangent with the LAC curve must necessarily be on the downward section of that curve, that is left of the minimum point of the LAC curve. Consequently the firm's output (Q_2) will be less than the 'ideal' output (Q_3) where the LAC is a minimum. Because the firm is producing less than the output which would keep long-run average costs to a minimum, this means that the firm did not build the plant size that would reduce long-run average costs to a minimum, but instead built a smaller plant. The difference between Q_3 and Q_2 in Figure 7-2(b) is known as *excess capacity* (and could probably better be described as unused economies of scale). According to critics this is indicative of the inefficient utilisation of resources. They contend that there are too many firms in a monopolistically competitive industry, all with plants that are smaller than the optimum size – a situation which is referred to as overcrowding in the industry. A smaller number of firms with bigger plants (more to the right on the LAC curve) would result in lower average costs. (To refresh your memory about different plant sizes and the LAC curve take another look at Figs 4-16 and 4-18 in Chapter 4.)

However, recent research seems to indicate that this view of excess (surplus) capacity and inefficient utilisation of resources has another side to it. The fact that there are many firms in a monopolistically competitive market does have the major advantage for society of guaranteeing greater product variety. Most consumers set great store by having a wide choice of products and services and are prepared to pay slightly higher prices for the privilege. If consumers are prepared to pay a premium for variety, then monopolistic competition is not necessarily having the effect of reducing society's economic welfare.

Product variation and sales expenditure (nonprice competition)

Because the products in a monopolistically competitive market are differentiated this makes it possible for a firm in this kind of market to use marketing campaigns and further product variation not only to cause the demand for its product to increase but also to make it less price-elastic. This is known as nonprice competition. *Product variation* (or product differentiation) has already been discussed (see 'Characteristics' on p 193). This refers to changes which a monopolistic competitor may effect in the properties of a product to make it more attractive to consumers and to distinguish it from other products. For example, the producer of a certain foodstuff could reduce the sugar content of the product and increase the fibre content to make it more attractive to health-conscious shoppers. We mentioned previously that product differentiation may involve

Product variation

Sales expenditure

real differences, or differences that are mainly imaginary. *Sales expenditure* refers to the expenditure incurred by a firm to advertise its products, increase its sales staff, provide a better service for the product, etc. Product variation and sales expenditure can boost a firm's sales figures and profits but they obviously have additional cost implications at the same time. A firm can go on increasing its expenditure on product variation and sales promotion as long as the resulting marginal revenue (MR) exceeds the marginal costs (MC); however, when MR = MC it is time to stop increasing this type of expenditure. (This is another application of this well-known rule in micro-economics.) Although expenditure on product variation and sales promotion can boost the profits of a monopolistic competitor in the short run, the firms in the industry will only make normal profits in the long run, because other firms will imitate the monopolistic competitor's product and new firms will enter the industry.

Advertising

Two important questions arise with regard to sales expenditure in general and advertising in particular. Does advertising persuade consumers to buy more of the product and does it create artificial needs? Second, do advertisements lead to more competition in a market or less? The argument regarding persuasion has been strongly advanced in the past. A writer such as John K Galbraith contends that firms would not keep on spending large sums on advertising if it was not having the desired results. Recent studies on the consumption of beer and cigarettes in the USA and Canada, however, have shown that although advertisements have an influence on consumers' choice of brand names, they do not appear to be very effective in increasing the total consumption of beer and cigarettes. With regard to the second question, a study of 150 industries in the USA found that industries in which the proportion of advertising expenditure to turnover is higher than average had smaller price rises and bigger increases in output. It would therefore appear that advertising promotes competition rather than impeding it. Although some advertisements are of a persuasive nature, they can also be informative to a large extent and enable consumers to make rational choices.

The very interesting debate on the advantages and disadvantages of advertising is by no means over. It falls outside the scope of our syllabus, however, and the discussion will therefore not be pursued here.

Practical problems for the monopolistic competitor

Non-price competition, which was discussed in the previous section, has the effect of making the attainment of the equilibrium situation more complicated for the monopolistic competitor than it might appear from the graphic analysis, at least at first glance. In the explanation based on Figures 7-1(a) and (b), a particular product and level of sales expenditure were accepted as given. This is not so easy in practice, where the monopolistic competitor has to keep three variables continually in mind – price, product and sales promotion – in his attempt to maximise profit. He needs to obtain answers to the following questions:

- Which specific variation of the product is the best?
- At what price should the product be sold?
- How much money should be spent on sales promotion?

The monopolistic competition model, although a very useful one, is essentially (like all models) a simplification and does not fully reflect the complexity of this problematic situation. Every possible combination of price, product and sales promotion strategy results in a different demand and cost situation for the firm, only one of which would lead to maximum profit. In practice the optimum combination cannot be predicted in advance, but must be worked out by trial and error. Also, the possible actions of competitors do not make the situation any easier for the monopolistic competitor.

Despite these comments, the theory of monopolistic competition does provide important insights, especially into product differentiation and non-price competition.

OLIGOPOLY

Characteristics

Few firms

Under the conditions of oligopoly the market is dominated by a few big firms. There could even be just two firms, a situation known as a duopoly. The product manufactured could be homogeneous (eg cement and aluminium) but is usually heterogeneous (eg cigarettes or toothpaste). When the product is homogeneous the market is described as a pure oligopoly and when the product is heterogeneous (ie differentiated), the market is described as a differentiated oligopoly. Entry to an oligopoly market is unrestricted, but that does not mean that it is easy, as is shown because there are only a few firms in the market.

The oligopoly is the market structure most commonly found in all the modern economies of the world. Table 7-1 shows examples of industries in which only a few firms are found, or in which a couple of firms dominate the market. This table shows the number of firms that were responsible for over 75% of the sales of certain goods in the South African markets during the eighties.

In South Africa, as in most other countries, the major portion of the total value of manufactures is produced by oligopolies. A researcher who analysed the South African manufacturing sector in the seventies classified 181 industries in seven market structures. The results of his investigation appear in Table 7-2. It can be concluded from this table that by far the majority of industries are characterised by oligopolistic conditions.

Table 7-1
Examples of oligopolistic markets in South Africa

Product	Number of firms that supply over 75% of the market
Aspirin	2
Sugar	2
Breakfast oats	3
Cement	3
Maizemeal	3
Fertiliser	3
Washing powder	4
Petrol	5
Toothpaste	5

Source: Finance Week 45(12), 21-27 June 1990:34, as quoted in P Mohr *et al*, 1996, *Ekonomie vir Suid-Afrikaanse studente,* Pretoria: Van Schaik.

Table 7-2
Market structures in the South African manufacturing industry, 1972

Market structure	Number of industries in each market structure
Monopolistic	12
Duopolistic	16
Highly oligopolistic	87
Moderately oligopolistic	20
Slightly oligopolistic	6
Unconcentrated	23
Competitive	17

Source: P G du Plessis, Concentration of economic power in South African manufacturing, *Tydskrif vir Studies in Ekonomie en Ekonometrie,* 3 (September):15.

Because only a few firms sell a homogeneous or differentiated product in a oligopoly, each firm is affected by the actions of other firms in the industry. Every oligopolist should therefore always bear in mind the possible reaction of his competitors to any action he may take. The chief characteristic of an oligo-

Inter-depen-dence

poly is therefore the *interdependence* between the firms of which it consists. The term 'interdependence' refers to the extent to which the actions of one firm are determined by the actions of other firms. For example, we frequently find that when one South African motor vehicle manufacturer starts a sales campaign and sells motor vehicles at a special discount or on very favourable terms (eg no interest on the loan) his immediate competitors follow suit with a very similar offer. Because price competition can lead to destructive price wars, oligopolists normally prefer to compete on the basis of product differentiation and good service, backed by advertising. Even then, when one oligopolist launches an advertising campaign his competitors often swiftly follow with campaigns of their own.

Clearly interdependence and competition are the most important characteristics of an oligopoly. This is the natural consequence of there being only a few firms in the market. As a result of this interdependence, policy decisions by firms are more complicated under an oligopoly than under other market structures. Because every oligopolist knows that his actions will have a significant influence on other firms in the industry, every firm has to take the possible reactions of its competitors into account when taking decisions on prices, product differentiation, advertising, service, etc. Because competitors may react in many different ways (depending on factors such as the type of product and the nature of the industry, etc), it is impossible to formulate a single, general theory on the price and product decisions of a firm in an oligopoly. The behaviour of oligopolists cannot be predicted with any certainty, because virtually anything can happen in an oligopoly. Instead of a single general theory that would be applicable to a firm under an oligopoly, we therefore find a number of theories, each of which depends on different assumptions about the reactions of competitors to the price and product decisions of the firm which is the subject of the study. These theories include those of economists such as Cournot, Bertrand, Chamberlin, Sweezy and Stackelberg. Remember, though, that all these models apply only to particular circumstances and are not generally valid. In the rest of this chapter we will concentrate only on the most important models.

The characteristics of an oligopoly can be summed up as follows:

- There are only a few firms in the market.
- Interdependence and competition are very important.
- Uncertainties in the market create the need for collaboration.
- The product may be homogeneous or heterogeneous.
- Entry to the market is unrestricted, but difficult.

- It has not proved possible to formulate a single, general theory on oligopoly, because the reactions of competitors may differ.

Origins of oligopolies

The reasons that oligopolies develop are similar to those for monopolies. They can be summed up as follows:

- Economies of scale may apply right up to such large production volumes that only a few firms are able to supply the entire market.
- Large-scale capital investment and specialised equipment are often required if a firm wishes to enter an oligopoly, as in the motor industry and the steel manufacturing industry. This creates a 'natural' barrier to entry.
- A few firms may possess a patent for a manufacturing process or the production of a certain product.
- Established firms may have a loyal following as a result of the quality of their product or the service they provide; this may be such a strong factor that new firms do not feel able to penetrate the market.
- A few firms may possess most or all of the raw materials required for the production process.
- The government may have granted a concession to a few firms only.

These are not only the reasons that oligopolies develop, but they also reflect the obstacles to entry encountered by other firms. If entry were not relatively difficult, the industry would not have remained an oligopoly over a long period.

The formation of cartels within an oligopoly

Collusion

We have already mentioned that no firm within an oligopoly can ever be certain about the policy and actions of its competitors. Companies therefore operate in a very uncertain environment. In order to reduce or eliminate this uncertainty, oligopolistic firms often collude; that is to say they agree on the prices they will charge and the quantities they will produce. The advantages of such collusive agreements are obvious: higher profits, less uncertainty, and the means to make it even more difficult for other firms to enter the market. Collusive agreements are difficult to sustain because there are always some participants who break the agreement in the hope that the others will not find out, or will do nothing about it if they do. For obvious reasons governments often legislate against collusion between firms.

Cartel When collusion takes place openly and formally, this is known as a *cartel*. A cartel may be defined as *an organisation of oligopolistic firms in an industry which has been formed with the specific aim of creating a collective monopoly*. Cartels are fairly common in many European countries, where they are not forbidden by the governments. In the United States of America most forms of collusion, both overt and covert, are illegal. Naturally this does not mean that such agreements do not exist. South Africa has a statutory Competition Board, which investigates the actions of companies and proceeds against them if necessary. The best-known example of a cartel in South Africa was formed by the three principal cement producers, Pretoria Portland Cement (PPC), Anglo-Alpha and Blue Circle, which are jointly responsible for over 90% of the total cement sales in the country. These three firms have colluded over a long period in price fixing and market share. The firms obtained official permission to continue to collude after practices of this kind were prohibited in 1986. In October 1994 the government withdrew its permission and the cartel was given until September 1995 to end its collusion. The best-known international example of a cartel is the Organisation of Petroleum Exporting Countries (OPEC), which includes a number of important oil-producing countries.

The operation of a cartel

The easiest way to explain the operation of a cartel is to start by supposing that a large number of firms (say 100) initially functioned in a perfectly competitive market. The firms produced a homogeneous product and were all equally efficient. Study Figure 7-3(b). The price at which each firm sells its output is equal to the market price P_0. The market price is determined by the point of intersection F of the market demand curve D_m with the market supply curve (that is the industry's supply curve) ΣSMC; the latter is the horizontal summation of the 100 marginal cost curves (SMC) of the firms (the assumption that input prices are not rising therefore applies). The matching MR curve also appears in Figure 7-3(b). The typical firm's short-run average cost curve (SAC) and short-run marginal cost curve (SMC) are shown in Figure 7-3(a). Because perfect competition applies, the demand curve for the individual firm shows a horizontal trend and the market price P_0 is equal to MR. Since the firm wants to maximise profits it will produce at point E (where $P_0 = MR = MC$) and will therefore produce an output of q_1 at the market price P_0. (Only normal profits are made.) The industry as a whole will function at point F in Figure 7-3(b), that is a total output of Q_1 will be produced at the market price P_0. (The output Q_1 is the sum total of the output of the 100 individual firms.)

Suppose that the 100 firms get together and form a cartel with a head office from which the price and production decisions of the firms are coordinated. The object of the collusion is to maximise the cartel's profits and so increase the members' profits. In order to determine the profit-maximising price and production quantity, the cartel acts like a monopolist and applies the marginal principal (MR = MC). To achieve the aims of the cartel, the management would fix the cartel's total production quantity at Q_c in Figure 7-3(b); the latter is determined by the point of intersection of the MR with the ΣSMC curve at point G. At G MR = MC and the profit of the cartel as a whole is therefore maximised. To ensure that the joint production of the members of the cartel does not exceed Q_c, the management will prescribe a quota q_c for each firm, which means that each firm's production decreases from q_1 to q_c. (If the 100 firms were all the same size, the quota $q_c = Q_c/100$.) Point G also determines the cartel price P_c, which is higher than the original price P_0. To sum up: for the cartel the profit-maximising output and quantity are Q_c and P_c respectively. Each firm produces q_c, which means that its production has decreased from q_1 to q_c; this production will be sold at the cartel price P_c which is higher than P_0.

Quota

Figure 7-3

The operation of a cartel

With perfect competition the market price is determined by point F, which is where the market supply curve and the market demand curve intersect. The total supply on the market will be Q_1 and each firm will offer q_1; only normal profit will be made at E. In a cartel point G (where MR = MC) determines the market price P_c and the quantity offered Q_c; each firm will produce the quota q_c and make economic profit.

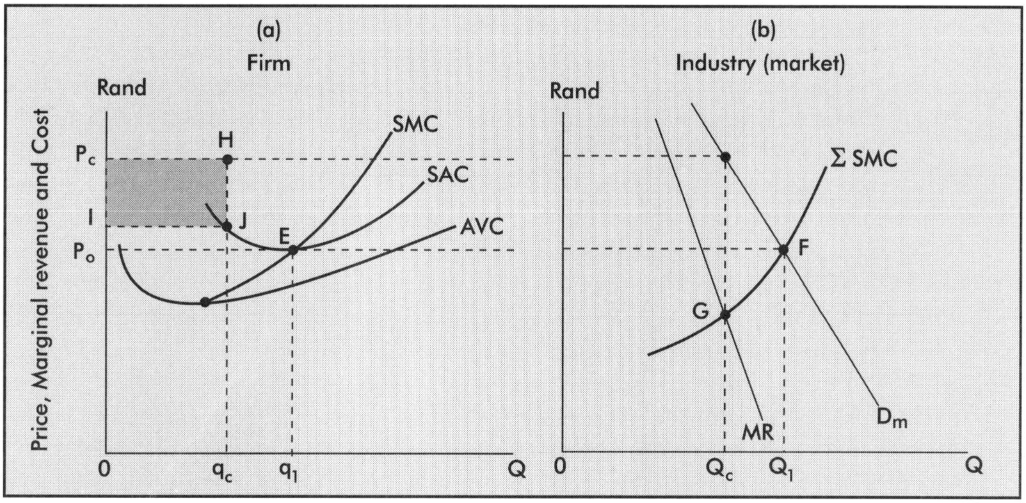

Before the cartel was formed, each firm made only normal profit. After the establishment of the cartel each firm makes economic profit – which is apparent because the total revenue $0P_cHq_c$ exceeds the total costs $0IJq_c$. The economic profit each firm earns is indicated by the shaded area IP_cHJ. It is quite clear that all the firms have been placed in a better position after the establishment of the cartel than when each firm operated under conditions of perfect competition. Naturally the assumption is that all the firms cooperate and do not exceed their quotas.

The rationale behind the formation of a cartel is obvious. It provides an opportunity to make more profit than under conditions of perfect competition. Cartels are not established for unethical reasons but are merely organisations that arise as a result of entrepreneurs' pursuit of maximum profit. The final result achieved by a cartel in terms of price, output and profit is the same as the result achieved by a monopolist, as discussed in the previous chapter. For this reason cartels, like monopolies, are not regarded in a favourable light by the authorities and measures are taken to curb their activities.

Although cartels are able to increase the profits of their members, in the past they have usually been unsuccessful in the long run, even in the absence of government action against them. The reasons for this will be discussed in the following section.

Why cartels fail: cheating by members

There is a big temptation for an individual member of a cartel to cheat and not to stick to the cartel agreement. Similarly, there are good reasons that a firm might choose not to become a member of a cartel. This is explained with reference to Figure 7-4. This figure shows the cost structure of a typical member of a cartel – the same as that in Figure 7-3(a). At the production quota q_c which is fixed by the cartel management the typical firm makes an economic profit which is represented by the unshaded rectangle A. If the firm acts *independently* of the cartel (in other words, cheats) it can see itself as a price taker – that is to say it can regard the cartel price P_c as constant as long as the other members of the cartel do not cheat or become aware of the activities of the firm in question. This firm, which intends to cheat, will then determine the output at which its profit is maximised, given that the price is P_c. The optimal output will be that at which MR = MC. Because P_c is constant, P_c = MR (as under perfect competition) and the profit-maximising position for the firm will therefore be at point L, where P_c = MR = MC. The profit-maximising output is indicated as q_{cheat} in Figure 7-4. The cheating firm therefore produces more than other members of the cartel ($q_{cheat} > q_c$). (At q_c, the production quota prescribed by the cartel, $P_c >$ SMC, which means that if the firm produces additional units, these units will generate more revenue than they cost to produce; the cheating firm therefore has a good reason to increase its output to q_{cheat} where P_c = MR = MC.) At an output of q_{cheat} the firm would earn an economic profit equal to the rectangle A *plus the shaded area* which is indicated as B. The firm that cheats can therefore make more economic profit than a firm which honestly adheres to the cartel agreement.

Cheating members

Because far more economic profit can be made by cheating, the members of the cartel are continually tempted to break the cartel agreement. There is therefore a very strong possibility that a cartel will collapse after a while. If the members of the cartel start acting independently and producing more than the prescribed quota, the total market supply will increase, which will cause the market price to drop. Higher production volumes and lower prices will reduce the economic profit. There is also a strong possibility that firms will build up extra stocks as a result of the increased production volumes. Competition among the firms will increase with the passage of time and practices such as selling products at 'secret' discounts will emerge. Such practices do not remain secret for long, however, and the firms which are still sticking to the cartel agreement get wind of the cheating – and then start breaking the agreement themselves. Before long the entire cartel will collapse and firms will find that their situation is the same as before the establishment of the cartel, when only normal profits could be made.

Figure 7-4

The reason that members of cartels often cheat

If the member of the cartel sticks to the prescribed quota q_c it would produce at point H and make an economic profit equivalent to the rectangle A. If the firm exceeds the quota and produces at point L (where $P_c = MR = MC$) it would make an economic profit equivalent to the rectangle A plus the shaded area B.

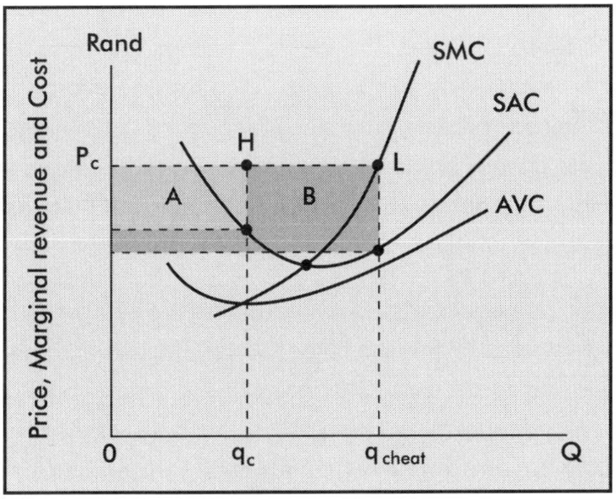

It is possible for a cartel to fail even if none of the members cheat. A successful cartel which secures economic profit for the members is likely to attract firms from outside the industry. If this happens, the market supply will also increase, which will reduce the economic profit. There is a strong possibility that the members of the cartel would then start to cheat in an attempt to counteract the decrease in their economic profit, and this would eventually lead to the downfall of the cartel.

As is apparent from the above discussion, the history of cartels does not contain many success stories. Ironically, the reason for the establishment of cartels (the pursuit of maximum profit) usually also leads to their downfall.

To conclude our explanation of how cartels operate, we shall discuss the best-known international example of a cartel, namely OPEC, in Box 7-1.

Box 7-1

THE ORGANIZATION OF PETROLEUM EXPORTING COUNTRIES (OPEC)

The Organization of Petroleum Exporting Countries is the best-known international example of a cartel. Although there have been problems from time to time, OPEC has succeeded in surviving since the seventies.

The cartel attracted worldwide attention for the first time in 1973 when it curtailed oil exports and took steps to raise the price of crude oil. The price of Saudi Arabian crude oil rose from $4 per barrel in 1973 to over $10 per barrel in 1974, for example. In 1979 OPEC raised the price of crude oil to over $30 per barrel.

What is OPEC and how does the organisation function? The cartel has thirteen members, all of whom are leading oil-producing countries. The members include Saudi Arabia, Iran, Venezuela, Libya and Nigeria. The OPEC countries levy an excise duty on every barrel of oil produced; that duty is seen as a cost item by the international oil companies that trade in those countries. The OPEC countries can raise the price of crude oil by increasing the excise duty, because no company can afford to sell the oil for less than the production costs plus the duty. According to the cartel model discussed, one would expect that the price of crude oil would be increased to around the level it would have been at with a monopoly. This is what happened and it is estimated that the OPEC countries obtained hundreds of billions of dollars from consumers in this way.

The economic power of OPEC declined during the eighties, however, as shown by the drop in the price of oil to below $15 per barrel. The downward pressure on the oil price, however, was partly because of a decline in the international consumption of oil. As a result of the recycling of oil, economical use of oil and competition from other sources of energy (partly as a result of the huge price rises), the demand for oil decreased. Also, the oil production of the non-OPEC oilfields (eg in Mexico and the North Sea) greatly increased, which placed further pressure on OPEC.

The OPEC cartel has a very interesting way of proceeding against countries that exceed their quota. Saudi Arabia, OPEC's biggest producer, often increases its oil production temporarily in order to force the world price of oil down so that any members of the cartel who may be cheating derive no benefit from their actions. When their profits suddenly drop, the guilty parties usually apologise and ask for new quotas so that the world price of oil will rise again.

Price signals and price leadership in an oligopoly

In oligopolies firms have a big incentive to collude in order to eliminate or reduce the uncertainties which are characteristic of this market form. Because formal collusions among firms (ie cartels) are generally forbidden and also quite often meet with failure, instead of entering into formal collusions oligopolists often do so tacitly. Without formally communicating with one another or concluding agreements they try to find a way of reducing uncertainties in the market.

Price signals

One of the problems of tacit collusion is that it is difficult for firms to reach agreement on the price of the product (without discussing it with one another). For this reason price signals often form an important element in tacit collusion. For example, a firm can announce that it intends to increase the price of its product and hope that its competitors will take this as a sign that they should fix their prices at a higher level as well. If the competitors fall in with this, this could give rise to a pattern of price leadership that would solve the problem of how to agree on a price. One firm fixes the price and the others act as price followers.

The price leader is usually the biggest or the dominant firm in the industry. Occasionally it is the firm with the lowest production costs; it could merely be the firm which is regarded as the best interpreter or barometer of demand and cost conditions in the marketplace. (Then it is known as barometric price leadership.) Examples of price leadership are often found in the steel and food industries.

In the next section we discuss one of the best-known models of price leadership, namely where the dominant firm in an industry acts as the price leader.

Price leadership by the dominant firm in an oligopoly

Dominant firm

Suppose that there is one large, dominant firm together with a number of smaller firms in an industry. Let us also assume that the dominant firm sets the price in the industry and allows the smaller firms to sell as much as they like at that price. The quantities the smaller firms cannot supply are produced for the market by the dominant firm. Given these assumptions, it is fairly easy to determine the price the dominant firm will set as the market price for the industry, if the dominant firm wants to maximise profits. Since each small firm accepts the

Small firms

price as a given and is permitted to produce as much as it wants to, the small firms would behave in the same way as under conditions of perfect competition and produce an output at which the price is equal to the marginal costs. We know that under perfect competition price is also equal to marginal revenue, therefore the small firms will produce at the point where $P = MR = MC$. A combined supply curve for all the small firms could be drawn by making a horizontal summation of their marginal cost curves. This supply curve is represented as ΣSMC in Figure 7-5. The output that the small firms are unable to supply is produced for the market by the dominant firm; the demand curve for the dominant firm can therefore be derived by subtracting the quantity the small firms offer at each price from the total market demand. This means that if D_m represents the total market demand in Figure 7-5, the dominant firm's demand curve D_{dom} can be determined by calculating the horizontal difference at each price between D_m and the supply curve (ΣSMC) of the small firms.

Figure 7-5

Price leadership

The dominant firm will set the price at P_1 and produce the quantity Q_{dom}. The small firms will produce Q_1 (which is equal to $Q_3 - Q_{dom}$).

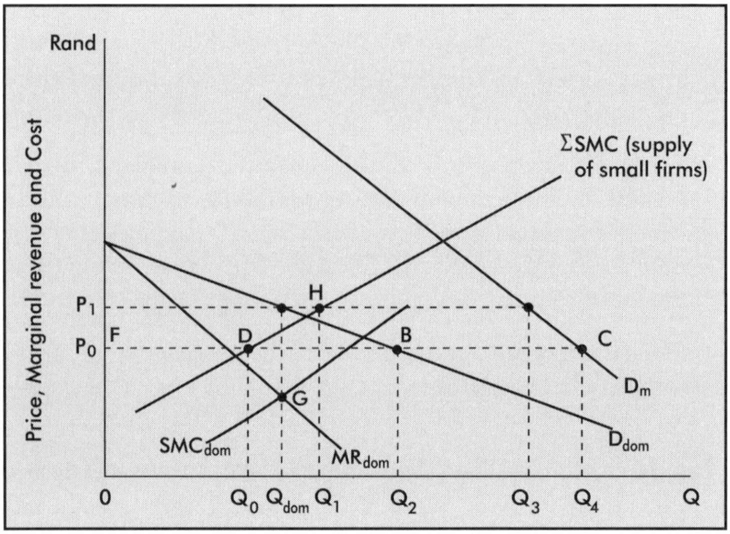

The graphical derivation of the demand curve (D_{dom}) for the dominant firm may be explained as follows. Suppose the dominant firm sets the price of the product at P_0. The supply curve ΣSMC shows that at the price P_0 the small firms will offer the quantity Q_0 (see point D), whereas the market demand curve indicates that the total quantity for which there is a demand will be Q_4 (see point C). The quantity the dominant firm will have to supply to the market is therefore $Q_4 - Q_0$, which is indicated at the price P_0 at point B and represents one point on the demand curve D_{dom}. In other words: Q_2 is equal to $Q_4 - Q_0$ (or, differently stated: FB = FC – FD = DC). Other points on the demand curve D_{dom} are determined in the same way by repeating the calculation at different prices.

Given that the demand curve D_{dom} for the dominant firm has been derived as above and that the marginal cost curve for the dominant firm, SMC_{dom}, is known, it is fairly easy to determine the price and output at which the dominant firm would maximise profits.

The marginal revenue curve MR_{dom} of the dominant firm is derived in the usual way from its demand curve D_{dom}. The profit-maximising output for the dominant firm is determined by the point G where its marginal revenue is equivalent to its marginal cost (MR = MC) and will therefore be Q_{dom}. This output (Q_{dom}) is produced when the dominant firm sets the price at P_1. At P_1 the total output of the industry is Q_3, of which the small firms will supply Q_1 (ie $Q_3 - Q_{dom}$) (see point H).

Everyone satisfied

If the dominant firm fixes the market price at P_1 and the above solution is obtained, all the firms in the industry will be in equilibrium, that is to say they will maximise profits. The dominant firm produces at a point where the profit-maximising condition MR = MC (point G) is observed, whereas the small firms, which operate as if under conditions of perfect competition, are in the same position at point H (we are assuming that the small firms all have the same cost structure). This solution should therefore satisfy everyone in the industry.

An explanation for oligopolistic behaviour: the kinked demand curve

The need oligopolists have to collude in order to eliminate uncertainties in the market has been mentioned a number of times. Earlier we said that such collusion is frequently against the law and in any case often results in failure on account of cheating by the members. The need by oligopolists for stability, particularly in the price of their product, still applies, however. The result is that price rigidity (that is, relatively inflexible prices) can be a characteristic of an oligopolistic industry. Even if costs drop or the demand declines, firms are reluctant to reduce their prices for fear of giving competitors the wrong message and initiating a price war. When costs or demand increases firms are also reluctant to raise their prices for fear that their competitors might not follow suit.

Reason for kink

Price rigidity is the basis of the well-known model of the *kinked demand curve,* which was formulated in 1939 by the American economist Paul Sweezy. The model also illustrates the importance of interdependence and uncertainty, both of which are characteristic of oligopolistic markets. Refer to Figure 7-6. According to Sweezy's model, each firm is faced with a demand curve which shows a kink at the prevailing market price P_0 (see point S). Above the kink, that is at the prices above P_0, the demand curve is very elastic (see the section TS). The reason is that the firm believes that if it sets its price above P_0 other firms would not do the same, with the result that its sales would decline sharply and its market share would shrink. On the other hand the, demand curve below the kink, at prices below P_0, is very inelastic (see section SV) because the firm believes that if it were to price its product lower than its competitors they would immediately do the same to prevent losing part of their market share. Therefore the firm cannot increase its market share by reducing its price; its sales will increase at a rate which is no higher than that of its competitors.

Figure 7-6
The kinked demand curve

As a result of the kink in the demand curve P_0 remains the equilibrium price even if the marginal cost curve moves upwards or downwards (provided it intersects the MR curve in the discontinuous area).

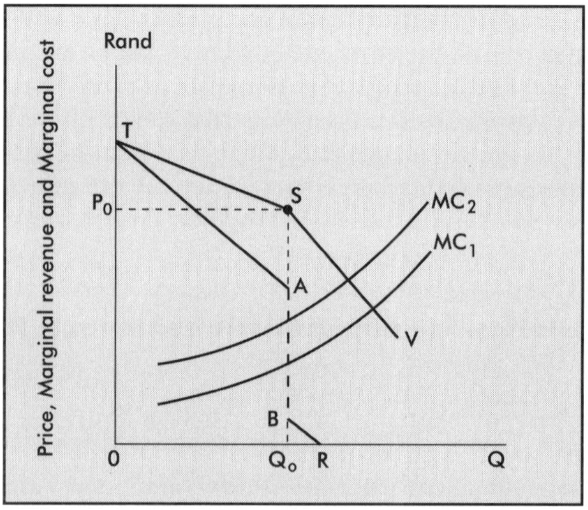

Discontinuous MR Because the firm's demand curve is kinked, the marginal revenue curve is not continuous, but shows a discontinuous section between points A and B. (As a result of the kink in the demand curve the total revenue of the firm, if calculated (P × Q), suddenly undergoes a major change at point S, which means that the marginal revenue, MR, also changes drastically immediately below point S – hence the 'fall' in the MR curve from A to B. The remainder of the marginal revenue curve, from B to R, is related to the demand curve between points S and V.) Profit is maximised at the production level where MR = MC. Suppose that MC_1 is the marginal cost curve of the oligopolist. MC_1 intersects the marginal revenue curve MR in the discontinuous section AB; profits are therefore maximised at the prevailing price and quantity (P_0 and Q_0).). However, Figure 7-6 shows that the firm's costs may change without the price changing. If the marginal cost increases from MC_1 to MC_2, it would still intersect the MR

P and Q unchanged curve at the same output level Q_0 and the price P_0 would also remain unchanged. The marginal cost curve MR can move either upwards or downwards but as long as it intersects the MR curve in the discontinuous section the equilibrium price and quantity will remain the same.

Sweezy's model was initially regarded by some economists as a generally applicable theory of oligopoly, but it is no longer so highly regarded. While the model is a visual method of illustrating the phenomenon of price rigidity, it does not provide a full explanation of price formation under an oligopoly. For instance, it does not explain how the firms arrived at the price P_0 in the first place; the model simply takes the prevailing price P_0 as given. Empirical research has also questioned the basic premise of the model – the indications are that competitors will imitate both price increases and price decreases. In that event the demand curve would not show a kink.

The model of the kinked demand curve is currently regarded as one of a whole range of theories to explain oligopolistic behaviour. The importance of this model is that it illustrates the underlying interdependence and uncertainty which are characteristic of oligopolistic markets and can be used to explain price rigidity, something which is often observed in practice.

Product variation and sales expenditure (nonprice competition) in an oligopoly

Most oligopoly models lead us to the conclusion that prices are fairly stable in this market form – and indeed observation in practice bears this out. Price wars do occur from time to time, but do not usually last long. In order to avoid price wars, oligopolists prefer to keep prices unchanged as far as possible and to compete by means of advertising, product differentiation and the services they offer (ie nonprice competition). (The attentive reader will immediately see the similarity to monopolistic competition.) Only when a price change is unavoidable as a result of changes in demand conditions and cost structures do oligopolists consider a price adjustment. If there is a price leader in the industry, a price adjustment of this kind can take place in a fairly orderly manner.

Like a monopolistic competitor, an oligopolist uses advertisements in an attempt to boost the demand for his product, that is to shift his demand curve to the right. If this is successful, the firm will be able to sell a larger quantity of the product at the same price. The problem, however, is that as soon as other firms see that their sales are dropping, they will probably react by expanding their advertising as well. It is possible that the only result will be an all-round increase in advertising costs, with each firm simply retaining its own market share and making less profit. This serves to emphasise how careful one has to be about advertising campaigns.

The same argument applies to product differentiation. Producers frequently differentiate their products in order to boost their sales, but this usually leads to a counter-reaction from other firms, the result again being higher costs and prices. Products are sometimes changed simply for cosmetic reasons – as when car manufacturers bring out different models. Other changes may involve real improvements which are to the advantage of the consumers – an example being a new kind of razor blade which is not only better but lasts longer as well. Product differentiation is sometimes aimed at a particular market segment, as when a car manufacturer brings out a model which is aimed specifically at young working people or at students.

The same arguments which arose with regard to advertising and product differentiation for the monopolistic competitor could well be repeated here. The principle that a firm's optimum expenditure on advertising and product variation is reached when the marginal revenue generated is equal to the marginal cost is equally valid here. That there are only a few firms in an oligopoly and that each firm must take the possible reactions of its competitors into account makes the marketer's task a bigger challenge.

Welfare effect of oligopoly

Because there is no general theory on oligopolies and we have discussed only a few models in this chapter, the welfare effect of an oligopoly cannot be compared in detail with that of perfect competition or a monopoly, for example. The following is a summary of the most important differences or similarities which can generally be identified:

- As in a monopoly or monopolistic competition, the producer in an oligopoly does not produce at the minimum point of the long-run average cost curve (LAC). The product is therefore not supplied to consumers at the lowest possible price.
- Firms in an oligopoly can make economic profit in the long run. This is in contrast to monopolistic competition and perfect competition, where only normal profit can be made in the long run. Note, however, that oligopolies use a large portion of their profits for research and development in order to find new and better products and cheaper production methods.
- As in monopolistic competition and monopoly, the price of the product in an oligopoly is higher than the marginal cost ($P > MC$), which also means that society attaches greater value to an additional unit of the product than to the resources required to produce it. This points to an inefficient utilisation of resources and a welfare loss.

Oligopolies – a worldwide phenomenon

As has already been stated, oligopoly is the market structure most commonly found in all the modern economies of the world. During the past decade the trend towards increasingly large oligopolies with international interests has increased, as is apparent from the fact that the biggest companies in the world are becoming even bigger as a result of mergers and internal growth.

Mergers

More and more small companies have merged with bigger companies, regarding this as the only way to survive. Impetus has also been given to the establishment and growth of international companies by the worldwide improvement in communications and transport, the disappearance of measures that impede international trade and the investments which originated from the formation of large trading blocs (eg in Europe and North America).

The sector where there has been the biggest growth in large corporations during the past few decades is banking. The growth of the world's largest banks has been described as spectacular. Another sector where rapid growth has taken place is communications. The merging of Time with Warner Communications and Japan's Sony with American Paramount Pictures are just two examples of this. The same trend has been evident in manufacturing. In the tyre industry three companies (Goodyear, Bridgestone and Michelin) have been responsible for more than half the world's total sales. At the time of writing of this chapter negotiations were taking place between Daimler-Benz and Chrysler which would lead to the establishment of the fifth biggest motor vehicle manufacturer in the world.

The movement in the direction of corporate expansion (and oligopoly formation) has not passed South Africa by. It was apparent from Table 7-2 that manufacturing in South Africa was already being dominated by oligopolies in the seventies. Reports appear regularly in the financial press on further mergers or proposed mergers. The banking and financial sector in South Africa has also seen a number of takeovers and mergers in the past few years. Various mergers of banks and building societies have taken place, such as between the Allied, Trust-Bank, United and Volkskas, to name one example. Brokerage firms have also merged their interests, acquiring international interests in the process. Auditing firms and advertising companies have done the same.

We should mention that mergers are not the only kind of operation that is taking place. In South Africa quite a few big companies have also been unbundled recently, that is to say they have split up into smaller enterprises. The unbundling has mainly affected companies with a wide variety of divergent, heterogeneous activities. As might be expected, mergers generally take place between companies conducting the same type of business, for example in the banking sector.

Because oligopolies are so widespread, it is a pity that no general economic theory has been developed for this market form. Further research in this field is still taking place; the emphasis appears to be on the expansion and application of what is known as 'games theory'. This is a challenging subject but unfortunately it is beyond the scope of the syllabus covered in this book.

IMPORTANT CONCEPTS

- Monopolistic competition
- Differentiated products
- Short-run equilibrium of the monopolistic competitor
- Long-run equilibrium of the monopolistic competitor
- Surplus capacity
- Non-price competition
- Sales expenditure
- Oligopoly
- Interdependence
- Collusion
- Cartels
- Price signals
- Price leadership
- Dominant firm
- Kinked demand curve
- Price rigidity

QUESTIONS

(1) Discuss the assumptions that make monopolistic competition as a market form unique. (10)

(2) Discuss equilibrium price determination of the monopolistic competitor in the short term. Use a figure to illustrate your answer. (20)

(3) In your opinion, does the greater variety that differentiated products offer, justify the higher price that the consumer has to pay? (4)

(4) Discuss the formation of a cartel. Use a diagram to illustrate your answer. (12)

(5) Discuss the reasons why cartels fail. (6)

(6) Discuss fully how the dominant firm divides the market between itself and the smaller firms. Use a diagram to illustrate your answer. (25)

(7) Explain why the kinked demand curve of Paul Sweezy has a kink in it. (5)

(8) Illustrate and explain how Sweezy's model can be used to explain the rigidity of prices and outputs in the case of an oligopoly. Refer to the effect of changes in cost on the price and output decisions of an oligopoly. (15)

(9) What criticism can be levelled against Sweezy's model? (4)

8

GENERAL EQUILIBRIUM ANALYSIS AND WELFARE ECONOMICS

In the previous chapters we analysed the reaction of producers and consumers to the economic problem of scarcity. We saw how consumers use their limited income to maximise utility, and firms allocate production factors and set prices to maximise profit. Because each agent (participant) and each market was analysed separately, it may appear as if microeconomics considers such agents and markets in complete isolation. However, this impression is false. It is also important for microeconomists to understand how various agents and markets interact with each other. In fact, one of the most interesting and stimulating fields of study in microeconomics concerns precisely the interrelationships between different agents and markets. This chapter will try to establish the theoretical underpinnings for studying such interrelationships in the economy.

After having studied this chapter, you should be able to

- describe the difference between partial and general equilibrium
- understand the criterion for Pareto optimality
- discuss consumption efficiency with the aid of an Edgeworth Box Diagram
- discuss production efficiency with the aid of an Edgeworth Box Diagram
- explain the interrelation between production and consumption efficiency with the aid of a diagram
- summarise the three Pareto conditions for general equilibrium efficiency
- describe the concept of welfare economics

PARTIAL VERSUS GENERAL EQUILIBRIUM ANALYSIS

The kind of analysis conducted in the previous chapters is generally known as *partial equilibrium analysis.* The effects of changes in a given market are confined to that specific market. No attempt is made to see what the repercussions are for other markets. This approach is like that of a film producer who, seated in a helicopter, is shooting a battle scene with his camera which has a telephotolens – first, he focuses on what the infantry is doing, then what is going on with the artillery and, finally, he homes in on what the generals are discussing. After all the scenes have been shot, he will have somewhat of a problem to integrate them in such a way that an outsider can gain a clear view of how the battle developed.

In a certain sense, economists have the same problem as this film producer, namely to present an integrated model of the economy as a whole. This chapter introduces the concept of *general equilibrium analysis,* which is a theoretical model which attempts to take account of the implications of changes in one market for other markets. The last part of this chapter will also touch on welfare economics, which is that aspect of economic analysis which studies the relative desirability of various distributions of wealth or productive resources.

General equilibrium analysis is also used to answer a question which has occupied economists for a long time, namely whether a perfectly competive market will yield a set of prices which will cause all markets simultaneously to clear. Recent research by mathematical economists seems to have confirmed such a notion, to which this chapter, however, will not be giving any further attention – it would require us to consider a set of mathematical equations which would make it too complicated. We will concentrate on presenting an introduction to general equilibrium analysis and welfare economics, leaving aside their mathematical technicalities.

The Pareto criterion

An important problem in economic analysis needs to be faced from the outset, namely the difficulty of making normative pronouncements about economic situations, that is whether one situation may be considered better than another. For example, is one distribution of production factors (or consumer goods) better than any other? The fundamental reason that it is so hard to decide such issues is that we cannot determine whether (say) a loaf of bread brings more satisfaction to Jones than to Smith, or whether Smith attaches greater value to an additional R100 income than Jackson. Subjective considerations play an unavoidable part in such interpersonal comparisons, which therefore cannot be decided without making value judgements.

Pareto optimality The well-known criterion for Pareto optimality, formulated in 1909 by the Italian economist Vilfredo Pareto, was designed to circumvent this problem. According to the Pareto criterion, any change which leaves at least one person better off without making anybody else worse off is desirable. Such a change is referred to as 'Pareto efficient'. When all possibilities for making such Pareto-efficient changes have been exhausted and we can no longer improve one person's position without worsening the position of someone else, a situation is achieved which is described as a 'Pareto-optimal distribution of resources'.

The Pareto criterion therefore steers clear of the problem of making interpersonal comparisons. The central question according to this criterion is: Can A's position be improved without making the position of B (or any other participant) worse off? A's position is compared with himself, whilst the position of B (or any other participant) stays the same.

The Pareto criterion is obviously not perfect either. For example, it is undecided about changes which make some individuals better off while leaving others worse off. Since most economic policy changes produce results of this kind, the Pareto criterion is clearly of limited use. Other more explicit methods have therefore been suggested to supplement the Pareto criterion, such as the Kaldor-Hicks criterion. Nonetheless, in spite of its limitations, the Pareto criterion is used in just about all the studies which attempt to measure the relative desirability of economic situations. It gives us a criterion to gauge the suitability of a specific changes in the distribution of production factors.

General equilibrium

As already mentioned, a general equilibrium model takes explicit account of the interrelationships between various sectors in the economy. To keep the complicity of such a model manageable, it is common to assume a simple economy in which only two consumers (Smith and Jones) play a role, only two goods (food and clothes) are produced, with the aid of only two production factors (capital and labour) – a so-called $2 \times 2 \times 2$ economy. First, we will investigate when consumption efficiency is achieved – for a given combination of goods produced, consumption efficiency requires that goods should be distributed among consumers in such a way that it is impossible to enhance the utility of one consumer without reducing the utility of the other. Second, we will look at production efficiency, which is achieved when it is impossible to increase the production of the one good without decreasing the production of the other good. Third, we will attempt to establish when production and consumption are compatible with each other, that is when that combination of goods is produced which consumers also wish to buy.

CONSUMPTION EFFICIENCY

Figures 8-1 and 8-2 show the indifference maps of the two consumers, Smith and Jones, of our simplified economy. We explained in a previous chapter how an indifference curve indicates a constant level of utility (or satisfaction) and how higher levels of utility are represented by higher indifference curves.

Figures 8-1 and 8-2

Indifference map of Smith; Indifference map of Jones

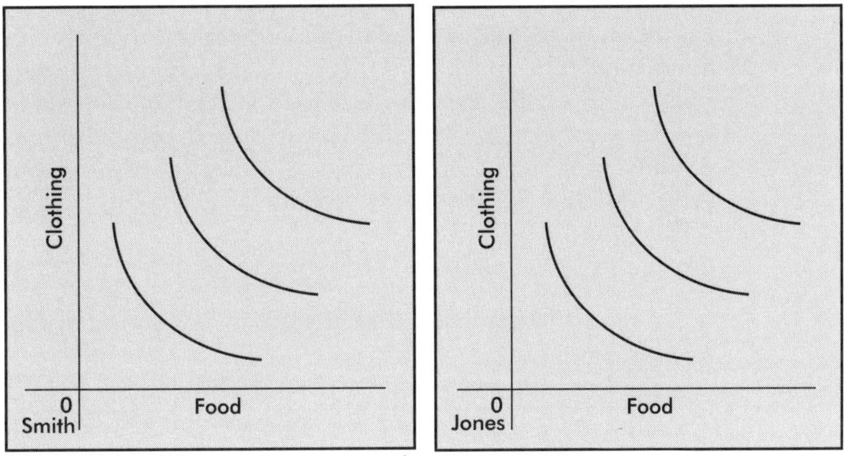

Edgeworth Box Diagram

The two indifference maps can now be combined to form an Edgeworth Box Diagram for consumption. This is achieved by rotating Jones's indifference map 180° and linking the two maps – see Figure 8-3. Jones's indifference map will now have to be viewed from the upper right-hand corner – for him, an indifference curve representing a low level of utility will lie close to the upper right-hand corner (eg J_1) and an indifference curve representing a higher level of utility further away from that corner (eg J_2). The 'bulge' of Jones's indifference curves also points towards the upper right-hand corner of the diagram. Smith's indifference map remains as in Figure 8-1 and can be interpreted in the normal way.

The dimensions of the Edgeworth Box Diagram are determined by the quantity of each product (food and clothing) available in the economy. In our present analysis, we assume that 12 units of food and 8 units of clothing are available, as in Figure 8-3. An arbitrary point H in the diagram (Fig 8-3) is now chosen, which is assumed to represent the initial distribution of goods among Smith and Jones. As can be seen from the figure, point H means that Smith receives 2 units of clothing and 10 units of food, while Jones obtains 6 units of clothing and 2 units of food. The question now arises whether the distribution at point H is optimal from the point of view of the economy as a whole, and also whether it would be possible to improve on this distribution. As we move from point H to point K, it is apparent that Smith reaches a higher indifference curve (from S_1 to S_2), while Jones remains on the same indifference curve (J_2). Smith thus experiences a higher level of utility, while the utility of Jones has remained the same. Therefore, according to the Pareto criterion, this is a desirable change or, in other words, a Pareto-efficient change. The economy as a whole (Smith and Jones) has been made better off by going from point H to point K. However, as we move further on, from point K to point E in Figure 8-3, it is clear that Smith can once again reach a higher indifference curve (S_3), with Jones's position not being compromised as he can stay on the same indifference curve (ie the same level of utility). The level of utility for the economy as a whole (and hence its welfare) has once more been improved by moving from K to E. If our two consumers, Smith and Jones, are clever enough (and it is assumed that they are) they will realise that the initial distribution of food and clothing at point H does not maximise their utility. They will therefore trade with each other until they reach the distribution at point E, in the process of which Smith gives up food and obtains extra clothing while Jones gives up clothing and obtains extra food.

Figure 8-3

Edgeworth Box Diagram for consumption

Smith's and Jones's indifference curves are combined.

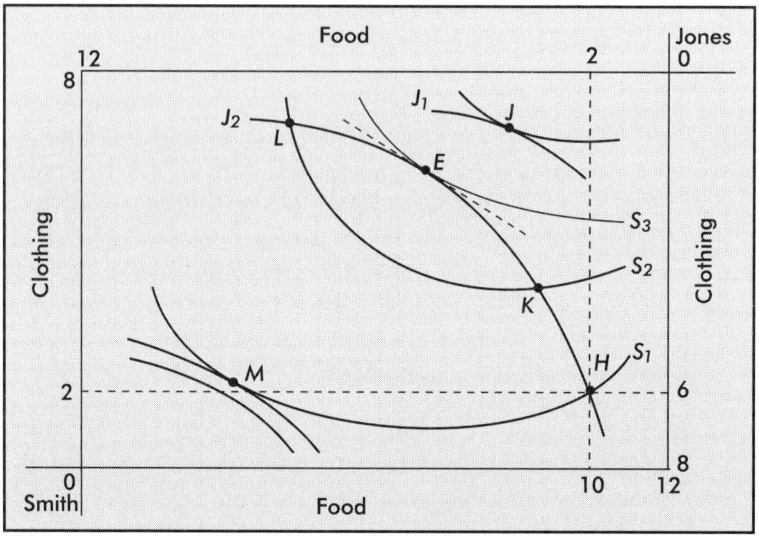

After Smith and Jones have exchanged goods to arrive at point E, they will have reached a Pareto-optimal distribution of goods. If, however, they were to move beyond point E to some other point in the diagram, say L, this would be at the expense of one of the consumers (in this case, Smith), who will move to a lower indifference curve (S_2) – this is therefore not a Pareto-efficient change. Given that we started off at a distribution at point H, it is impossible to improve on point E by way of exchange between the consumers. At point E, Smith and Jones's indifference curves just touch – a line through E (like the dotted line) will therefore be a tangent to both indifference curves, which means that at E the marginal rate of substitution of food for clothing (MRS_{FC}) is equal for both consumers. This is called the *first Pareto condition* for general equilibrium in the economy, which can formally be expressed as follows:

First Pareto condition

The efficient distribution of consumer goods requires that the marginal rate of substitution between any two consumer goods should be equal for all individuals using these goods, ie $(MRS_{FC})_{Smith} = (MRS_{FC})_{Jones}$ for the simplified economy of our example.

This condition can be stated more generally, namely

$$(MRS_{xy})_a = (MRS_{xy})_b = ... = (MRS_{xy})_n$$

with the letters after the brackets (a, b, etc) indicating consumers and the letters x and y referring to goods. If this marginal condition for consumption is not satisfied, at least one individual will benefit from further trade without harming the position of anybody else.

Contract curve

An Edgeworth Box Diagram for consumption does not just contain one point such as E where $(MRS_{FC})_{Smith} = (MRS_{FC})_{Jones}$ holds. In fact, an endless variety of such points exists. Two more are shown in Figure 8-3, namely M and J. If a line is drawn through all these points, we obtain a curve known as the *contract curve for consumption*. Figure 8-4 shows it as the curve which runs from the origin of Smith's indifference map to the origin of Jones's. Consumption equilibrium (ie a Pareto-optimal distribution of goods between individuals) is obtained at any point on the contract curve, while consumption equilibrium fails at any point away from the contract curve. The basic assumption of microeconomics is that consumers will always act to maximise their utility, which implies that consumers, if they are not already on the contract curve for consumption, will move towards it.

The question arises which of any two points on the contract curve for consumption, say E and J in Figure 8-3, is preferable from the point of view of the economy as a whole. A movement from E to J in Figure 8-3 means that Smith goes to a higher indifference curve and Jones to a lower one. Smith is therefore better off while Jones loses out. As mentioned earlier in this chapter, the Pareto criterion cannot be used to decide whether E or J is a better position for the economy as a whole. We will come across this problem again later in this chapter.

Figure 8-4

Contract curve for consumption

Points on the curve represent consumption efficiency (first Pareto condition).

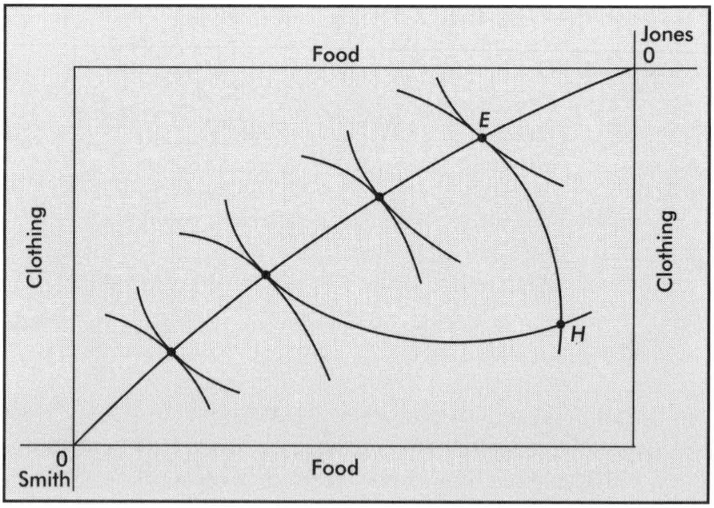

PRODUCTION EFFICIENCY

Edgeworth Box Diagram

The way an Edgeworth Box Diagram portrays production efficiency is similar to how it portrays consumption efficiency. We also start with two isoquants, one for the production of food and one for clothing, which are combined to form an Edgeworth Box Diagram for production. (In Figure 8-5, the isoquant map for the production of clothing has already been rotated 180° and combined with the isoquant map for the production of food to form a box diagram.) The dimensions of the box are determined by the amounts of inputs, that is, the amounts of production factors capital (K) and labour (L) available to the economy.

Assume that point A represents the initial distribution of inputs over the two producers (ie the producer of food and the producer of clothing). Again, the question arises whether, from the vantage point of the economy as a whole, these producers can improve on point A. It is once more apparent how a movement from point A to point B, and afterwards to point C, brings the production of clothing up to a higher isoquant (from C_1 to C_2 to C_3) while maintaining the production of food at the same isoquant (F_1). Hence the production of clothing increases, while food remains the same – this is therefore a Pareto-efficient change. It typifies an increase in the overall level of production of the economy, achievable with the given amounts of production factors available. The slopes of the isoquants at point C are equal, which means that the marginal rate of technical substitution of labour for capital ($MRTS_{LK}$) is the same for the production of clothing and for the production of food. This is called the *second Pareto condition* for general equilibrium in the economy, which can formally be expressed as follows:

Second Pareto condition

An efficient allocation of production factors requires that the marginal rate of technical substitution between any two production factors be equal for all production processes using both inputs, ie $(MRTS_{LK})_{Food} = (MRTS_{LK})_{Clothing}$ for the simplified economy of our example.

This condition can more generally be expressed as:

$(MRTS_{LK})_x = (MRTS_{LK})_y = ... = (MRTS_{LK})_n$

where x, y and n indicate production processes for food, clothing, etc.

Figure 8–5

Edgeworth Box Diagram for production

The isoquant maps of food and clothing have been combined. Points on the contract curve represent production efficiency (second Pareto condition).

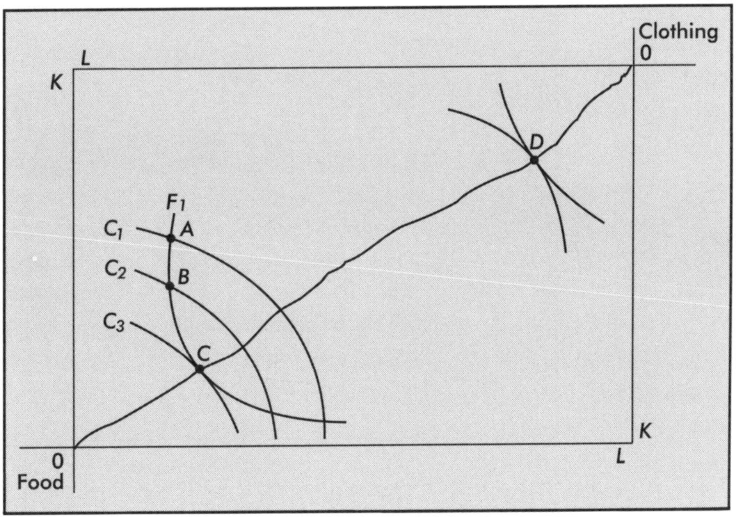

If this condition is not satisfied, the re-allocation of production factors over production processes can increase the production of at least one good without decreasing the production of any other good; hence, the overall level of production of the economy can be enhanced without employing any additional production factors.

Because each producer has an endless number of isoquants, there is an endless variety of points like C. All such points taken together form the contract curve for production (see Figure 8-5), which in accordance with the Pareto criterion reflects production-efficient input combinations.

The production possibility curve

The output levels represented by the production-efficiency points on the contract curve can be used to construe a production possibility curve (PPC) as in Figure 8-6. Such a curve shows the maximum attainable combinations of goods which the community can generate with the given amounts of production factors available. The PPC is derived under the assumption that all inputs are fully utilised as well as efficiently allocated, and that technology and the available inputs remain constant.

Figure 8-6
Production possibility curve
This shows the maximum attainable combinations of goods which the economy can generate with available production factors and technology.

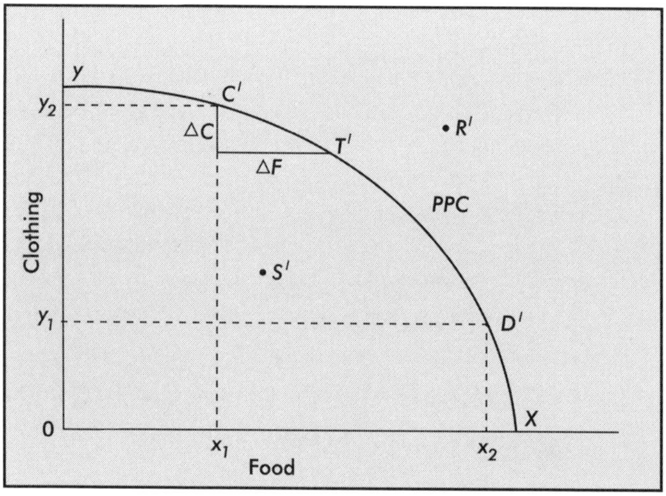

The following method is used to derive the production possibility curve. The isoquants in Figure 8-5 indicate production levels for food and clothing respectively. A point such as C in Figure 8-5 lies close to the origin of the isoquant map for food, but far from the origin of the isoquant map for clothing. Hence it displays a product combination where many clothes are produced (say, y_2 units) but little food (say, x_1 units). When we transpose this information to the PPC in Figure 8-6, it is represented by point C′ which reflects the same information. On the other hand, a point such as D in Figure 8-5 represents a product combination with a lot of food (say, x_2 units) but few clothes (say, y_1 units) – the same combination which in Figure 8-6 is depicted by point D′. By thus redrawing in Figure 8-6 all the product combinations on the contract curve in Figure 8-5, we obtain the production possibility curve.

The vertical and horizontal intersects of the production possibility curve (points X and Y) in Figure 8-6 depict situations where all available production factors are used to produce only food (at X) or only clothing (at Y). Point Y in Figure 8-6 corresponds with the origin at the lower left-hand corner of the Edgeworth Box in Figure 8-5, where only clothing is produced but no food. Similarly, point X in Figure 8-6 accords with the upper right corner of the Edgeworth Box in Figure 8-5, where only food is produced but no clothing.

Incidentally, two further points, S′ and R′, appear in Figure 8-6. Point S′ lies inside the production possibility curve and thus indicates that the production factors are not fully and efficiently used – subsequent analysis will disregard such points. Point R′ cannot be attained with the available amount of inputs and technology and will therefore also be ignored.

The PPC allows us to make a further deduction. A movement from C′ to T′ in Figure 8-6 means that the economy produces more food but fewer clothes. Hence, when all production factors are fully utilised, the economy can only produce more of one product (food) when producing less of the other (clothes). The rate at which one product is exchanged for another is called the *marginal rate of transformation* (MRT). The MRT denotes by how much the production of clothing needs to be reduced in order to produce one extra unit of food, which can be written as $\Delta C/\Delta F$. It can clearly be seen from Figure 8-6 that $\Delta C/\Delta F$ also measures the slope of the tangent to any point on the PPC. Hence, to obtain the marginal rate of transformation (MRT), one needs merely to calculate the slope of a tangent to the production possibility curve.

THE SIMULTANEOUS ATTAINMENT OF PRODUCTION AND CONSUMPTION EFFICIENCY

The previous two sections viewed consumption and production efficiency separately. It is now time to consider how the production and consumption sectors can be brought together. The consumption combinations of the model's two consumers are given in Figure 8-4. Production, however, is based on the available amount of capital and labour and the combined isoquant maps as pictured in Figure 8-5 – the contract curve in Figure 8-5 and the production possibility curve in Figure 8-6 reflect the same production combinations. The following questions now arise: What will the general equilibrium situation be? How can we make sure that the combination of food and clothing which producers produce corresponds with the combination of food and clothing which consumers wish to consume?

We have already pointed out how the production possibility curve (Fig 8-6) represents the combinations of food and clothing which the community can produce with the production factors available. It therefore also indicates the maximum attainable combinations of the two goods which are available for consumption (Fig 8-4) in the economy. By combining the production possibility curve in Figure 8-6 with the Edgeworth Box for consumption in Figure 8-4, the production and consumption sectors can be brought together. This is done in Figure 8-7. Point B in Figure 8-7 lies on the production possibility curve, indicating a combination of 12 units of food and 8 units of clothing *produced* in the economy. These 12 units of food and 8 units of clothing obviously also denote the maximum amounts of goods available for *consumption* in the economy. Hence, it stands to reason that the Edgeworth Box for consumption should fit exactly inside the production possibility curve. Note how point B was chosen to correspond with the combination (12 units of food and 8 units of clothes) with which we started. However, any other combination on the production possibility curve could be chosen, which would mean that the Edgeworth Box for consumption would have different dimensions (say, 15 units of food and 6 units of clothing), but would still fit exactly within the production possibility curve. Actually, in theory there is a separate Edgeworth Box for consumption for each production combination on the PPC, of which point B is only one. We pointed out above that each point on a contract curve inside an Edgeworth Box for consumption (eg points F and G in Fig 8-7) represents an efficient allocation of goods between consumers.

Figure 8-7

Simultaneous production and consumption efficiency

At point F, $MRS_{FC} = MRT_{FC}$ (third Pareto condition).

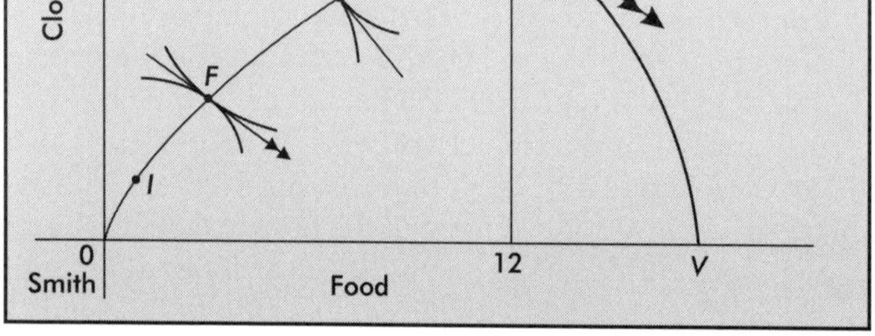

As already explained, at point B in Figure 8-7 the quantity of food and clothing *produced* is equal to what is available to be *consumed*. But that does not necessarily mean that this available *combination* of food and clothing corresponds with what consumers *wish* to consume. For *simultaneous efficiency* in both production and consumption a further condition needs to be met: consumers must be *willing* to substitute one good for the other in consumption at the same rate at which the economy *is able to* transform one good into the other in production (the latter rate being measured by the slope of the PPC). This means that the MRS between food and clothing of both Smith and Jones must be equal to the MRT between food and clothing. Hence, simultaneous efficiency requires that the slope of the indifference curves of both Smith and Jones should be equal to the slope of the PPC, which happens at point F in Figure 8-7. This is known as the *third Pareto condition* for general equilibrium in the economy, which is concerned with the relation between the consumption and production sector. This Pareto condition can more formally be expressed as:

Third Pareto condition

Simultaneous consumption and production efficiency require that the marginal rate of substitution between any two consumer goods for both consumers should be equal to the marginal rate of transformation between these consumer goods during the production process, ie $(MRS_{FC})_{Smith} = (MRS_{FC})_{Jones} = MRT_{FC}$.

A more general expression would read:

$$(MRS_{xy})_a = (MRS_{xy})_b = \text{.........} = (MRS_{xy})_n = MRT_{xy}$$

with the letters after the brackets (a, b, etc) indicating consumers and the letters x and y referring to goods.

The economic implication of the third Pareto condition is that the combination of goods produced in the economy must be optimal from the perspective of both producers and consumers. It is not sufficient that the conditions for economic efficiency in the production and consumption sphere should be met separately. These conditions have also to be met at a point where the mutually interdependent production and consumption decisions conform with each other.

The attentive reader will have noticed how, in a certain sense, the third Pareto condition presupposes the first two conditions. The satisfaction of the third condition automatically guarantees that the first two conditions are met. The third Pareto condition consists of two parts: $(MRS_{xy})_a = (MRS_{xy})_b$ and MRT_{xy}. If the marginal rate of substitution is the same for consumers (as required by the third Pareto condition), the first condition is automatically fulfilled. Also, the marginal rate of transformation reflects the slope of the

PCC, which is derived from the contract curve for production, which meets the second Pareto condition. By implication, therefore, points on the PPC fulfil the second Pareto condition. Hence, when the third Pareto condition is met, the first two conditions are met as well.

All three Pareto conditions are therefore satisfied at a point such as F in Figure 8-7. Point F, however, is by no means unique. There are many such points where all three Pareto conditions are fulfilled. (But a point such as G does not satisfy the third Pareto condition, because the slope of the indifference curves of Smith and Jones is not equal to the slope of the PCC; while $(MRS_{FC})_{Jones} = (MRS_{FC})_{Smith}$ holds, this is not equal to MRT_{FC}.) The next question is: Given that point F in Figure 8-7 is not unique, which point on the contract curve should then be regarded as optimal from the point of view of the community (Smith and Jones) as a whole? The next section will address itself to this question.

A further question is: What would the situation be like if MRT was not equal to the MRS? Since an answer to this question will interrupt the flow of our argument, we will relegate it to Box 8-1.

Box 8-1

THE EQUALITY OF MRS AND MRT

What is the underlying reason for the optimality rule according to which the MRT and the MRS have to be equal? Assume that the economy finds itself in a situation where the conditions for the MRS and MRT are fulfilled (ie production and consumption efficiency are achieved), but that $MRT_{FC} = 1{:}2$ (ie 2C/1F) while $MRS_{FC} = 1{:}3$ (ie 3C/1F). The economy therefore produces on its PPC and the two consumers consume somewhere on the contract curve. Because $MRT_{FC} = 1{:}2$, this means that to increase the production of food by one unit, the economy (Smith and Jones) needs to offer up two units of clothing – production factors need to be shifted from the clothing to the food producing sector. Assume that this is precisely what happens – the economy produces one additional unit of food but two units less clothing. Let us leave Smith's consumption basket unchanged, but give Jones this 1 additional unit of food produced, for which Jones is prepared to give up 3 units of clothing while remaining equally well off (remember that $MRS_{FC} = 1{:}3$). What has been achieved? The level of utility (welfare)experienced by both Smith and Jones is the same as before these changes, *but there is now one surplus unit of clothing.* (3C is removed from Jones' basket, but only 2C was necessary to produce the 1 additional unit of food.) By arbitrarily distributing this one unit of clothing over Smith and Jones, both can increase their level of utility (welfare). Hence, the original situation could not have been Pareto optimal. Such an advantageous rearrangement of production and consumption would not have been possible if the condition MRS = MRT had already been met.

Equality between MRS and MRT

If $MRS_{FC} = MRT_{FC}$, the third Pareto condition for simultaneous production and consumption efficiency is satisfied.

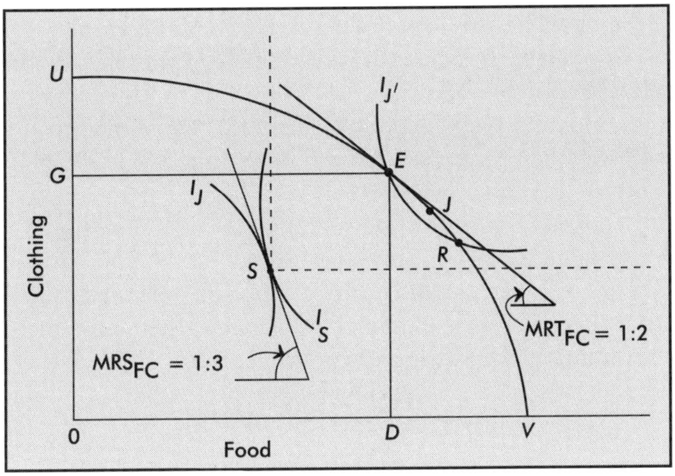

The above discussion can be further illustrated in a diagram. The economy produces at point E on the production possibility curve UV, where $MRT_{FC} = 1:2$. Construct an Edgeworth Box 0DEG and assume that Smith and Jones consume at point S where $MRS_{FC} = 1:3$. (0 and E are the origins for Smith and Jones respectively.) Freeze Smith's consumption at S. Draw Jones' indifference curve in its natural state as shown by the dotted axes running through S. Also draw indifference curve $I_{J'}$ corresponding with I_J. Because Jones' $MRS_{FC} = 1:3$ at S and the $MRT_{FC} = 1:2$ at E, the curve $I_{J'}$ will cut through the PPC from above, as can be seen from the figure. The economy can move its production to a point such as J (on UV), where Jones will find himself on a slightly higher indifference curve than $I_{J'}$, while Smith remains at S.

If the condition concerning the equality between MRS and MRT is fulfilled, Jones' indifference curve $I_{J'}$ will form a tangent to the PPC at E. As a result, it would not be possible to rearrange production and consumption in such a way that the welfare of one person can be improved without making another person worse off – thus increasing the welfare of the community as a whole.

SUNDRY REMARKS ABOUT THE STUDY OF WELFARE ECONOMICS

We mentioned in the previous section that a point such as F on the contract curve in Figure 8-7 is not unique. Hence the distribution of food and clothing between Smith and Jones is not unique either. It is even possible that a point on the contract curve in Figure 8-7 satisfies all three Pareto conditions, but that one consumer lies on an indifference curve representing a very high level of utility while the other lies on an indifference curve representing a very low level of utility. At point H in Figure 8-7, for example, Smith lies on a high indifference curve but Jones lies on a low one (or Smith gets almost all food and clothing but Jones is almost starving and virtually naked), while the situation is reversed at point I. The question is now: Which of the many possible points such as F on the contract curve in Figure 8-7 where all three Pareto conditions are satisfied, will the community (Smith and Jones) prefer? This question is very difficult to answer, because as we move from point F to, say, H, Smith becomes better off at the expense of Jones. Because utility cannot be measured, it is virtually impossible to make interpersonal utility comparisons. As a result, there is no easy way of determining which situation affords maximum utility to the community as a whole. The Pareto criterion cannot help us here either, as it cannot say anything about a change which makes one consumer better off while leaving another worse off.

Welfare economics

The problem as sketched in the previous paragraph falls within the field of study known as *welfare economics*. Welfare economics attempts to judge the relative desirability of economic situations from the point of view of the community as a whole. The central question of welfare economics is which allocation of economic resources yields the maximum welfare (utility) for the community as a whole. It goes without saying that welfare economics is essentially normative, meaning that value judgements are an integral part of any choice between alternative economic scenarios. Even if a model which could make such choices were to be built, it would necessarily contain some kind of welfare criterion according to which alternative situations are weighed up against each other. Undoubtedly such a welfare criterion would then reflect the value judgements of the model builder, be he or she a planner, state body, politician or whoever. Value judgements, unfortunately, cannot be scientifically determined, and there is consequently no guarantee that welfare criteria have an equal concern for the welfare of each individual (or group of individuals) in society.

There are theoretical models which determine which allocation of economic resources gives maximum welfare to a community, but it falls outside the scope of this course to discuss them in greater depth.

WELFARE ECONOMICS IN PRACTICE

It should be obvious that welfare economics is a difficult field of study whose practical applications are rather complicated. Nonetheless, many studies have been conducted to apply welfare principles. Without going into detail, we can mention some of these: a study to determine the welfare cost of monopoly; the welfare cost of extraordinary high medical care; welfare losses due to transactions outside the formal economy; as well as a study about the extinction of the Blue Whale as an example of the inefficiency which arises when prices do not reflect the marginal cost of a product – clearly, studies which cover a wide spectrum of issues.

The role of the government

Even in a perfectly competitive economy, it is unlikely that a Pareto optimum will ever be reached, because, when the supply and demand of a product do not reflect all the costs and benefits in producing and consuming a product, the 'right' price will not be set. In that case, competition will not bring about the adaptations to the market price necessary to achieve maximum welfare. The government will therefore also have an important role to play in the economy – as evidenced by the wide variety of government involvements that exist, from the provision of public goods (eg the protection of citizens against foreign aggression) to the regulation of monopolies or the enforcement of anti-pollution measures. This concerns a field of study which will receive attention in other economics courses.

IMPORTANT CONCEPTS

- Partial equilibrium analysis
- General equilibrium analysis
- Pareto optimality
- Edgeworth Box Diagram
- Contract curve
- Consumption efficiency
- Production efficiency
- Production possibility curve
- Marginal rate of transformation
- Simultaneous efficiency
- Pareto's three conditions
- Welfare economics

QUESTIONS

(1) Explain why, with regard to consumption, points that lie away from the contract curve are regarded as inefficient. (Also use a diagram to illustrate your explanation.) (6)

(2) Explain fully in your own words (without a diagram) what happens if an economy moves from a point that is not on the *contract curve for production* to a point that does in fact lie on the contract curve. (6)

(3) What does a *production possibility curve* represent? Explain the meaning of a point that lies within the curve. What do we know about a combination of goods that is represented by a point that lies outside the curve? (Also use a diagram to illustrate your explanation.) (8)

(4) Explain fully how a general equilibrium can be achieved *simultaneously* in production and exchange, given that factors of production are fully employed. (Also use a diagram to illustrate your explanation.) (15)

(5) Assume that Utopia has a 2 × 2 × 2 economy (ie two consumers, two products and two factors of production). Explain how the *contract curve for the production* of food and clothing in Utopia will be derived. Also explain the difference between efficient and inefficient production. Use an Edgeworth Box Diagram to illustrate your discussion. (15)

(6) Use the *contract curve for production* discussed in question 5 to derive the *production possibility curve* for Utopia. (Explain how you go about this.) Show common points between the two curves clearly. (5)

(7) Suppose that in Utopia it is found that the MRT_{FC} = 3:1, while the MRS_{FC} = 1:1. Define and discuss each of these concepts briefly and explain why, according to the Pareto criterion, there is room for improving welfare. (5)

(8) (a) *Name* only the three conditions that must be met in order to satisfy the Pareto criterion. (3)

(b) *Explain* in your own words the marginal conditions that must be met in order to satisfy the Pareto criterion. (9)

(9) Is each allocation of resources that satisfies the Pareto criterion also a social welfare optimum? Explain in your own words. (3)